The Radically Open Dialectical Behavior Therapy Workbook

Skills to Overcome the Paradox of Perfectionism, Anxiety, Depression & Other Disorders of Overcontrol

THOMAS R. LYNCH, PhD
J. NICOLE LITTLE, PhD

New Harbinger Publications, Inc.

Publisher's Note

This publication is designed to provide accurate and authoritative information in regard to the subject matter covered. It is sold with the understanding that the publisher is not engaged in rendering psychological, financial, legal, or other professional services. If expert assistance or counseling is needed, the services of a competent professional should be sought.

New Harbinger Publications is an employee-owned company.

New Harbinger Publications, Inc.
5720 Shattuck Avenue
Oakland, CA 94609
www.newharbinger.com

Cover design by Amy Shoup

Acquired by Catharine Meyers

Edited by Vicraj Gill

Library of Congress Cataloging-in-Publication Data on file

MIX
Paper | Supporting responsible forestry
FSC® C008955
FSC www.fsc.org

Printed in the United States of America

27 26 25

10 9 8 7 6 5 4 3 2 1 First Printing

"*The Radically Open Dialectical Behavior Therapy Workbook* is a powerful radically open dialectical behavior therapy (RO DBT) skills workbook that speaks directly to those trapped by rigid standards and chronic self-criticism. With compassion and clarity, it offers practical tools to break free from the exhausting pursuit of perfection. This workbook is a must-read for anyone ready to trade overcontrol (OC) for connection, flexibility, and true well-being—a game changer for clients and clinicians alike."

—**Karyn Hall, PhD, MSCP, APIT**, licensed psychologist; director of the Houston DBT Center and DBTWise; certified RO DBT supervisor; and author of *The Radically Open DBT Workbook for Eating Disorders*

"Readers will step onto a path toward greater freedom and fulfillment, guided by Tom Lynch and Nicole Little's compassionate, engaging, and entertaining writing, vivid examples, and practical exercises. *The Radically Open Dialectical Behavior Therapy Workbook* helps overcontrolled readers learn to practice openness, flexibility, and curiosity about themselves and others; find relief from emotional loneliness; build connection and intimacy; and navigate thorny aspects of relationships, such as giving and receiving difficult feedback. I strongly recommend this essential guide for consumers and clinicians alike, overcontrolled or not, and I look forward to using it with my clients (and myself!)."

—**Alexander L. Chapman, PhD, RPsych**, professor of psychology at Simon Fraser University; president of the DBT Centre of Vancouver; and coauthor of *The Dialectical Behavior Therapy Skills Workbook for Shame*

"This insightful and practical book offers powerful skills to loosen the grip of perfectionism and excessive control by helping readers build flexibility, develop close bonds with others, and find more joy in life. It's a compassionate guide for anyone seeking to thrive socially and emotionally while pursuing meaningful goals. And along the way, the reader will have a little fun, too, while working with this book."

—**Martina Wolf-Arehult, PhD**, psychologist, coordinator of the national highly specialized medical care unit for severe self-harm and eating disorders, cofounder of the Swedish DBT association, and author of *Out of Loneliness*

"*The Radically Open Dialectical Behavior Therapy Workbook* is a groundbreaking resource for anyone struggling with excessive self-control. Its structured approach, which includes self-enquiry practices and social signaling techniques, empowers individuals to embrace openness, flexibility, and social connectedness. Backed by robust research and clinical evidence, it provides a clear path toward reducing perfectionistic behaviors and enhancing overall well-being. I highly recommend it to anyone seeking freedom from OC and a more fulfilling life."

—**R. Trent Codd III, EdS**, clinician at Cognitive Behavioral Therapy and Assessment Associates, and author of *The Stoicism Workbook*

To Erica—who makes all things possible.
—Tom

With gratitude for the wisdom of my clients, the mentorship of Tom and Erica, and the love of Deanne.
—Nicole

Contents

CHAPTER 1

The Paradox of Perfectionism

People strive for perfection. The perfect figure. The perfect performance. The perfect plan. But what makes perfection such an attractive goal? It's at best a momentary experience and, like beauty, "in the eye of the beholder." Plus, being perfect at anything takes time and is hard work.

So, why bother?

Well, for one, our species' survival depended on the efforts of individuals who worked hard to meet or exceed expectations. For example, tribes highly valued individuals who practiced shooting an arrow until they could hit almost any target—both as hunters and warriors. Plus, being correct matters—for both individual and species success. Determining accurately whether that furry thing in the bush is a tiger or a bunny made a big difference when it came to whether one was going to be eating dinner or *be* dinner. Indeed, mastery of almost anything involving complexity—like learning French, physics, or how to make a decent *crème brûlée*—takes time and is hard work. It requires perseverance, effortful control, and attention to detail. Indeed, most societies depend on individuals with superior, detail-focused brains to find the errors others may have overlooked—like the seemingly innocent missing word in a trade agreement or the frayed wire in a jet engine.

Despite these advantages, most people don't aspire to be called "perfectionists." Why? Because it implies a fussy control freak who can't relax (oh, my!). It implies someone who's hard-driving, uncompromising, and relentless—and often not much fun to be around, despite how successful they may be.

Ultimately, possessing high personal standards isn't inherently bad. As research shows, perfectionism can be healthy or unhealthy. Healthy perfectionists are those who strive for greatness; their standards are high but realistic. They're not devastated by being less than perfect or making a mistake every now and then. They're motivated to do their best without being paralyzed by a fear of failure. They're conscientious, but not to a fault. They can flexibly adjust expectations about performance or precision depending on the situation. They can celebrate their own success and others', appreciate a job well done, and evaluate personal failures without falling apart.

Problems emerge when striving for perfection becomes an obsession.

When Perfection Becomes an Obsession

People with maladaptive, unhelpful perfectionism are never satisfied, even with their best efforts; they always feel that they could do better (or at least appear to do better). They consider anything less than the absolute best a failure. They strive for a higher level of performance than is possible to attain, making it hard to feel good about the work they've done or themselves. They learn to avoid taking risks to avoid making mistakes, become highly sensitive to perceived criticism, and base self-worth on how well they're performing relative to others. Because their self-worth comes from impossibly high standards, they aren't satisfied with what others might see as superior achievement—nothing's ever good enough.

An obsession with perfection makes mistakes intolerable. *If someone feels terrible about making a mistake, they may come to believe that it's terrible to make a mistake.* Blue moods and panic about making mistakes only serve to prove that anything less than perfection is simply wrong. Decreased productivity, lethargy, and lack of drive resulting from repeated episodes of depression provide further evidence of innate inadequacy and worthlessness—feelings they dare not share with anyone, because it would imply that they're less than perfect.

Interestingly, for many, it's not about actually winning the race, but *appearing* to win. Thus, while perfectionism can be understood as the desire to be perfect, it can also be understood as the desire to *look* perfect: to portray a flawless image to others (Hewitt & Flett, 1991). This may help explain why so many perfectionists avoid treatment. It requires you to admit that you've got a problem, not only to yourself—but also to someone else. It also explains why so many perfectionistic people downplay problems or claim all is well ("I'm fine") even in crisis.

Of course, when winning or being correct is what matters most, relationships suffer. People characterized by unhelpful perfectionism are often highly successful in achieving personal goals—but not a lot of fun to be around. Moreover, compulsive over-striving often results in a narrow, imbalanced set of life experiences where chances for social relations are missed or avoided (Frost et al., 1990; Graham et al., 2010). To the maladaptive perfectionist, relationships are more likely to be valued according to how much another person helps or hurts the achievement of personal goals ("you're either with me or against me"). The result is a range of interpersonal problems, including lower perceived social support, intense interpersonal conflicts and marital difficulties, greater daily interpersonal hassles, and high disagreeableness or hostility (e.g., Hewitt et al., 2006; Mackinnon et al., 2012; Molnar et al., 2012; Sherry et al., 2013).

A hyperfocus on performance and achievement is also exhausting. It requires frequent social comparisons to verify the extent your performance is superior or adequate. When comparisons are unfavorable, envy and bitterness are soon to follow, which can negatively impact close social bonds. As one person described her perfectionistic mother: "It's difficult to be around her… She's always raining on someone's parade." Thus, maladaptive perfectionism is a painful personality style to possess—not only is being good never good enough, social ostracism and loneliness also become more likely.

Does any of the above resonate with you? Let's take a moment to reflect on high standards. Take some time to answer the questions below.

- *To what extent are your high standards directed towards yourself? For example, "When I'm working on something, I cannot relax until it's perfect."*
- *To what extent are your high standards directed towards others? For example, "I have high expectations for the people who are important to me."*
- *To what extent do you believe your high standards result from unrealistic demands or expectations placed on you by others? "I've always felt pressure from my parents to be the best."*
- *What consequences have your excessively high standards resulted in? How have they impacted relationships?*

____

____

____

____

____

____

____

The Perfectionism Trap

The paradox is that perfection is perfectly fine and helpful, as long as you don't take striving too seriously. But when being good means being good *all the time*, it becomes a trap: being perfect all the time is an impossible task. For one, no one knows everything, nor ever could, regardless how long or hard they tried. And because we don't know what we don't know, we're bound to make mistakes. Plus, what's considered "the truth" or "the best" today may be considered "false" or "inferior" tomorrow. Things are constantly changing; our perceptions and beliefs about standards of excellence differ widely and vary according to family, environmental, and cultural experiences. Moreover, the wide variety in how our brains are "hard-wired" further affects how we perceive the world, often without us being aware of it—which extends to perfection: what you see as perfect may not be seen as perfect by another. The trap begins when you start thinking your definition is best.

The paradox of perfection also presents a conundrum. Most societies value and reward individuals who meet or exceed expectations. Doing well, not making mistakes, and achieving long-term goals lead to job promotions, not jail time. And thus, perfectionism becomes hard to change; it's so often rewarded. Unfortunately, accomplishment and its positive mood states can reinforce overly optimistic beliefs in our abilities that become a suit of armour, protecting us from the pain of indecision, fears of making a mistake, or feelings of incompetency by steering us to automatically reject anything that makes us feel uncomfortable. This armour ends up numbing us to new information, differing perspectives, or new learning, which keeps us stuck in old patterns that may no longer be effective. Thus, part of the trap of maladaptive perfectionism is that you tend to pay attention only to things that advance your goals and ignore or dismiss anything that doesn't. You become stubborn to a fault. For example, someone with maladaptive perfectionism may insist that items on their desk are always at perpendicular and 45-degree angles before any work can be done, or refuse to hear a different way of doing things before they finish what they had planned first.

Yet another aspect of the perfectionism paradox is that admitting to unhelpful, perfectionistic traits can feel like failure. Sometimes it just feels easier to pretend everything is okay—but the downside is that this can keep us stuck in misery. Moreover, although the drive for perfection makes it easier to predict and control the environment, others, and oneself, it becomes a trap when it captures the majority of your attention and time. Maladaptive perfectionism's fundamental axiom is "When in doubt, try harder," irrespective of circumstances or potential consequences. Thus you might work obsessively on completing an important but uncomfortable task even when it's clear you'd be better off resting or avoiding it altogether. A heightened sense of urgency can emerge, manifesting in compulsive attempts to quickly resolve problems (or potential problems) and then just as quickly move on to the next one, with no rest in between. Such compulsive striving is exhausting. It requires willpower, depleting our energy resources (Gailliot et al., 2007); and it makes life feel like a burden, demanding constant vigilance for potential problems and relentless, effortful control that leaves little space for rest, play, or intimacy with others.

That said, striving for perfection can become such an automatic way of being that you don't see it as a problem. It's a bit like asking a fish to notice the water they're swimming in. For example, *have you ever noticed that the more perfectionistic a person is, the less likely they seem able to identify it as a problem?* But being blind to perfectionistic traits is easy when perfectionism is part of your sense of self—your unique identity that sets you apart from others. You might see compulsive striving, exceptionally high standards, and self-sacrifice to achieve goals as what makes you special. Your exceptionally high standards and self-sacrifices are a badge of honor (not a problem)! Of course, when "I'm not like most other people" means "I'm better than most other people"—as can happen with maladaptive perfectionism—you can slip into contempt for those who don't meet your standards, and avoid social situations that won't help you achieve personal goals. You might also ignore critical feedback you receive because "my problems are fundamentally different" or "so complex that no one could ever possibly understand them". The downside, of course, is that this often signals superiority that—even when expressed surreptitiously, or when it represents some truth—can trigger feelings of resentment in others, or envy, or even secret desires that you fail. What's more, most people innately recognize self-assessments of personal superiority as subjective and potentially biased or self-serving. It assumes one's self-assessment represents truth—yet, when it comes to living, there are many ways to live well and effectively. And not all of them have to do with achieving perfection (tee hee). Consequently, the major consequences of maladaptive perfectionism are primarily social in nature—aloofness and distance from others—and this often leads to a socially isolated and lonely existence, even if you've enjoyed considerable personal achievement.

This points to another trap: the pursuit of excellence can become addictive. After all, winning feels good. But maladaptive perfectionism considers pleasure justifiable only if it's worked for. Happiness must be earned; leisure time must be self-improving; pleasures unrelated to achievement (e.g., enjoying a sunset) are dismissed as irrelevant or decadent extravagancies. But at what cost? For one, if you can only experience pleasure or reward if you've put a lot of effort into something—successfully resisted temptation, detected errors, or defeated rivals—your field of attention becomes self-centered: focused on *you* and *your* needs, wants, or beliefs, and hyper-focused on *your* mistakes, *your* performance, and how *you* can do better. Your high standards also become "truth" that can be used to judge the performance of others. You end up signaling to others you're focused on what they're doing wrong or how they should behave according to your standards. In this way, people high in maladaptive perfectionism move toward a self-preservation orientation wherein individual competition, beating others, and being the absolute best are paramount (Flett et al., 1998; Sherry et al., 2007). The trap is forgetting an essential fact about our species. We depend on others for our success. And striving to be special derives meaning primarily from the extent it contributes to the tribe or one's community.

Lastly, the perfectionism trap is also a little sneaky—which is why we call it a trap (tee hee). Trying to rid yourself of perfectionist tendencies can reinforce beliefs that you need to be better by not being a perfectionist, feeding a core belief you're never good enough as you are (yikes!). It's similar to the dilemma of the Chinese finger trap, in which a victim's fingers are trapped in both ends of a small cylinder woven from bamboo. Your initial instinct to pull your fingers outward only tightens the trap. To escape, you must stop *trying* to escape and move towards the middle instead—which enlarges the openings and frees your fingers. Similarly, the aim of this book is to introduce a new way of thinking about maladaptive perfectionism, and some evidence-based skills that can help loosen up this dynamic. Our journey begins in the section below. In the meantime, practice loving your perfectionistic tendencies—even if it's only a little bit *(tee hee)*.

Maladaptive Perfectionism Is About Being in Control

If perfectionism can be so maladaptive, why do we experience it? In many ways, it's about self-control. A survey among thousands of people across fifty-four countries (Park, Peterson, & Seligman, 2006) asked how much respondents exhibited twenty-four different virtues, including self-control. Of all the virtues, people rated themselves lowest on self-control. It seems that almost everyone thinks they need more self-control. No wonder why: self-control allows us to resist giving into that impulse to eat more ice cream, to exercise even when we don't want to, avoid saying that angry thing we want to, or to make ourselves finish an important project even though we don't feel like it. Self-control includes things like self-discipline, the elimination of bad habits, overcoming temptation, focusing on long term goals, not letting feelings dictate our choices, persisting through pain, and willpower. It's all about keeping your feelings, your thoughts, and your behavior in check. Interestingly, a number of researchers have linked effortful control with the personality factor of conscientiousness (e.g., Kochanska & Knaack, 2003; MacDonald, 2009; MacDonald et al., 2007). Conscientiousness refers to "socially prescribed impulse control that facilitates task and goal-directed behavior" (John & Srivastava, 1999, p. 121) and it's generally a good trait to possess.

Just as with perfectionism, individuals with high self-control—who are able to delay gratification, make plans, persist in onerous activities to achieve long-term goals, and behave conscientiously—are highly valued in most communities. They're the doers, the savers, the planners, and the fixers—the people you see working late at night and then rising early to ensure that things work properly. A thriving society needs people who can exert self-control, inhibit destructive and selfish impulses, think about long term goals, and take planful action toward them. As a result, high self-control is often seen as a virtue that we should try to cultivate. Indeed, research shows that high self-control is generally related to occupational and educational success.

But can there be too much of a good thing? Can we be overcontrolled?

The answer is yes. A growing body of research shows that some people suffer from excessive and rigid patterns of self-control, or *overcontrol*. Excessive self-control is associated with social isolation, poor interpersonal functioning, perfectionism, rigidity, lack of emotional expression, and severe and difficult-to-treat mental health conditions, such as anorexia nervosa, chronic depression, autism, and obsessive-compulsive personality disorder (Lynch & Aspnes, 2001; Lynch & Cheavens, 2008; MacLean et al., 2014; Morse & Lynch, 2004; Zucker et al., 2007; see also Lynch 2018a, 2018b.)

Overcontrolled (OC) individuals are quintessential perfectionists. They don't need to learn how to be more serious, try harder, or do better; they're already experts at doing this. Instead, they need to learn how to chill out and attend to their relationships—yet often feel clueless about how to go about achieving this. This counterintuitive idea—*that you can have too much self-control*—is the heart of this book and the skills it teaches, all informed by an evidence-based treatment known as radically open dialectical behavior therapy (RO DBT; Lynch, 2018a, 2018b).

The Self-Control Spectrum

Just like every other trait, self-control lies on a spectrum. Most people exhibit what's called *flexible control*. They're able to inhibit or disinhibit, as needed, to respond adaptively to the ever-changing situations of life. People who are flexibly controlled can inhibit impulses and emotions to serve longer-term goals—such as inhibiting the desire to watch TV and exercise instead, or suppressing the desire to yell at their boss in order to keep their job—and also disinhibit to freely express emotion when the situation calls for it: playing, joking around, relaxing with friends, or having a meaningful conversation. Both working hard and having a good time are important in life. Flexibly controlled people are able to generally maintain a mixture of self-control and disinhibition that, as Goldilocks might put it, is "just right."

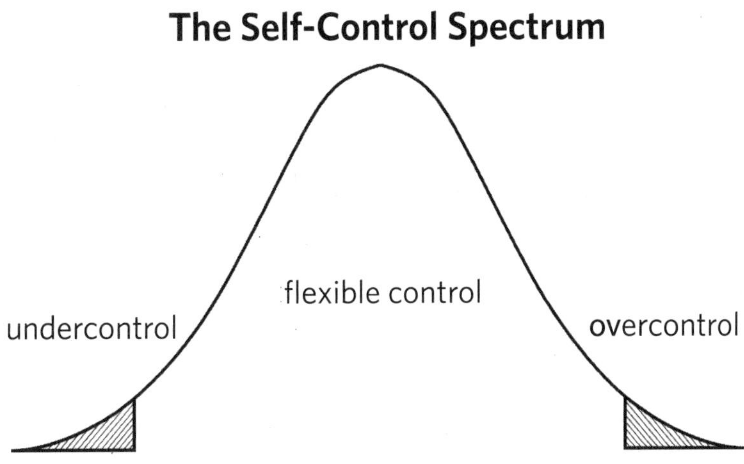

Figure 1.1. The Self-Control Spectrum

Problems tend to occur on the tails of the self-control spectrum (see figure 1.1). Problems on the undercontrolled (UC) end of the spectrum tend to be pretty obvious. When people lack sufficient ability to inhibit their immediate impulses and emotions when under stress, they're likely to cause a ruckus. UC individuals possess low distress tolerance, and will do almost anything to stop or blunt current-moment distress, making them appear unpredictable, dramatic, impulsive, and, depending on their mood state, insensitive to others' social signals and needs. They may disregard social norms and damage relationships to feel better in the moment, only to regret it later. It's not that they don't care or aren't trying. They were born with biologically lower capacities to tolerate distress, delay gratification, and inhibit impulses, compared to most people. They lack the inhibitory capacities to prevent an emotional outburst from occurring when under stress or conflicting demands. And they're often painfully aware of their inability to control their expressions of emotion. On the plus side, UC individuals rarely attempt to control or inhibit expressions of positive emotion—it just happens! When UC individuals say they like something, they really mean it—at least for the moment—making them often fun and exciting to be around. Genuine laughter, for instance, is highly contagious.

In contrast, problems related to overcontrol (OC) are expressed discreetly. OC people tend to be serious about life, make personal sacrifices to help others, and strive to achieve important goals. They often have a high sense of moral obligation to do "the right thing" even when it's very difficult or unpleasant. They're "good citizens" who strive to manage their life without burdening others. However, OC individuals struggle to cope with unpredictable situations or events requiring spontaneity. They're intolerant of uncertainty and thus will do almost anything to prevent problems from occurring in the future (to a fault). Where UC people might avoid an impending threat, to escape emotional distress, OC people will more likely *approach* an impending threat to eliminate it, making them compulsive fixers. Their difficulties are more about "doing too much" (e.g., compulsive fixing, cleaning, correcting, straightening, planning, or rehearsing) than "not doing enough." Which makes it hard to find time to enjoy the present moment until "all the chores" have been completed—which is essentially never, in "OC Land" (yowsers!).

Plus, although they often experience high levels of anxiety and arousal, they usually downplay any distress they are feeling, simply saying "I'm fine" instead. Avoidance of public displays of emotion make it less likely for their problems to be noticed; and consequently, they're less likely to receive psychological help when it's needed (Morse & Lynch, 2004; Lynch & Aspnes, 2001). Oftentimes no one outside their immediate family is aware of their inner psychological distress. As a result, problems associated with OC receive less attention and OC individuals are likely to quietly suffer in private and alone. The resulting social disconnection is central to what makes OC so painful, and a big part of what we want to address in this book.

Now let's take a moment to assess which style best fits you.

Assessing Your Style of Coping

The focus of this book is on the overcontrolled end of the spectrum—because as a personality style, it's the one most associated with maladaptive perfectionism. But note that overcontrol isn't just one trait; it's a confluence of traits that all come together in an overarching pattern of coping. As people go further out onto the tail ends of the distribution of self-control, they tend to have more of the corresponding traits. So, while there are a number of things that overcontrolled people usually have in common (see "OC Behavioral Themes and Traits"), some will have more of them than others. Take a moment to ask yourself the questions in box 1.1. The more you say yes to (i.e., check off), the more likely you are to have an overcontrolled style of coping.

OC Behavioral Themes and Traits

(Lynch, 2018a)

- Inhibited and/or disingenuous (insincere) emotional expressions
- Hyper-detail-focused and overly cautious behavior
- Rigid and rule-governed behavior
- Aloof and distant style of relating to others
- High social comparisons, envy and bitterness

Box 1.1. Common Features of Overcontrol

More yeses mean more overcontrol.

- ☐ *Do you believe it is important to do things properly or in the right way?*
- ☐ *Are you a perfectionist?*
- ☐ *Are you cautious and careful about how you do things?*
- ☐ *Do you prefer order and structure? Are you organized?*
- ☐ *Do you like to plan ahead? Do you think before acting?*
- ☐ *Are you able to delay gratification? Are you able to easily inhibit an impulse?*
- ☐ *Do you consider yourself conscientious? Are you dutiful?*
- ☐ *Are you quiet, restrained, or reserved by nature?*
- ☐ *Is it hard to impress you?*
- ☐ *Does it take time to get to know you?*
- ☐ *Are you likely not to reveal your opinion immediately but wait until you get to know someone better?*

Knowing whether you lean toward overcontrol or undercontrol matters because your personality style impacts how you perceive and respond to the world and the particular skills you may need when problems emerge.

Before we continue our self-assessment, a few caveats:

1. UC individuals are likely to express strong emotions regardless of context—at home, at work, with friends or strangers, at the gym or in the street, and so on—and they're often oblivious of its impact on others. OC individuals, by contrast, strongly dislike public displays of emotion, and are expert at inhibiting impulses or behaviors that may attract unwanted attention or criticism—with what extreme displays of emotion do occur being rare, and usually in private, at home or among family. That said, dramatic expressions of emotion in public settings (aka emotional leakage) do occasionally occur in OC people—especially in situations that feel anonymous or where displays of emotion are socially sanctioned (such as a political demonstration).
2. Similarly, UC individuals can sometimes exhibit behaviors that on the surface "look" like OC behavior. Those who've achieved success in school or work often develop perfectionistic tendencies; indeed, the areas of their life where their behavior is most controlled are usually the areas

they have been most successful. The difference between OC and UC perfectionism has to do with how widespread it is in a person's life. Because a UC person has poor distress tolerance skills, they find it extremely difficult to maintain discipline and self-control over long periods of time and in all contexts, so their displays of superior self-control and competence are often contained within one or two areas of their life (see Linehan, 1993). The perfectionistic OC individual is capable of maintaining discipline and self-control not only for long periods of time but also in most contexts—regardless of how distressing a situation might seem.

3. As we'll explore in chapter 2, when threatened or overwhelmed, all humans lose their expressive capacities; we become flat faced and our voices go monotonic. But OC individuals are likely to display inhibited, constrained, and disingenuous emotional expressions in all or most situations—even those that others would consider non-threatening (e.g., at work, at home, with family, with friends, at the gym, at a party), whereas UC individuals will return to their naturally (and often overly) expressive way of being, once the threat has passed or they have reregulated.

4. The final caveat to consider, in the self-assessment, pertains to risk taking. Although OC individuals are generally risk-averse, many OC individuals describe themselves as "rebels" or risk takers. And indeed, they often are. However, the difference between OC and UC risk taking has to do with planning. UC risks are typically impulsive and spontaneous—they occur without much forethought. The types of risks OC individuals report almost always involve some form of planning, practice, or training beforehand (e.g., skydiving is a carefully planned risk).

Okay, now that we have covered the major caveats, let's return to our self-assessment (phew!). For this, we'll use the RO Word-Pair List. It's useful and interesting to complete, even if you're already confident about which style best describes you. Importantly, this measure is *not a measure of pathology or poor mental health.* It's simply a measure of personality that helps you determine whether you lean toward overcontrol or undercontrol. Ultimately, you could score very high on either domain and not be psychologically distressed or unhappy. And having a particular personality style doesn't necessarily mean there's something "wrong" with you—which is probably a good thing, since everyone has a personality (tee hee). As we've been learning, it's when your habitual style of coping becomes rigid and inflexible that problems arise.

RO Word-Pair List

To complete the word-pair list, consider the pair of words or phrases in each row. Then, pick the descriptor (word) that best describes you and place a checkmark in the box next to the word you chose. For example, the first word-pair in the list is *impulsive–deliberate*. To answer, simply ask yourself which word best describes you: overall, do you see yourself as more impulsive or more deliberate? Then move on to the next word-pair and do the same thing, until you've picked one word from each pair in the entire list.

Remember to pick only one word per pair. Pick the word that describes you as you are—*not* how you want to be or hope to become in the future, or how you were in the distant past. If you're unsure which word to pick, simply make your best guess (wow!) or imagine which word a friend or work colleague might choose to describe you. And don't agonize over this exercise; that would be very perfectionistic and OC (tee hee). Finally, to get your score, simply add up the number of checkmarks in each column. The column with more checkmarks represents your overall personality style. A higher score in column A indicates a tendency to be more undercontrolled; a higher score in column B indicates a tendency to be more overcontrolled.

Remember, a high score for either column does not necessarily indicate your coping is maladaptive. Also, sometimes a person reports nearly equal scores for both columns—for example, the total for column A is 23 and the total for column B is 24. The measure's been designed to account for this. Simply look to the column with the higher score.

A		B	
Impulsive	☐	Deliberate	☐
Impractical	☐	Practical	☐
Naïve	☐	Worldly	☐
Vulnerable	☐	Aloof	☐
Risky	☐	Prudent	☐
Talkative	☐	Quiet	☐
Disobedient	☐	Dutiful	☐
Fanciful	☐	Realistic	☐
Fickle	☐	Constant	☐
Acts without thinking	☐	Thinks before acting	☐
Animated	☐	Restrained	☐
Changeable mood	☐	Stable mood	☐
Haphazard	☐	Orderly	☐
Wasteful	☐	Frugal	☐
Affable	☐	Reserved	☐
Impressionable	☐	Not easily impressed	☐
Erratic	☐	Predictable	☐
Complaining	☐	Uncomplaining	☐
Reactive	☐	Unreactive	☐
Careless	☐	Fastidious	☐

A		B	
Playful	☐	Earnest	☐
Intoxicated	☐	Clear-headed	☐
Self-indulgent	☐	Self-controlled	☐
Laid-back	☐	Hard-working	☐
Unconventional	☐	Conventional	☐
Dramatic	☐	Modest	☐
Brash	☐	Unobtrusive	☐
Obvious	☐	Discreet	☐
Vacillating	☐	Determined	☐
Unrealistic	☐	Sensible	☐
Gullible	☐	Shrewd	☐
Unpredictable	☐	Dependable	☐
Dependent	☐	Independent	☐
Improper	☐	Proper	☐
Chaotic	☐	Organized	☐
Susceptible	☐	Impervious	☐
Unstable	☐	Steadfast	☐
Volatile	☐	Undemonstrative	☐
Excitable	☐	Stoical	☐
Lax	☐	Precise	☐
Unsystematic	☐	Structured	☐
Thoughtless	☐	Thoughtful	☐
Inattentive	☐	Attentive	☐
Short-lived	☐	Enduring	☐
Perky	☐	Despondent	☐
Passionate	☐	Indifferent	☐
Immediate gratification	☐	Delayed gratification	☐
TOTAL score A		**TOTAL score B**	

Okay, so how'd it go?

As we noted earlier, knowing whether you lean toward overcontrol or undercontrol matters; your personality style impacts how you perceive and respond to the world. And we all lean one way or the other on the UC-OC spectrum. But if you remain uncertain about which way you lean, even after completing the word-pair list—that's OK. Why? For one, it would be arrogant (and anti-RO DBT) for us to insist otherwise or believe that the word-pair list is the best, most definitive, or only way for a person to understand themselves or their personality style. Moreover, although this book is designed specifically for perfectionistic OC individuals—that doesn't mean the skills we will cover in later chapters won't help people who are more UC. Indeed, we're all likely to benefit from training and practice in skills designed to enhance openness, flexibility, and social connectedness. But before we move on, take some time to reflect on what it was like to complete the word-pair list.

To what extent did I like or not like my result (total score) on the word-pair list? What might this tell me about my openness for change?

____

____

____

To what extent did I choose words describing how I wish to be—over those that might describe me as I am? What might this tell me about the way I live my life?

____

____

____

Did I use this exercise as another way to get down on myself? Or alternatively, did I experience secret pride or pleasure in knowing my style? What might my answers to these questions tell me? Is there something here to learn?

____

____

____

____

Well done! Hopefully you now have a better sense of which personality style best fits you. Again, although RO DBT was developed for problematic OC, that doesn't mean OC coping is always problematic. People with high self-control and detail-focused brains are most likely the ones who made it possible for our species to land on the moon! So, we don't want to throw the baby out with the bathwater. Now, let's find out more about RO DBT.

What Is RO DBT?

RO DBT is an evidence-based treatment emerging from over thirty years of research into how to help people suffering from excessive overcontrol. It's based in evidence and informed by ten clinical trials and one multi-center clinical trial that was one of the largest trials ever conducted on treatment-resistant depression (Lynch et al., 2020). A recent independent systematic review concluded that RO DBT has been shown to be effective for both adolescents and adults for a variety of conditions characterized by excessive self-control, such as autism, anorexia nervosa, and obsessive-compulsive personality disorder, as well as for longstanding or treatment-resistant conditions, in particular treatment-resistant depression (Hatoum & Burton, 2024). So, it's been shown to help a wide range of people with various overcontrolled disorders.

RO DBT's core principles and skills can help loosen the grip of maladaptive perfectionism and overcontrol. It does so by recognizing what OC individuals really need. Because they're perfectionists, OC individuals tend to see mistakes everywhere (including in themselves), and work harder than most others to prevent future mistakes from occurring. They don't need to learn how to take life more seriously, try harder, plan better, or behave more appropriately in public. They have too much of a good thing—their self-control is out of control, and they suffer as a result (Lynch, 2018a). So, rather than falling into the trap of asking what's "wrong" with an individual struggling with maladaptive perfectionism, RO DBT begins by asking what it means to be psychologically healthy (for all of us) and then uses this as a guide to know where to go. According to RO DBT, psychological health and well-being consists of three core features (Lynch, 2018a):

1. *Receptivity and openness* to new experience and disconfirming feedback, so we can learn
2. *Flexible control*, so we can adapt to the ever-changing situations and events we encounter in life
3. *Intimacy and connectedness* with at least one other person, based on the premise that our survival as a species depended on our ability to form long-lasting bonds and work together in groups.

Before we dig deeper into the points above, take a moment to reflect using the questions below.

Can you think of an example of a person (or three different people) who has each of these features?

___

___

___

What do you admire about that person?

___

___

___

What might your answers tell you about yourself or what you might need to learn?

___

___

___

___

Receptivity and openness. Our brains are pattern-matching machines that are constantly making predictions about the world and acting based on those predictions. If our mental models are working well, they don't need to be updated. But when they aren't, it's important that we're open to disconfirming feedback so that we can update our beliefs, goals, and behaviors. Openness also models humility and willingness to learn from what the world has to offer. It signals to others that you're willing to hear their opinions without automatically discounting them, enhancing relationships. Plus, openness is the only way to learn something new. Whether it's learning to play the piano or to maintain a marriage, learning anything new or improving how we behave always requires openness. While closed-mindedness usually has short-term gains, it tends to cost us in the longer term. Refusing to listen to feedback from a coworker may protect your self-esteem now, but it'll likely harm your relationship with that person over time—as you won't be able to modify your behavior in ways that are helpful to the relationship—and it may impact your job performance, too. Importantly, as we'll learn in later chapters, openness does not mean approval, naively believing, or mindlessly giving in.

Flexible control. Our behavior needs to be flexible and responsive to the situations we're in, including to the needs of others. Life presents ever-changing circumstances, to which we must respond flexibly to be consistent with our values. Problems arise when we respond rigidly to change or when our responses are governed by rules or past learning, not our present-moment experience. For example, context matters when it comes to emotional expression. Having a flat facial expression when playing poker makes winning more likely. Displaying that same flat facial expression or using a monotonic voice when, say, praising a child likely sends the opposite message to what was intended.

Healthy living requires a balance of inhibition and disinhibition. It involves learning how to appreciate your default style of coping with a willingness to relinquish it when the situation calls for it. This enhances relationships, because you're doing what's needed in the moment to effectively manage a situation, but in a manner that accounts for the needs of others. RO DBT aims to help us celebrate diversity by recognizing that there are many ways to live, behave, or think, not just one "correct" way; for instance, there are innumerable ways of expressing love, and countless ways to cook carrots. Plus, context matters when it comes to emotional well-being and living by your values alike. For example, you might pride yourself on complying with rules, but not when breaking a rule is needed to prevent harm; you might strive for perfection, but not when doing so will damage an important relationship. Learning how to flexibly adapt your behavior to fit the circumstances you're in is a core part of the skills taught in this book.

Intimacy and connectedness. The third part of the definition acknowledges our tribal nature. We need others and suffer when we're not connected to a tribe. From an RO DBT perspective, what really matters, in terms of relationships, is quality, not quantity. Thus, a "tribe" can consist of as few as two people. And a central aspect of psychological health is having at least one person in your life that you know will be there when you need them. Research suggests that we only need one relationship that involves strong feelings of attachment, love, or mutual caring to reap the positive psychological benefits for well-being. It's not the number of people in your social network that's important, but the perceived quality of the relationship (e.g., Palinkas et al., 1990; Lynch et al., 1999).

Individual well-being and success are highly dependent on other people. For example, the chair you're presumably sitting in while reading this sentence wasn't made by you; nor was your smartphone, likely sitting nearby (you know, the thing that keeps distracting you from reading this book, tee hee). Indeed, humanity's success has always been highly dependent on our capacity—unique among animal species—for forming long-term social bonds with unrelated others and working together in tribes. For our early ancestors, exclusion from the tribe meant almost certain death. Indeed, research shows that non-human primates socially isolated from their tribe die of exposure, lack of nourishment, or predation in a matter of days to weeks (Steklis & Kling, 1985). In the long run, we're tribal beings, and we yearn to share our lives with other members of our species (see box 1.2).

Box 1.2. A Note About "Tribe."

In the context of this book, "tribe" refers to the evolutionary roots of our species. As noted by Lynch (2018b, p. 168):

> *"Tribe" is not a common word used to describe the importance of community in the clinical world. The use of the word "tribe" in RO DBT strategically smuggles the evolutionary importance of our need for others (that is, our species' survival required capacities to form long-lasting bonds and work in groups). Thus, tribe matters—not only because it highlights a core feature of psychological well-being but also because the word itself helps remind us of our ancestral beginnings that still strongly influence us today.*

Ultimately, who will look after us when we fall ill, tell us we're loved when we feel unsure or alone, make us laugh when we feel sad, and kindly tell us when we've done wrong or help us learn what we don't know? The answer is: only those with whom we've formed strong social bonds, committing to make self-sacrifices to benefit each other's well-being without always expecting something in return (Lynch, 2018a). Our tribe is what makes us feel strong and confident in facing the world. And being rejected by a tribe hurts; research shows that social ostracism triggers the same areas of the brain triggered when we experience physical pain (Eisenberger & Lieberman, 2004). In modern times, the consequence of not feeling part of a tribe is a pervasive sense of loneliness, which has been linked to poor mental and physical health outcomes like heart disease, depression, or suicide. The good news: growing research shows that when we feel part of a tribe, we naturally feel safe and worry less (Lynch, 2018a), and feel less agitated, anxious, depressed, and hostile (yowsers!).

But if you're suffering from maladaptive perfectionism and overcontrol, knowing this doesn't necessarily make you feel any better. Like the trap of maladaptive perfectionism, loneliness isn't something you can fix on your own by striving harder. And when you're lonely, it's hard to feel happy, no matter how hard you try to accept yourself, distract yourself, stay busy, or take the latest pharmaceutical solution—loneliness sticks like glue (Lynch, 2018a). Loneliness is a conundrum: it means no one is around, but you need someone around to cure it. What's more, for someone suffering from maladaptive perfectionism and overcontrol, being dependent on another person is often considered a sign of weakness: *If I can't solve a problem by myself then I must be inadequate*. Or, you might think, *If I don't do it myself, it'll never get done, or done properly*. The problem is that loneliness is the type of problem that can only be *solved properly* with another person—that is, via friendship. Overcontrolled, perfectionistic individuals are often great at convincing themselves and others that change is unnecessary—contending, for example, that love is fake, feeling detached and alone is normal, and no one can ever truly understand another person. They may insist that change is impossible, or believe *I am not like other people* or that *Being correct is more important than being liked*. They may consider the risks of intimacy, like obligation or disappointment, too great or not worth it. Making friends can also feel, for OC individuals, like losing control; interpersonal interactions are unpredictable, because you can never know for certain how another person will respond.

Moreover, friendship, like love, is a gift that must be given willingly. You cannot force someone to love you or become a friend. Furthermore, true friendship begins when two people are able to share not only their successes but their secret doubts, fears, and past mistakes with each other. It requires vulnerable self-disclosure, and openness to feedback and differing opinions (yowsers!). That can feel terrifying when you're OC. You might fear that if you reveal your true feelings or show vulnerability to another person, they'll use it against you or take advantage of you. Perhaps the biggest fear of all is: what if a friend discovers your "dirty little secret"—that you're not as perfect as you might pretend to be? Spoiler alert: you can relax. Your friends already know you're not perfect (tee hee).

RO Fun Fact: Why Do We Like Our Friends?

This may seem like a silly question, but it's important to know why we like our friends—at the very least for reasons of personal understanding. Ask yourself this: Do I like my friend because they've just returned from Hawaii with a great suntan after purchasing their second yacht and they're about to complete their third PhD after being nominated for a Nobel Prize for humanitarian work with impoverished children? Maybe so, but it's more likely that your friendship is based not just on knowing the good things about them.

It's more probable that you like your friend because they've revealed to you things they may struggle to share with others or are less proud of—for example, their doubts, their fears, their past mistakes, secret desires, as well as their successes. When we signal vulnerability without falling apart, we automatically make relationships more intimate and equitable because revealing weakness opens us up to being hurt by the other but also to the possibility of new learning when our friend provides us with helpful advice or a differing perspective. True friends with close bonds know things about the other person that could hurt them, but they don't use it against them. (Lynch, 2018b, p. 206)

What's double cool is that good friends know each other's imperfections and personality quirks—and love each other for them anyway. The reason this works is because revealing personal information to another person is a powerful social safety signal. It essentially says, "I trust you"—we don't reveal vulnerability to those we distrust—and "You and I are the same," meaning we share a bond of fallibility. Essentially, revealing vulnerability is the foundation of true friendship.

Yet, if you're lonely or you've struggled to establish close social bonds, knowing how, when, and with whom to reveal vulnerability can feel impossible. Plus, since making friends can seem so easy for others, not knowing how can become another reason you get down on yourself (for not being perfect), making giving up and nonparticipation feel like a viable alternative. Unfortunately, this only makes loneliness and feelings of isolation more likely—especially when we realize that we're the only one not participating.

The good news is that RO DBT introduces a novel way of thinking about overcontrol and maladaptive perfectionism that's wholly different from other approaches to date (Codd & Craighead, 2019).

According to RO DBT theory, inborn differences in our biotemperament (the biogenetic predispositions that influence how we perceive and respond to the world), combined with family, cultural, and environmental experiences emphasizing the importance of self-control, performing well, and not making mistakes, lead to the development of a maladaptive, overcontrolled style of coping that interferes with the formation of close social bonds, resulting in social isolation, loneliness, and distress (phew!). In other words, it's not lack of contact, but lack of intimate connection—often from quite early in life—that OC people struggle with. Importantly, OC people's reports of social ostracism and beliefs about being unlikeable aren't cognitive distortions; they're accurate observations of the real-life social consequences associated with social-signaling deficits. So, rather than focus on changing beliefs about being unlikeable, RO DBT aims to help you change the social-signaling deficits—the micro-expressions, body postures, gestures, and voice-tones—that've been shown to exacerbate social ostracism and make a person less likeable. For example, robust research shows that behaviors like displaying a flat face when praising someone, or mismatches between outward expression and inner experience (like smiling when angry) will make it more likely for others to perceive one as untrustworthy or inauthentic (Boone & Buck, 2003; English & John, 2013; Kernis & Goldman, 2006), reducing social connectedness and exacerbating psychological distress (see Mauss et al., 2011). Indeed, RO DBT is the first treatment in the world (Codd & Craighead, 2019) to prioritize changing social-signaling deficits so that one's emotional expression is more appropriate to the social context. More appropriate emotional expression results in increased trust and desires for affiliation from others, and thereby increases social connectedness—making "being perfect" less of a driving force, and mistakes less of a crisis. When we feel part of a tribe, we naturally feel safe and worry less.

> RO DBT differs from most other treatments by positing that individual wellbeing is inseparable from the feelings and responses of the larger group or community.
>
> (Lynch, 2018a, p. 378)

But what is a social signal? A *social signal* is any behavior a person exhibits in the presence of another person, regardless of its intention (e.g., yawning during a conversation is commonly interpreted as a sign of boredom, even if you're actually just sleepy) or conscious awareness (e.g., an involuntary sigh can communicate as much as a conscious sigh). We are constantly socially signaling when around others (via our micro-expressions, body movements, and voice tone), even when we're deliberately trying not to (silence can be just as powerful as nonstop talking).

Another major difference between RO DBT and most other approaches is that RO DBT, by targeting the biotemperamental predispositions linked to perfectionistic overcontrol, accounts for individual differences in biotemperament (Lynch et al., 2015). What does this mean? Again, biotemperament refers to the inborn genetic and biological tendencies that affect how we perceive and respond to the world. For example, most OC folks are born with an innate biological propensity to focus on the details (such as asymmetry or a missing comma in a sentence) rather than on the big picture. They're great at noticing the trees, but struggle seeing the forest—which can lead to problems, because sometimes seeing the big picture is what's needed to cope effectively. And as we'll learn in chapter 2, detail-focused processing isn't the only OC biotemperament (Spoiler alert: There are three others, tee hee).

Biotemperament powerfully influences a person's perception, learning, and actions, at the sensory-receptor (or preconscious) level of responding. The problem with being born with an extreme biotemperamental predisposition, as occurs in OC, is that you cannot think or talk yourself out of a genetically based predisposition; your brain is hardwired to respond to certain stimuli in a particular way. OC biotemperamental predispositions, like heightened threat sensitivity, also exacerbate over-learned tendencies to inhibit, constrain, or mask feelings, interfering with the formation of close social bonds. To address this, RO DBT teaches skills to reduce or alter the potential negative influences of biotemperament—informed by experimental research showing neuroinhibitory relationships between the parasympathetic nervous system (PNS) and the sympathetic nervous system (SNS; see Berntson et al., 1991; Porges, 1995). Broadly speaking, the brain system that arouses us (the sympathetic nervous system, or SNS) and the brain system that calms us (the parasympathetic nervous system, or PNS) operate as antagonists; when one is on, the other is off (Berntson et al., 1991). For example, *have you ever noticed that you cannot feel both calm and fearful at the same time?* Similarly, we cannot simultaneously experience genuine joy and real anger at the same time. RO DBT capitalizes on this by teaching skills to activate different areas of the brain associated with PNS or SNS activity —in particular those areas associated with social safety (see Porges, 2011). This enables an overcontrolled person to override biotemperamental predispositions to constrain facial expressions, exhibit tight gestures, or use a monotonic voice during interactions, and naturally relax facial muscles and other areas of the body needed to signal friendly intentions. Others are then much more likely to signal similar cooperative responses, such as smiling back, and that maximizes the chances that social interactions become rewarding experiences.

The third major difference between RO DBT and most other approaches is the emphasis placed on openness. Indeed, radical openness is the core philosophical principle and skill in RO DBT. Radically open living impacts not only how we see the world—making us more receptive to critical feedback—but also how others see us: people like people who are open-minded. As you'll learn, radically open living is considered both a state of mind and a powerful social signal that influences personal and other perception. As a state of mind, it involves actively seeking our personal unknown to learn from an ever-changing environment. Rather than assuming the world needs to change for us to feel better, radical openness posits that we most often learn from those areas of our life that we find most challenging. Thus, practicing radical openness involves purposeful self-enquiry and a willingness to be wrong, with an intention to change when change is needed. The benefits for dealing with maladaptive perfectionism are enormous. When you start asking "What do I need to learn?" instead of "What did I do wrong?" every time things don't go your way, perfection is no longer the metric by which you judge success. Your sense of purpose becomes less about how well you're performing relative to others, and more about how receptive you are to new learning (yowsers!). Don't feel compelled to just take us at our word here; discover for yourself the benefits of openness by practicing the skills outlined in later chapters. Ultimately, of course, the decision to practice is entirely up to you. Indeed, RO DBT considers it arrogant to tell others how to live. But practice anyway (tee hee)—you may be delighted by what you discover.

Lastly, but not leastly, another major difference between RO DBT and other approaches pertains to silliness (yowsers!). Indeed, in RO DBT, silliness is no laughing matter! We take silliness seriously, because perfectionistic overcontrolled individuals take life too seriously. Rather than learn how to be more serious, strive harder, or do better, people suffering from unhealthy perfectionism and maladaptive overcontrol need to learn how to chill out and have a little fun! Indeed, the shared positive feelings most people experience when socializing with friends is similar to the combination of joy and interest commonly seen during interactions between mothers and infants in healthy attachment bond formation (Depue & Morrone-Strupinsky, 2005; Schore, 2021). And being able to nonjudgmentally chuckle, as adults, when we make a mistake is a sign of positive mental health, signaling to the world that we don't take ourselves or life too seriously, and that we'll likely be open to feedback. It also, often, *feels* better, in the long term, than punishing yourself.

Okay, you might think, *but you can't really be serious about being silly—can you? I mean, do I really have to practice being silly? Really?*

Of course, you don't. After all, it's your life, right? It would be silly for us to insist that you practice being silly. But do it anyway (tee hee)—you may be surprised by what you find. More seriously, silliness is truly helpful. Purposefully behaving in a nonsensical manner around another person can make it clear to them you mean them no harm. It can lighten up tense social interactions and signal that you're not taking things or yourself too seriously. Ultimately, silly behavior automatically signals friendly intentions, regardless of how it's expressed or what you feel or think inside. It's so powerful that it gets its prosocial message across even when you might be convinced the other person believes you're being a "total wacko" (yowsers!). RO DBT teaches specific skills that can help someone not only feel chilled out but also signal a little levity to others when the situation calls for it. And—for readers out there who are squirming (tee hee)—the good news is that, as you'll learn, because our brains are hardwired to read the social-signals of others in milliseconds, you only need be silly for a second or two to reap its social benefits. So, hang in there, and don't mind any unusual language you might find in the chapters ahead (tee hee!).

A Look Ahead

What can you expect from the chapters ahead? Well, in our next chapter, we'll outline how perfectionistic overcontrol develops, using a biosocial theory that accounts for both biological and environmental influences. Chapter 3 will introduce a novel neurobiological model of emotional responding that's linked to many of the skills in RO DBT. Chapters 4 and 5 will outline social signaling as the core mechanism of change in RO DBT, providing explicit instructions on how to activate and signal social safety. Following this, in chapter 6, we'll explore radical openness and the specific skills needed to practice being radically open. Chapter 7 will teach you how to make friends and maintain close intimate bonds with others. From there, you'll learn how to be open to feedback from others (chapter 8) and how to provide others feedback without harming the relationship (chapter 9).

We also hope to enrich your reading by sharing some personal stories or anecdotes when relevant. Spoiler alert: Nicole has an advantage over Tom when it comes to anecdotes about overcontrolled coping—because she self-identifies as overcontrolled, meaning her personality style leans toward OC. So, expect some tidbits and stories derived from Nicole's personal experience, including an occasional chuckle about her OC antics. Tom, on the other hand, leans toward undercontrol—despite being the developer of a treatment for overcontrol (yowsers!). But you can expect some personal stories and anecdotes from him, too.

Lastly, before we move on, we'll introduce two OC characters, Tula and Elijah, whom we'll use to illustrate teaching points in each chapter. They represent composites of clients we've worked with over the years who've blessed us with their stories, insights, challenges, and triumphs. So, let's begin by having them tell us a little about themselves—starting with Tula.

• *Tula*

I am the kind of person who looks really good on paper. If you were to read my CV, you'd be like, "Wow! This person's going places!" I have a couple of good degrees from respected schools, excellent references from my internships, a few scholarships and awards, and a strong social media presence. My old schoolmates would sometimes say they envied me because everything I did looked so effortless. Ha! If only they knew the truth. In reality, I've struggled with anxiety my whole life. And I feel like I missed out on some basic "How to Be a Human" instruction guides, like how to make real friends, relax at work, act on a date, or spend money without freaking out. It took me a long time to decide if I wanted to go to therapy, because what would I say? My life is nothing to complain about in the big scheme of things, and I felt like it was my fault I was so anxious and lonely all the time. But I researched different therapies and found a RO DBT program in my area. Even in the first session, it was like a lightbulb went off. I wasn't crazy, I was wired differently. And I was finally in a place to learn how to harness that uniqueness and let go of what wasn't working—and maybe let go of working all the time!

And now to Elijah.

• *Elijah*

I was raised in a very serious family whose motto was "never air your dirty laundry," and I vowed that I would live my life differently than having to be capital-S serious all the time. But it's like I didn't really ever get the hang of being easygoing or open. Instead, I learned to be "the nice guy"—you know, the person you can depend on at work, who never complains or rocks the boat. Inside, however, I noticed I was growing resentful that people didn't notice how hard I worked or how helpful I was. And I'm not always the nice guy at home. There, I can be downright passive-aggressive, which has really impacted my relationships. One time, at a family birthday gathering, my sister-in-law said to me, "You know, Elijah, you've been part of this family for ten years and I feel like I don't know anything personal about you!" When I started learning about RO DBT, things started clicking—my fake cheery persona, born out of a desperate desire to fit in, was actually getting in the way of getting closer to people or feeling less depressed. I wouldn't say changing lifelong habits is easy, but it's getting easier!

OK, well done on getting through this chapter. By now, we hope you have a sense of which personality style (OC or UC) you lean toward. And if it's OC, that's great, because in our next chapter we describe the biosocial theory of overcontrol—including its biological underpinnings (wow!).

CHAPTER 2

Perfectionistic Overcontrol: A Biosocial Theory

In our last chapter (which, for this book, was our first; tee hee) we learned that *maladaptive perfectionism is about having too much of a good thing*—namely, too much self-control. The paradox of maladaptive perfectionism is that you can't use your superior capacities for self-control to control your perfectionism (yikes!)—partly because it's biologically based. This chapter will introduce a novel biosocial theory (Lynch, 2018a) to delve deeper into the biotemperamental roots of perfectionistic OC, and it'll examine how these features interact with the socio-biographic environment a person lives in to yield an overcontrolled style of coping (phew, that's a mouthful!). That is, we'll explore how *nature* influences *nurture*, and vice versa—and its impact on *coping*. Here's a little story to get us started (Lynch, 2018b, pp.88–89):

> *There once was a man who believed no one liked him. His friend said, "Just go to the village and spend time in the square. You will see that none avoid you."*
>
> *The man said, "You don't understand—people really hate me. They look at me as if something is wrong with me. I don't see how this would work."*
>
> *Finally, his friend convinced him to try, and so he did.*
>
> *The next week his friend asked, "How did it go at the village?" The man replied, "I did just as you said. I went to the village with my three hunting dogs—restrained of course—my shield on my back, and my sword in my belt. You never can be too cautious! What might you think happened? The mothers in the village picked up their children and took them inside. The fathers glared at me with contempt, and not a soul came to speak to me on the bench I sat on in the center of the square. My dogs weren't even barking that much! And you think people like me?"*

So, what does this story have to do with problems of overcontrol? For one, it illustrates how habitual ways of perceiving the world bias our responses to it. It also provides an example of how overcontrolled individuals bring moods and behaviors ("hunting dogs, swords, and shields") into social situations that can make the situation worse. These can range from relatively subtle social signals, such as neutral facial expressions and fake smiles, to more obviously problematic behaviors, like accusing others of nefarious motives. It shows how hunting dogs, swords, and shields often function as overlearned defensive responses—responses designed to protect us from harm that damage relationships instead. The story also illustrates how the reactions of others to our swords, shields, or barking dogs can reinforce negative beliefs we have about ourselves and the world, making defensive responding on our part more likely in the future (yikes!).

What types of hunting dogs, shields, and swords do you carry with you when you visit your village? For example, do you

- usually stay on the outskirts of conversational circles,
- look away when someone compliments you,
- habitually display a flat facial expression,
- rarely smile during greetings or interactions,
- report you're fine when you're not,
- smile when feeling anger,
- block offers of help,
- try to avoid eye contact,
- change the topic when emotions are discussed,
- rarely apologize—even when you're in the wrong,
- frequently check your phone during conversations,
- redo other people's work,
- downplay other people's success,
- agree with someone while inwardly disagreeing, or
- tell others how they should think or feel?

How have these social signaling habits impacted your interpersonal relationships? Is there something here to learn?

____

____

____

____

However you answered the questions above, the point of the story is to illustrate how perfectionistic, overcontrolled individuals often unintentionally see and respond to the world, especially in social situations, in ways that function to isolate them from others. And as we'll learn next, biotemperament may be a driving force behind this.

The OC Biotemperament (Nature)

Biotemperament refers to inborn predispositions or tendencies that affect how we experience the world and how our brain processes information at a pre-conscious level. We're all born with biotemperaments, which act like a lens that affects how we perceive and respond to the world from the moment we're born. And since we all have a biotemperament, this means that at a very basic level, we all have a biased view of the world. A core principle in RO DBT (Lynch, 2018a) is that *we don't see the world as it is, we see the world as we are.*

Biotemperamental predispositions are powerful because they impact perception and regulation at the preconscious, sensory-receptor level of awareness (often in milliseconds). When extreme, they make our responses more rigid and less adaptive to change. For example, OC biotemperamental predispositions for heightened threat sensitivity makes it more likely for OC people to feel and appear uptight regardless of context—e.g., at work, at home, at the gym, or at a party (yowsers!). People with less intense or fewer biotemperamental sensitivities can more easily modify their behavior to match the context they are in. They can tease and laugh with friends, dance with abandon at a party, and appear inscrutable when negotiating tough terms at work or sombre when delivering disappointing news.

According to RO DBT theory (Lynch, 2018a), four biotemperamental predispositions are typical of OC people:

1. High inhibitory control
2. High detail-focused processing
3. Low reward sensitivity
4. High threat sensitivity

High inhibitory control. This refers to superior capacities in inhibiting emotion-based action or expressive tendencies (Lynch, 2018a).* This biotemperamental predisposition enables an OC person to inhibit overt expressions of emotion—for instance, suppressing an overt display of disgust, or masking an expression of disappointment. It also enables OC people to delay gratification, avoid temptation, tolerate distress, persist, and plan for the future to achieve long-term goals. For example, you can keep from eating every doughnut purchased for your family on the drive home, or remember that company sales vary depending on the time of year and plan your marketing strategy accordingly. Thus, the capacity for high self-control is highly adaptive in many situations. It becomes a problem when you're unable to *relax* your inhibitory control in situations that are safe or call for light-heartedness, laughter, or free and open expression of emotion and thoughts, such as casual conversations, going for drinks with colleagues after work, going on a date, playing a silly game with friends, vacationing with your family, praising a valued employee, trading jokes with friends, dancing with your child at their wedding, talking with a teenager about their favorite subject at school, or other interactions that are an essential part of close social bonds and intimate connections.

Individuals characterized by excessive inhibitory control are also over-reliant on strategic rather than hedonic means of achieving desired goals (Lynch, 2018a). That is, their behavior isn't driven by current mood or dysregulated emotions; it's often the consequence of non-emotional executive processes involving reasoning, logic, prediction, and rules. Thus, you might be likely to attend a party out of a sense of duty or obligation—not because of anticipatory pleasure. High biotemperamental inhibitory control is also thought to be linked to desires for structure and order. Research on individuals exhibiting excessive needs for structure and control reveals that, when stressed, they're more likely to try to quickly fix uncertainties and use solutions that have worked in the past, instead of developing new ones—which often results in *more* errors, because they find it difficult to let go of old solutions or rules even when a prior solution no longer applies (Brand, Schneider, & Arntz, 1995; Neuberg & Newsom, 1993; Thompson, Naccarato, Parker, & Moskowitz, 2001). Furthermore, one of the biggest problems with an information-processing and problem-solving style that favors reason and logic over emotion and intuition is that pure

* Biotemperamental self-control is supported by research showing individual differences in *disinhibition versus constraint* (DvC; see Clark & Watson, 2008; Watson & Clark, 1993), widely known in the developmental literature as *effortful control* (e.g., Kochanska et al., 2009; Rothbart et al., 2007).

logic often fails when it comes to human relationships. For an example of this, see the box "The Logical Romantic."

"The Logical Romantic"

There once was a very logical person who decided that it would be advantageous to get married. Since they did not have a lot of experience in this area, they decided to begin this process by generating a list of the attributes they considered most important in a spouse—for example, conscientious, a hard worker, doesn't smell, is orderly, likes long walks, has good teeth, and so on. Next, they set about looking for their ideal mate. After some time, they finally located someone who matched all of their search criteria (checked all the boxes on their list). They then proposed marriage. And after the other person agreed, they married! But within two years they were divorced. Why? Because the very logical person discovered that they had never really liked their spouse in the first place! The moral of this story is that emotions matter when it comes to human relationships (Lynch, 2018b, p. 143).

High detail-focused processing. This refers to a disposition to focus on details (such as asymmetry or small discrepancies) over more global perspective taking (i.e., noticing the big picture). This disposition can foster success in careers (such as accounting or data analysis) or hobbies that depend on a strong ability to focus on details and strong pattern recognition. Indeed, research examining individuals diagnosed with anorexia nervosa and autism (two common OC conditions) reveals poorer performance on tasks demanding global processing (Happé & Frith, 2006; Lang et al., 2014; Lang & Tchanturia, 2014) and superior capacities for detail-focused or local processing (Aloi et al., 2015; Lopez et al., 2008; Lopez et al., 2009; Losh et al., 2009). Plus, when detail-focused processing combines with the other predispositions, it can exacerbate maladaptive perfectionism and interfere with the ability to get work done in a timely manner. When you're so good at finding flaws, nothing is ever good enough to be considered finished (yikes!).

Superior biotemperamental capacities for detail-focused processing can also cause difficulties in relationships. You might criticize (directly or indirectly) or appear disapproving of those who fail live up to your standards for precision and thoroughness.

Low reward sensitivity. This refers to the tendency for OC people to be less responsive to the positive things in life. Low temperamental reward sensitivity (or positive affectivity) has been linked primarily with depression (Clark & Watson, 1991; Durbin et al., 2005) and to a lesser extent, schizophrenia and social phobia (see Mineka et al., 1998; Watson & Naragon-Gainey, 2010). In OC people, this manifests in their being generally less excitable, having less positive emotion and enthusiasm, and finding rewarding experiences to be generally less emotionally powerful, pleasurable, or enduring. Low reward sensitivity also means that OC people often find social situations less rewarding compared to others. This, when combined with high threat sensitivity, tends to result in OC people being less motivated to engage in social interactions, or approaching them with dread rather than anticipation. As a result, social situations are often engaged out of a sense of duty or obligation, rather than because they look forward to the company of others.

High threat sensitivity. This refers to a tendency to interpret situations that are actually neutral or ambiguous as threatening. When combined with high detail-focused processing, it means that OC people are likely to notice small changes in their environment and interpret those to indicate potential danger. For example, an OC individual might be more likely to notice small changes in someone's facial expression and interpret them as a sign of rejection. As a result, OC people tend to be extremely sensitive to signs of social rejection and often expect to be ostracized or rejected. Heightened threat sensitivity also means that rejection is often felt more intensely and anticipated with anxiety and worry. For example, research examining behavioral inhibition among anxious, solitary children characterized by shy, timid, standoffish, or verbally inhibited behavior has shown that they may be biotemperamentally hypersensitive—hardwired to experience social rejection more negatively (London et al., 2007). But since OC people also tend to have strong inhibitory control, they rarely display their apprehension openly or directly ask for help. Instead, they quietly suffer alone. Plus, as we'll learn in the next chapter, heightened threat sensitivity neurobiologically impedes capacities for the prosocial, friendly social signaling that's essential for social connectedness.

To summarize, when you're OC, you may be biologically predisposed to be threat sensitive (e.g. when you're walking into a rose garden, you might be more likely to notice the thorns first, flowers second), experience lower reward sensitivity (e.g., you're not particularly excitable and hard to impress), exhibit high detail-focused processing (e.g., you're likelier to notice minor discrepancies or errors in the environment—a tilted frame, a typo, or misaligned wire in a jet engine), and possess superior capacities for inhibitory control (e.g., you can keep it together and plan ahead even under high stress). These biological predispositions are often adaptive. Yet, as we've learned, they can also cause problems when they're extreme or context-inappropriate. But biotemperamental predispositions are only part of the story when it comes to understanding OC. There are also transactions within the socio-biographic environment (*nurture*) that are posited to exacerbate biotemperamental predispositions (*nature*)—and vice versa. The next section outlines how socio-biographic environment plays a role in the development and maintenance of OC tendencies.

Sociobiographic Influences (Nurture)

Your sociobiographic environment encompasses a wide range of external events, settings, or experiences that can impact your perceptions and responses—including family, peers, culture, workplace, educational settings, and historical events or experiences, such as trauma and loss, as well as environmental stressors, like famine, pollution, or natural disasters. RO DBT posits that family and cultural expectations prioritizing performance, high achievement, and not making mistakes function to reinforce maladaptive perfectionism and OC coping (Lynch, 2018a). As we have learned, the OC brain not only possesses innate capacities for superior self-control; it's hardwired to be detail-focused and to notice the potential for threat over the potential for reward.

Imagine an OC brain growing up in an environment where it received messages like:

- Never let them see you sweat.
- Mistakes are intolerable.
- Expressing emotions is undignified.
- Being correct is more important than being liked.
- Winning is imperative.

Chances are that their biotemperamental predispositions would be reinforced. For example, repeated family or cultural messages stressing mistakes as unacceptable may inadvertently communicate to a child that they're never good enough and result in risk-avoidant behavior, hypersensitivity to perceived criticism, maladaptive perfectionism, and self-worth that's based solely on how well they perform compared to others (Lynch, 2018a). Maladaptive perfectionism has been linked to extreme family enmeshment and authoritarian parenting styles (Craddock et al., 2009). Longitudinal research using a community-based sample found mothers' reports of childhood emotional distance (e.g., "I do not praise my child") to be associated with an increased risk of avoidant, paranoid symptoms among their children, even after controlling for physical or sexual trauma, physical neglect, and other personality disorder symptoms (Johnson, et al., 2000).

Family and cultural values of high performance can reinforce notions that a child already is or should be special, different, or superior compared to their peers (e.g., more intelligent, compliant, responsible, diligent, or skillful)—and *that's a lot of pressure!* A strong family focus on performance also tends to trigger a lot of social comparison, as the child needs to constantly check whether they're doing well enough compared to others. Moreover, childhood experiences with peers are also a powerful influence. For example, children with inhibited temperaments early in life have been shown to be more prone to bullying by their peers (Gladstone et al., 2006). Bullying may exacerbate OC behaviors associated with avoidance, risk aversion, and aloof interpersonal styles (Perren & Alsaker, 2006). Plus, overcontrolled kids are often ostracized and rejected (e.g., not being picked for the team or invited to a party; other children not wanting to sit next to them, and so on).

Note the examples listed above are only a small subset of the wide range of possible sociobiographic experiences that can impact a person's life. And BTW, trying to list all that are possible—is impossible (boo hoo). It's also important to recognize that sociobiographic experience can generalize to other areas of one's life unrelated to the original experience—and not always in helpful ways. When a previously neutral stimulus, like being asked for an opinion, becomes paired with extreme fear—for example, every time you shared an opinion your mother disliked, she locked you in a closet—the fear can generalize to other situations: being asked for an opinion by anyone comes to feel scary. The problem is that, in most situations, opinion sharing is an important part of healthy interactions—and avoiding this functions to maintain the original fear, since you never learn that most people don't consider a different opinion a bad thing. Let's hear an example of this principle from Elijah.

I remember when I was about eight or nine, I took a book out of the school library about how an entire library was eaten by a book and this adventurous reader eventually saved the day. I was reading the book in the living room and my dad came in because he heard me laughing. He said, "Nothing is so funny that you need the neighbors hearing you laugh like an idiot. You sound like a braying donkey." He then took the book from me and read the title, and said with a sneer, "You think this is funny? You need to grow up and quit acting like a child." I'd never thought about my laugh before, but let me tell you, I never laughed like that again.

Elijah's story is a good example of how a perfectionistic OC child learns "If I inhibit my expressions of emotion, I can avoid being criticized." Unfortunately, suppressing emotional expression (e.g., inhibiting laughter) when the context calls for emotional expression (e.g., having a laugh with friends)—is not a good way to avoid criticism (or keep friends). For example, Elijah's inhibited social signaling habit, originally learned at home, generalized to other settings. His peers came to see him as "uptight" or "no fun," because he never laughed heartily at their jokes. That eventually resulted in him receiving fewer invites from friends for shared time together. Indeed, robust research shows that we not only become anxiously aroused when interacting with a non-expressive person, but we also prefer not to spend more time with them (e.g., Gross, 2002; Butler & Gross., 2003). The point is, Elijah's interaction with his dad impacted how he behaved—not just at home when around his father, but also elsewhere and with other people.

What types of social signaling habits have you picked up from your sociobiographic environment? How have they impacted your relationships and your social environment?

____

____

____

Would you teach a child to signal or behave in a similar manner? If not, why not?

____

____

____

What might your answer tell you about these signals' prosocial utility?

____

____

____

And for fun (tee hee), pick one of your habits, ideally something you do everyday—like checking your phone during conversations, answering a question with a question, or changing the topic when emotions are discussed. For the next week, monitor its frequency, when and where it occurs, and with whom. (For a worksheet version of this exercise, visit http://www.newharbinger.com/50782.) Immediately after you display the signal, observe how it impacts the behavior of others. For example, do they appear *more* or *less* engaged, interested, pleased, or attentive? Or do they suddenly apologize, look away, change the topic, or start to talk faster? And BTW, don't feel like you need to do anything about what you observe. Meaning, don't try to fix it (that's what perfectionists do, tee hee). Watch what happens instead, and record your observations below at the next opportunity. (And if nothing seems to happen, that's okay too.) Do save your observations for later; in future chapters, we'll be teaching you some skills to change those social signaling habits that are likely to damage relationships (kinda cool, eh?).

The social signaling habit or behavior I'm tracking: ______________________________

When and Where It Happened	With Whom	How It Impacted Others' Behavior	Other Observations

Sometimes, however, the negative consequences of a sociobiographic experience are not particularly apparent—or may even seem like a good thing. Here is an example of this from Tula.

> *When I think about my childhood, what stands out is how structured my life was. I don't really remember a lot of free play or imagination time. Even today, days off work stress me out. Plus, everything I was involved with as a child—Girl Scouts, chess club, sports—seemed to value structure, achievement, rules, conformity, and behaving properly. When I started babysitting as my first job, I remember my parents being really impressed by my "maturity." Word soon got out that I was "a very responsible young lady." But what people didn't know was that my demeanor of responsibility was actually a cover. More babysitting jobs made it easier for me to justify not having time to interact with my peers or avoid social events. And what's interesting is, over time, no one seemed to notice my absences. Eventually I decided that no one really cared—which, I now realize, resulted in me isolating from others even more.*

The point of Tula's story is that families or environments that emphasize rule following or being orderly—like never missing deadlines, or setting punishments for being unruly or late or not keeping one's room tidy—can inadvertently encourage OC coping. Sociobiographic messages prioritizing dutifulness, discipline, persistence, and self-sacrifice can help children strengthen innate capacities for self-control, build a sense of self-efficacy, and achieve long-term goals—but for kids already biologically predisposed to be self-controlled or inhibited, they may foster the development of maladaptive perfectionism and overcontrolled coping.

Take a moment now to consider your own environments as a child. What type of messages did you receive that may have steered you toward an overcontrolled coping style?

Messages my environment sent me:

1. ____

2. ____

3. ____

4. ____

Now, let's step back a moment, and imagine how a child might learn how to cope, depending on the type of message received from their environment. For example, if a child is told that mistakes were intolerable, they might learn to avoid taking risks. What's the upside to this? You avoid appearing vulnerable or making mistakes. And the downside? You're less likely to feel the thrill of uncertainty and spontaneous joy—which often come from taking chances. Plus, never taking risks makes it less likely you'll learn anything new! That said, as we learned in chapter 1, many OC individuals consider themselves risk takers—and they are, with certain types of risk. For example, they might skydive, they might do stand-up comedy, or they might go on roller coasters. However, all these risks are calculated risks, which require planning, rehearsal, and often, mandated safety measures.

What types of risks do you take?

____

____

____

OC coping is also often encouraged by sociobiographic messages valuing performance and achievement—which can lead to compulsive striving, and never resting between achievements. As previously noted, there's an upside: perseverance and achieving goals often leads to job promotions, awards, and financial success. But the downside of compulsive striving is that you're exhausted most of the time and rarely stop to relish your success—it's always time for the next task on your list.

Use the following exercise to get a sense of where you stand when it comes to having fun. (And, to make the exercise more fun and memorable—tee hee—share your answers with a friend!)

Exercise: Are We Having Fun Yet?

(Adapted from Lynch, 2018b, pp. 133–144.)

How many of my recreational activities are competitive in nature? If I'm not winning, do I still find the activity enjoyable?

____

____

____

How serious am I about my recreational activities? How often do I engage in recreation, relaxing, or fun that doesn't require any preplanning or preparation?

____

____

____

How much time each day do I allow myself time to rest, play, or do nothing? Do I ever take a nap?

____

____

How often do I read a book or watch a TV program that's not teaching me something or about self-improvement?

____

____

Have I ever been given feedback that I work too hard or that I need to relax? Do I find it hard to self-soothe, relax, or experience pleasure without guilt?

____

____

To what extent do I believe it immoral or selfish to engage in behaviors that are for pleasure or have no obvious productive value? To what extent do I believe that relaxing, playing, or recreation must be earned?

____

____

____

What do I find amusing? What's so amusing about what I find amusing?

____

____

How often do I find myself laughing, chuckling, or giggling, without trying?

____

____

The sociobiographic environments OC people grow up in also often convey values of stoicism, fortitude, and perseverance, which are intended to bolster their abilities to tolerate distress. But because OC individuals already possess superior capacities for self-control, they naturally tolerate physical and emotional pain longer and without complaint, compared to most other people. It's a great skill to have—but it can also lead to problems. For example, never complaining is not a very good idea when things are seriously wrong. Say your finger is about to fall off because of gangrene, or say you delay going to the doctor only to find you have cancer that would've been curable if you'd sought help earlier. Negative health consequences, injury, and exhaustion are often the consequence of overtolerance of distress. OC people might exercise despite a nagging pain or injury, put off booking the dentist or doctor despite intuitive concern or persistent pain, or continue to work ridiculous hours or in toxic working conditions despite being burned out. *Are there areas in your life where you tolerate distress too much or in an unhealthy way?*

____

____

____

Another consequence of sociobiographic influences are family and cultural expectations about always appearing self-controlled and never revealing weakness. The ways these expectations are communicated can vary widely. There might be messages valuing the importance of being correct over being connected, that people can't be trusted, or that being dependent on someone is foolish. Such messages reinforce emotional reserve and an aloof and distant style of relating. Indeed, as noted in chapter 1, masking (e.g., smiling to hide anger) and inhibiting expressions of emotion are core features of OC coping. In the short term, pervasive masking and inhibition of emotions may help you feel safe or avoid unwanted embarrassment—but in the long run, they make it harder for people get to know who you really are, making loneliness and isolation the most likely outcome. Plus, if you never reveal vulnerability, people may come to think of you as arrogant. And, if you never ask for help, not only will you never get any; you may start to feel burned out. Ultimately, masking and inhibiting expressions of emotion will strongly impact how you engage with other people and the types of relationships you form.

Interestingly, how an OC individual's aloof and distant relationship style might manifest can vary considerably. It might be covertly changing the topic of a conversation to avoid revealing personal information, or issuing stern glances of disapproval whenever others joke, laugh, or tease, or controlling the topic of conversations, or providing vague answers when asked for your opinion, such as "I don't know," "Probably," or "It just depends." Other ways aloofness can manifest include:

- Rarely using terms of endearment or expressions of love
- Appearing bored or indifferent to other people's problems

- Lack of reciprocity (e.g., mutual smiling, laughing, or crying) during social interactions
- Feigning interest by asking questions but not really listening to the answer
- Pretending to be engaged by frequently smiling and nodding when others speak
- Answering questions with a question to avoid a genuine answer
- Phony and conspicuous displays of excessive concern or flattering behavior that are unnecessary, unasked for, or inappropriate for the context or nature of the relationship

What is the upside to this? Well, people leave you alone. And the downside? You end up alone. Although masking and inhibited emotional expressions are intended to avoid criticism and keep you safe, in the long run, they do the opposite. Because your social signaling style feels phony or impossible to read, people avoid interacting with you, leading you to feel more and more like an outsider and increasingly unsure how to connect with others.

Okay, we've now covered all the core features of RO DBT's biosocial theory—how *nature* influences *nurture*, and vice versa—and its impact on *coping*, See figure 2.1 for a visual summary of the model.

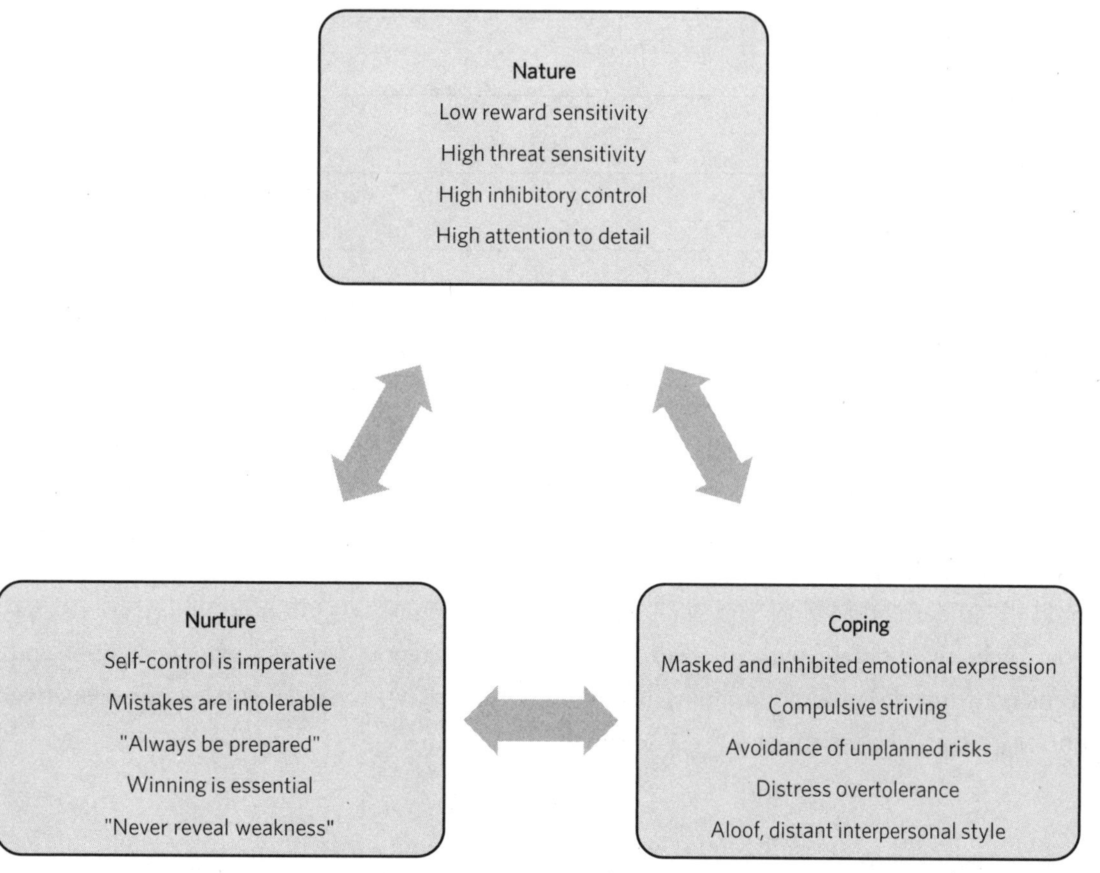

Figure 2.1. Biosocial Theory of Perfectionistic Overcontrol (adapted from Lynch, 2018a)

Now, take a moment to consider all that you've just learned regarding the biosocial model. And think about the key ways these coping strategies may have manifested and been reinforced in your own life. Here are a few examples to get you started:

- ☐ If I'm always the hardest worker, no one can complain about me.
- ☐ By keeping people at arm's length, I can avoid embarrassment.
- ☐ If I just tell everyone "I'm fine," I can avoid conflict.
- ☐ By keeping relationships superficial, I can avoid feeling obligated to anyone but myself.
- ☐ If I amass enough achievement, I will finally feel adequate.
- ☐ By not complaining, I won't burden those around me.

Now for yours:

- ☐ ______________________________
- ☐ ______________________________
- ☐ ______________________________
- ☐ ______________________________
- ☐ ______________________________

If you pause and take a look at your list, you might also ask yourself what valued goals may be blocked by your ways of coping. But before you answer, let's take a look at what we mean by valued goals.

Values are the principles or standards that a person considers important in life, which help guide how they live. They help us determine our priorities in life and assess the degree to which our life's turning out the way we envisioned it. When we fail to live by our values, we often feel an underlying dissatisfaction or discomfort. *Goals*, on the other hand, are the means by which a value is expressed or achieved (Lynch, 2018a). Thus, if you *value* having a family, your *goal* might to be find a romantic partner. OC folks tend to "underreport values and goals that have obvious links to interpersonal relationships (such as a goal of being intimate with another person) and overreport valued goals associated with self-improvement (to work harder), autonomy (to live independently), achievement (to be productive), and self-control (to think before they act)" (Lynch, 2018a, p. 123).

Overcontrolled Individuals Value Self-Control

Examples of common OC values linked to self-control include competency, achievement, restraint, temperance, fairness, politeness, self-sacrifice, accuracy, integrity, service, responsibility, dedication, self-improvement, honesty, accountability, and discipline.

Yet all of these values depend upon a social context for meaning; that is, they are virtuous not just because they are difficult to live by, but also because they function to contribute to the well-being of one's tribe. For example, values for service, fairness, and honesty are cherished because they place the needs of others over the needs of the individual. (Lynch, 2018a, pp. 123–124)

Regardless, identifying valued goals can be difficult. Many struggle with knowing *what they want* or *desire out of life* because they've spent a lifetime focusing on *what they don't want*. Use the questions below (also available at http://www.newharbinger.com/50782) to help clarify your values.

1. When it comes to family, friends, and work, what are the things you consider most important?

   ____

   ____

2. What attributes do you admire in others?

   ____

   ____

3. What ideals would you consider important to teach a child?

   ____

   ____

4. What attributes would you hope others might use to describe you—e.g., at your funeral?

   ____

   ____

Below are some examples of values and goals. Check any that might apply to you and then add more of your own:

Example of Value	Example of Goal	My Goals
• Honesty, integrity	☐ To admit when I am wrong or have harmed another without falling apart ☐ To stand up for injustice, with humility	
• Kindness	☐ To make sacrifices for another person, without always expecting something in return ☐ To recognize that it is arrogant to expect the world or others to conform to my personal beliefs ☐ To celebrate others' success without resenting their advantage	
• Flexible responding	☐ To ask for help when I need it ☐ To openly reveal my feelings when the situation calls for it ☐ To let go of plans when they're not working	
• Family, friends	☐ To work out misunderstandings rather than walk away or hold grudges ☐ To notice what was done well when correcting my kids ☐ To start dating ☐ To apologize when I've been unkind and repair any damage that may have occurred	

Example of Value	Example of Goal	My Goals
• Openness, learning	☐ To nonjudgmentally listen to opinions from people who hold different values or morals than me ☐ To be open to feedback even when it hurts ☐ To take a risk when I don't know the outcome	
• Other possible values?	• Other possible goals?	

Okay, well done! Now take a look at your list of valued goals. *To what extent are they about self-improvement, independence, productivity, or planning ahead—versus about relationships, intimacy, friendship, openness, or flexible responding? What might your answer tell you about yourself or what you might need to learn?*

____

____

____

BTW, it's okay to add to your list over time. Although values generally don't change very much, your goals, or how your values are expressed, often change or need to be adjusted to match changing circumstances. And don't lose your list of valued goals, because—spoiler alert—we'll be referring to them again in later chapters. Which brings us to the end of this chapter (boo hoo).

So, Now You Know

In this chapter, we've learned more about RO DBT's biosocial theory: how perfectionistic, overcontrolled coping likely results from transactions between innate biological predispositions (nature) and family, cultural, and environmental experiences (nurture). OC folks are born with brains hardwired to *notice the potential for harm* over the potential for reward in any given situation; to *automatically notice minor errors*, like a misplaced comma (but don't tell our editors—tee hee!); and *inhibit impulses and emotional expressions*, making it possible for them to feel highly anxious on the inside but not show any emotion on the outside. Family, cultural, and environmental experiences that emphasize the importance of self-control, performing well, and not making mistakes can exacerbate OC biotemperamental predispositions and stoke the development of a maladaptive, overcontrolled style of coping. Though OC people can control impulses and expressions of emotion, delay gratification, and tolerate distress for long periods of time, they often feel lonely and isolated from others. Lastly, we learned the importance of living by your values, and practiced identifying our valued goals, which we'll revisit in later chapters.

Our next chapter takes theory a step further. We'll show you how RO DBT uses findings from brain-behavioral science to understand and help people change emotional responses, to really live by valued goals and create a life worth sharing. Yowsers!

CHAPTER 3

Understanding Emotional Responses

When Nicole was a kid, her family's television set didn't have a lot of channels—way fewer, if you counted only the Canadian ones. And when Tom was a kid, it was just live footage of dinosaurs (tee hee). Fast forward to today, where we have seemingly endless options for what we watch and when. When it comes to our brains, we tend to think we have endless options too. But unlike TV programming, our evolutionary programming hasn't changed all that much. Our modern brains are the same as our primordial ancestors'. From an evolutionary point of view, there hasn't been much need for change. Our original programming still gets the job done—it maximizes individual and species survival.

The aim of this chapter is to update your understanding of your neural programming by introducing a novel *neurobiological model of socioemotional responding* (Lynch, 2018a). We'll also show how this theory will be practically applied, linking as it does to skills we'll be teaching in later chapters (Yowsers!).

The Five Emotionally Evocative Channels

Unlike the nearly limitless channel-surfing capabilities built into modern TVs, our brains come with a mere five channels of programming. That is, they have five *neural substrates*—which is fancy brain language for areas of our nervous system that respond to differing classes of emotional stimuli important for survival (Lynch, 2018a). In other words, each class of stimuli is associated with its own unique neural substrate and pattern of bodily responses, which influence our desire to connect with others and our nonverbal social signaling, such as our facial expressions, voice tone, and body posture (Lynch, 2018a; Porges, 2003). The five classes of emotionally evocative stimuli, or *cues*, are:

- Safety
- Novelty
- Reward
- Threat
- Overwhelm

Our neurosensory system constantly scans the world and ourselves for the presence of cues, or stimuli relevant to our well-being. When we detect something new or unexpected, we quickly evaluate or judge it as safe, novel, rewarding, threatening, overwhelming, or some combination of these, such as when a stimulus has both rewarding and threatening aspects (e.g., a hive dripping with honey and swarming with bees; Lynch, 2018b).

Cues, which most often occur outside of our awareness, can be internal, external, or contextual. *Internal cues* are inside the body, such as thoughts, sensations, or memories (e.g., a sensation of nausea, a memory of a mistake you made years ago, a craving for a cigarette). *External cues* occur outside the body, such as noises, sights, or odors (e.g., a dog barking; a warm, gentle breeze; seeing someone we love; the scent of jasmine in the air). *Contextual* factors include things like time of day or year, physical fatigue, substance use, or food deprivation. They indirectly impact how we evaluate other cues. For example, an apple will more likely be evaluated as a potential "reward" when a person is hungry. They can also vary depending on age or type of experience. For example, toddlers often cry—whereas school-age children laugh—when a circus clown or Halloween "monster" approaches.

Okay, you might be thinking. *Why does knowing all this matter?*

The short answer: if you know which neural substrates are being activated at any given moment, you'll know how to change it (that is, if you wanted to; tee hee). It also matters, because when one of the five neural substrates is fired up as a result of a cue, it not only changes physiology in milliseconds; it also changes your desires to spend time with others, as well as how you socially signal.

Let's dig a little deeper and discover how each channel shows up for you.

Safety cues are stimuli associated with feeling protected, secure, loved, fulfilled, cared for, and part of a community or tribe. Our natural set point (ideally) is a state of safety, and calm readiness and openness—which includes an ongoing, low-level processing of environmental inputs or stimuli. Safety cues trigger a calm-friendly state, linked to a brain-neural substrate known as the ventral vagal complex (VVC; Porges, 2011), which is part of the parasympathetic nervous system (PNS). The VVC constitutes our social safety system. Its nerves govern the muscles in our body needed to communicate and form close social bonds (Porges, 2007). Middle-ear muscles help us hear better what others are saying by tuning into the higher-frequency sound vibrations associated with human speech; voice box muscles help us communicate warmth and friendliness to others via a musical tone of voice; facial muscles signal authenticity and trustworthiness by openly revealing (not hiding) facial expressions of emotion (Porges, 2011). According to our model, social safety responses trigger social engagement signals. Our body is relaxed, our heart rate slows, and our breathing slows and deepens; our facial expressions match our inner experience; we can effortlessly make eye contact and accurately listen to others, and we're likely to want to be touched or touch another (Lynch, 2018a). Yet when social safety cues are withdrawn or not present, the social safety system's regulation of the muscles of the face and head is downregulated, automatically impairing our capacity for empathy or friendly prosocial signaling (Porges, 2011).

Social-safety cues vary widely. Possible examples include a warm cup of milk, a stroll in the park, a laughing child, a smile or hug, a person's voice, stroking a beloved pet, a happy memory, an image of a loving parent, time with a good friend, and so forth.

Take a moment to reflect: *What cues trigger feelings of safety in you? How often do you experience social safety?*

____

____

____

____

____

Novelty cues are discrepant or unexpected stimuli that trigger an automatic process by which we determine whether the cue is important for our well-being. Our social safety system's calm-friendly state is briefly withdrawn. We freeze, hold our breath, and turn our attention towards the novel cue (Bracha, 2004; Schauer & Elbert, 2015). Our body is immobile but prepared to move, we are alert but not aroused (Lynch, 2018a). An automatic appraisal process begins.

• *The Story of Two Friends, Episode 1: "What Is It?"*

(Adapted from Lynch, 2018b.)

Imagine you're walking with a friend down your neighborhood street, having just finished a nice cup of tea. You both comment on the unusual quiet— traffic seems nonexistent. You notice ahead in the distance, on the other side of the street, what looks like a large crowd of people. Both of you stop and stare, holding your breath as you strain to discern what's happening. Something is peculiar; many of the people are standing in the middle of the street. Some are laughing as if something's hilarious; others are shaking their heads as if in disapproval. You continue to stare—your brain is trying to figure out the significance of this unexpected event. Is this a good thing or a bad thing? Will it be helpful or harmful to move closer?

The above episode illustrates how, when unexpected, discrepant, or novel things happen, the brain quickly tries to determine whether what's happening is important to our well-being. Essentially, it's trying to determine, often in milliseconds, whether the novel stimulus is safe, threatening, rewarding, or overwhelming.

Take a moment to reflect: *What are recent examples of novelty cues in your life? When you encounter something new or unexpected—do you tend to see the potential for reward or the potential for harm? What might this tell you about your way of responding to the world?*

____

____

____

____

____

Rewarding cues are stimuli we appraise as potentially gratifying or pleasurable. Our sympathetic nervous system (SNS)'s excitatory approach system is activated. We experience a sense of anticipation that something pleasurable is about to occur. Let's return to our story of two friends.

• *The Story of Two Friends, Episode 2: "It's a Parade!"*

As you recall, our first episode concluded with you and your friend unexpectedly encountering a crowd of people in the middle of your street. Your novelty-evaluation system was triggered by this event, which momentarily deactivated your social safety system. You both stopped and stared intently at the crowd, trying to ascertain its significance. Now let's imagine that your friend is delighted by this new discovery! They want to approach it. They smile broadly, turn to you, and excitedly exclaim, "Wow, it's a parade! Let's go see!" They begin tugging on your sleeve and urge you to move closer.

Episode 2 shows what happens when a novelty cue (an unexpected crowd of people) is evaluated as a *potential reward*. When our reward system is activated, we feel excited and elated; our heart rate goes up and we breathe faster. Our conversations are more animated, making us more fun to be around. However, there are some downsides to reward states. The more extreme they are, the harder it is for us to respond from a stance of calm readiness and openness; our social-safety system becomes deactivated or inhibited. Even as we feel on top of the world, we lose our ability to empathically read the subtle social signals displayed by others, and we're less aware of how our behavior may impact them. For example, we may fail to notice that another person appears to be in pain, or angry or sad about something, or bored, wanting to change the topic. We may also be unaware that we're speaking more rapidly in conversation, not allowing time for others to speak, or frequently talking over or interrupting them. We're more likely to be arrogant and opinionated, and to overestimate our abilities, while underestimating the abilities of others.

What cues trigger rewarding or pleasurable experiences for you? How often do you feel excited and animated? What might your answers tell you about yourself?

____

____

____

____

____

Threatening cues are stimuli appraised as potentially dangerous or harmful. When we feel threatened, we experience a sense of anticipation that something bad might happen or a desired goal might be blocked. Sympathetic nervous system (SNS) defensive arousal is activated, triggering feelings of anxiety or irritation, and an urge to flee or attack (fight or flight). Our social safety system is turned off or inhibited; we lose our ability for empathy and empathetic perception and prosocial friendly signaling becomes impaired. We can only force a fake smile; our facial expressions are constricted, our voice tone becomes monotonic, our gestures are tight and non-expansive, and we're more likely to avert our gaze or stare with hostility, and misinterpret what another person says.

• *The Story of Two Friends, Episode 3: "No, It's a Riot!"*

Recall that our last episode ended with your friend's SNS reward and excitatory approach system being activated, leading them to excitedly encourage you to join them in their pursuit of what they believed was a parade. Now let's imagine that your appraisal of the situation is different. Your brain perceives this mass of people as potentially dangerous, not rewarding. While your friend excitedly smiles and urges you to approach the crowd, your body tenses, your heart begins to race, and your facial expression becomes flat. Your easy manner disappears. You grab your friend and earnestly shout, "NO! It's not a parade—it's a riot. We need to get out of here! RUN!" You pull your friend towards you and begin running away from the crowd. You are sweating and breathing hard, and desperate to escape.

Episode 3 shows what happens when a novelty cue (an unexpected crowd of people) is interpreted as a *potential threat* and fight/flight responses are triggered. It also illustrates how two people can interpret the same cues in exactly opposite ways! Bodily sensations make each evaluation "feel like truth" to the person making the evaluation—which is one reason differing perceptions of same events often lead to arguments.

How often do you interpret things differently from other people? To what extent do you think your disagreements with others pertain to differing interpretations about events?

What types of cues trigger defensive reactions on your part or feelings of threat, anxiety, or irritation?

Put a checkmark next to the cues you wrote about that involve people, relationships, or social interactions. What might this tell you about your life, your way of being, or what you need to learn?

Overwhelming cues trigger our emergency shutdown system. When higher-order, emotion-based action tendencies are overwhelmed—when fleeing or fighting don't work, and it looks like we might be dinner for that bear—our brain-body copes by "turning everything off" in order to conserve energy and maximize survival. Shutdown responses involve activation of the PNS's "old vagus," or dorsal vagal complex (DVC; Porges, 2007), a neural pathway innervating the gut that, in the day-to-day, functions to regulate digestion. In shutdown, our heart rate, breathing, and body movements slow down; fear, anger, and other powerful emotions fade away. We become immobilized and experience pain less intensely. We may dissociate or faint. Social safety signaling is deactivated—and, like zombies, we look and feel emotionally numb. DVC activation and shutdown responses have been linked to behaviors common in chronic depression, like loss of interest, lethargy, and social withdrawal (Marvel et al., 2004).

Interestingly, overwhelming reward can be the eliciting cue for a shutdown response no less than overwhelming stress or pain, like boarding a plane when you're afraid of flying or being involved in a bad accident. Although experiences of overwhelming reward are rare, the brain responds to them the same way it would to overwhelming threat (Lynch, 2018b). For example, imagine being next to a very famous person you have longed to meet—but being blocked by three bodyguards—just as your smiling idol turns to greet you. Your reward feels so close, yet impossible to reach—overwhelming your SNS excitatory approach system and triggering your older evolutionary PNS-DVC shutdown system, which is designed to inhibit or turn off fruitless approach efforts. When this occurs, you suddenly lose interest in meeting your idol. You stop smiling; your face and voice go flat. You feel increasingly detached, numb, and light-headed—just before you faint (wow!). Film clips from the 1960s, showing teenagers fainting during press conferences given by the Beatles, show exactly that. Let's see an example of DVC activation in Episode 4 of our story of two friends (yippee!).

• *The Story of Two Friends—Episode 4: "The Collapse"*

Recall that our last episode ended with your friend ignoring your warnings and excitedly approaching the unexpected crowd—while you were sweating, breathing hard, and running away. As you fled, you glance backwards. You can no longer see your friend—but you do see three very large people wearing identical white uniforms and masks, break from the crowd and point in your direction. They start running towards you—chanting "Teeth! Teeth! Glorious teeth!" You try to run even faster—but your pursuers are faster still. One of them grabs you from behind. You turn and try to knock them aside. But to no avail, because they are too strong. And before you know it, all three are upon you. They throw you into the back of a van and tie you to a reclining chair with a bright light overhead. You freeze in terror but continue to seek a means of escape. You are still able to move, but the bonds are too tight, and there appears to be no means of escape. You feel helpless and an urge to give up (a PNS-DVC flag response). To make matters worse, the villains force your mouth open and begin poking and prodding your teeth with pointy objects and tubes, their efforts accompanied by low-level whirring and gurgling sounds. But you don't feel any pain. Instead, you feel increasingly detached from the situation and can barely hear what your abductors are saying—right before you lose consciousness and faint (PNS-DVC shutdown is fully activated).

Epilogue

When you regain consciousness, you find yourself sitting in a police car next to a kindly officer who is attempting to explain what happened. It seems you've been the latest victim of the Order of Maleficent Flossing Gurus (OMFG), a reprobate cabal of dental hygienists gone rogue (OMFG, indeed!). You smile weakly and take a deep breath. You feel a bit worn out but are pleasantly surprised to discover that your teeth feel exceptionally clean and your breath minty-fresh (social safety [PNS-VVC] system has started to reengage).

Episode 4 shows what happens when your SNS defensive-arousal system doesn't work as intended. You're being chased by a group of people; you try to run away, but they're too fast. You try to fight them off, but they're too strong. So, what does your brain-body do? It shuts down, to conserve energy, making survival more likely. Episode 4 illustrates how shutdown processes include initial flagging responses involving disinterest, apathy, and urges to give up (i.e., partial DVC activation), followed by numbing, pain insensitivity, and loss of consciousness (full DVC activation) when escape is impossible. The epilogue, in turn, illustrates how our neuroregulatory system adjusts to changing circumstances—in this case, by re-activating the social-safety system when you woke next to that kindly police officer and it became clear that the threat had passed.

Take a moment to reflect. *Are there times that you feel numbed out, shut down, or unresponsive to events or people around you? What cues trigger a shutdown response in you? How often do they occur? Are they more likely to occur when you are around other people or when you are alone? How do they impact other people? What might your answers to these questions tell you about yourself or the way you see the world?*

____

____

____

____

____

____

Putting Theory into Practice

Okay, now that we know more about our socioemotional programming, it's time to put theory into practice. As we learned in chapter 1, compulsive striving and perfectionistic overcontrolled coping are exhausting habits. *So, how does one find the energy to change a habit that is perpetually energy-depleting? (Yowsers!)* Plus, as we learned in chapter 2, maladaptive perfectionistic overcontrol is partially biologically based, and OC biotemperamental predispositions often influence perception and regulation at the preconscious level, in milliseconds. So, how do you change something that you don't even know has occurred? (Double yowsers!) RO DBT addresses these conundrums by teaching bottom-up regulatory skills, moving from body to brain, that conserve energy and reduce the potential negative influences of biotemperament.

These skills are informed by experimental research showing neuroinhibitory relationships between the parasympathetic nervous system (PNS) and the sympathetic nervous system (SNS; see Berntson et al., 1991; Porges, 1995). What this means: the brain system that arouses us (i.e., the SNS) and the brain system that calms us (i.e., the PNS) operate as antagonists; when one is on, the other is off (Berntson et al., 1991). For example, *have you ever noticed that you cannot feel both calm and fearful at the same time?* Similarly, we cannot simultaneously experience genuine joy and real anger at the same moment in time. Plus, our neuroregulatory system is bidirectional, meaning our brain (how we think) influences our body (how we act), and vice versa: our body (how we act) also influences our brain (how we think). What's double-cool is that we can *use* the contradictory relationship between the PNS and SNS to regulate emotional experience from the bottom-up—meaning, we can use our facial expressions, gestures, and body movements to alter how we feel or think on the inside.

Consequently, rather than trying to think yourself out of a biotemperamental predisposition—which is impossible—RO DBT teaches you skills to turn on or turn off antagonistic neural substrates linked to PNS and SNS activity by activating different muscle groups in your body linked to social safety. This approach enables an overcontrolled person to override biotemperamental predispositions and overlearned social signaling habits (like a flat facial expression, monotonic voice tone, and so on) during interactions, and naturally relax facial muscles and other areas of the body needed to signal an easy manner and friendly intentions. Others are then much more likely to signal similar cooperative responses, such as smiling back, which in turn maximizes the chances that social interactions become rewarding experiences. Plus, since these techniques don't require much effort to produce beneficial effects, they also provide your brain a much-needed minibreak to replenish energy reserves (which can so often be depleted when you feel you have to be "perfect" all the time). Suddenly, life can start to feel less like a burden and more like an adventure (kinda cool, eh?).

A graphic overview of the entire neuroregulatory model and how each channel impacts social signaling can be seen in the figure on the next page (adapted from Lynch, 2018a, pp. 44–45).

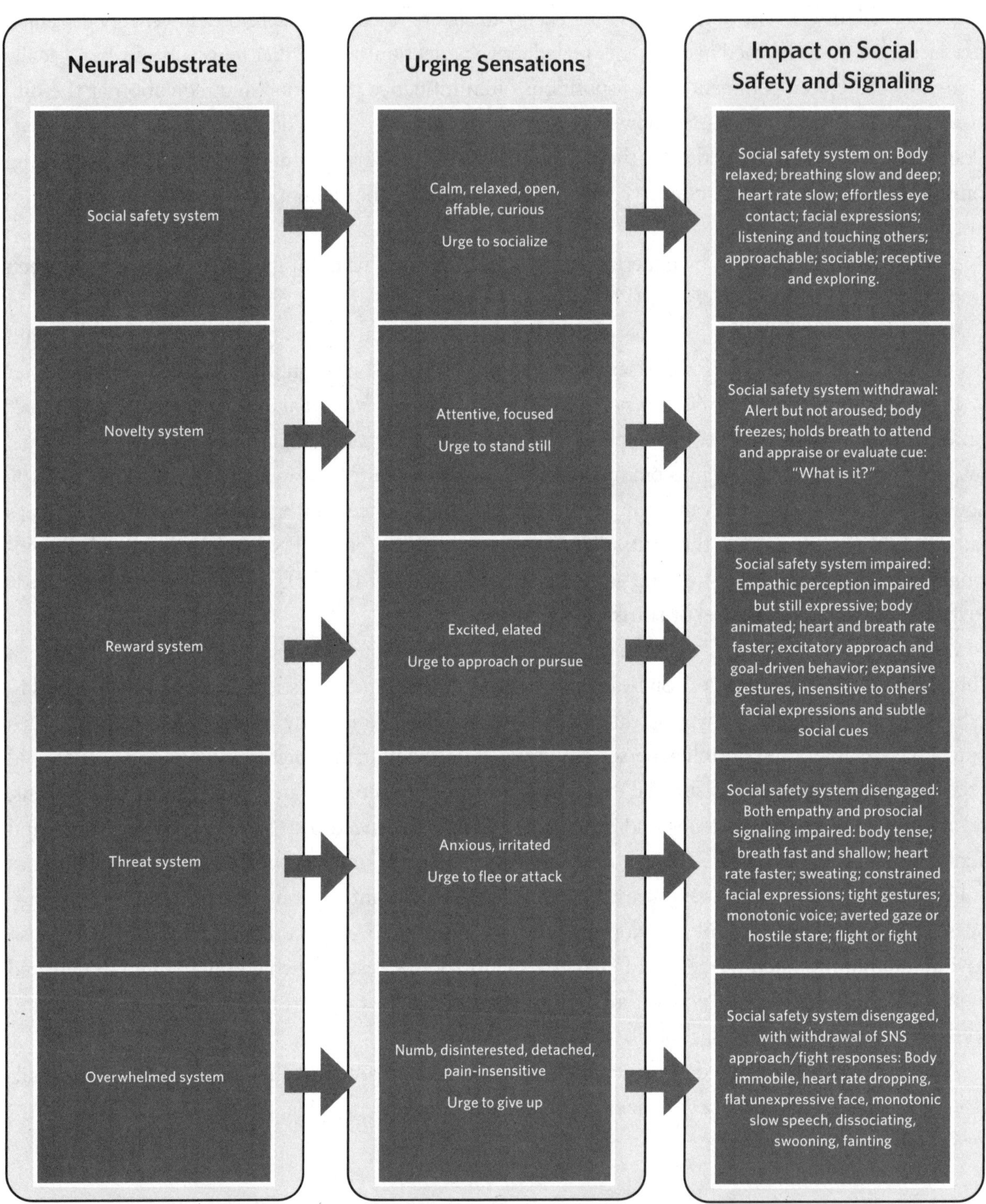

Figure 3.1. The RO DBT Neuroregulatory Model

Let's hear how this model might work from Elijah and Tula's perspectives.

• *Elijah*

I pride myself in knowing everyone in our neighborhood and strive to always be seen as helpful and caring to all. I've also been an active member of our neighborhood watch program for years. After all, to get ahead, you must get along. But sometimes I get fed up, especially when people ignore rules of etiquette or take advantage of my politeness. For example, just the other day, after a pleasant meal and nice cup of tea (social safety system on), I was out with my dog on our usual evening neighborhood stroll. I unexpectedly encountered an unfamiliar person who was also walking a dog. Since I know everyone in our neighborhood, I froze in place, and my first thought was, Who's this? *(novelty system activated). The stranger kept walking and passed me with a smile, saying, "Good evening," and then just carried on as if nothing was out of the ordinary—they didn't even explain their presence! I felt my body go tense and my mouth dry. I was barely able to reply without stuttering, saying "Yes, yes…a very pleasant evening" (threat system activated). They were gone before I had my wits about me. So, I decided to alert the neighborhood watch committee just to be on the safe side. Later I found out they were a new neighbor that had just moved in—whom I hadn't yet had a chance to meet. Oops!*

What about Tula?

• *Tula*

A couple of days ago at work, while taking a break to read a new novel by my favorite author and enjoy my favorite yogurt (social safety system on), my supervisor texted me and asked for a private meeting to discuss the current project I was working on. I froze and held my breath (novelty system activated). My mouth went dry and I started to think I was likely in big trouble, since there'd been a few delays on the project (threat system activated). When I got to his office, I was sweating, and my jaw was tight; I swear he could hear my heart pounding. I sat down and he said "Tula, is everything okay?" I sounded like a robot when I answered "Yes" and could not meet his eyes (overwhelm system partially activated). Turns out that my supervisor wanted to tell me that the delays on the project had been a blessing in disguise, because it'd allowed time for our customer to make some important adjustments in the project that would benefit everyone involved. And here I was, acting like I was about to get fired.

Both Elijah and Tula's examples are the stuff of everyday life. Notice how both stories begin with them being in a state of calm readiness and openness (social safety system on). Whereupon both then encounter an unexpected or novel cue—for Elijah, an unknown person; for Tula, an unexpected text message—cues that were quickly appraised as potentially threatening, and for Tula, eventually as overwhelming, which led to shutdown responses. Yet later, both their initial appraisals of danger were discovered to be non-threatening, or even potentially rewarding. Interestingly, the very cues Elijah and Tula appraised as threatening, other people might've read as potentially rewarding or safe. The main point is that Elijah's and Tula's stories are prototypical examples of how most OC individuals respond to novel events or unexpected stimuli—partly as a function of heightened biotemperamental threat sensitivity, but also often a function of prior learning as well.

Pulling It All Together

Knowing which neural substrate is most active at any given moment can be extremely helpful. Not only does it help you understand what you're feeling and why you're behaving the way you are; it also helps point to the types of skills you may need to practice if you wish to change the neural substrate you're currently in. The good news: a core part of the RO DBT skills taught in the upcoming chapters will focus on how to do this. But before we can change, we first need to know where we are.

Practice noticing the emotional substrate you're in and how this changes over the course of a day. *Which types of cues elicit differing substrates for you? To what extent does the activation of a particular substrate depend on the time of day, person, or type of situation you are in?* Use the checklist below (adapted from Lynch, 2018b, pp. 86–87, and available as a worksheet at http://www.newharbinger.com/50782) to help in your identification. Place a checkmark in the box that *best* describes your body sensations and social signaling style in a given scenario. BTW, it's okay to check more than one box, because sometimes neural substrates are coactivated—for example, we may feel both scared and excited on a first date—but typically, one system dominates.

- ☐ **My body felt relaxed and calm.** Were you able to easily make eye contact or express your emotions with little self-consciousness? Did you smile or laugh without feeling phony? Was your voice-tone easygoing or musical? Did you desire to reach out to or touch the person you were with, say on the arm? *When you check this box, it's most likely that your social safety system is on.*

- ☐ **My body felt alert and focused.** Did you suddenly find yourself standing still and gazing intently? Or listening carefully? *When you check this box, it's most likely that your novelty system is on.*

- ☐ **My body felt energized and powerful.** Were you more expressive, talkative, or liable to use expansive gestures than what might be typical for you? Was your speech louder or faster than normal? Did you talk over others or find it harder to pause to allow another to speak? Did it require effort to listen to others? *When you check this box, it's most likely that your excitatory reward system is on.*

- ☐ **My body felt tense, agitated, or hot.** Did you find it difficult to smile without feeling phony? Was your facial expression flat or stony? Did you avert your eyes or stare intensely? Did your voice tone sound flat or strident? Were your gestures tight and constrained? *When you check this box, it's most likely that your threat system is on.*

- ☐ **My body felt numb and detached from reality.** Was your face and body expressionless? Were your body movements slow? Did you feel numbed out or unresponsive? Was it hard to talk or attend to the environment? Was your speech rate slower than normal? Did you stare vacantly? Did you feel like fainting? *When you check this box, it's most likely that your overwhelmed or shut-down system is on.*

So, Now You Know

According to the RO DBT neuroregulatory model, our stress-regulation systems evolved to enhance our survival but also—importantly, for our species—to enhance our survival by connecting with others (Lynch, 2018a). We naturally feel calm when we feel part of a tribe or close to someone, whether they're related to us or not. In this chapter, we learned that because our neuroregulatory system is bidirectional, meaning our brain (how we think) influences our body (how we act) and vice versa, we can use our facial expressions, gestures, and body movements to alter how we feel or think on the inside. For example, differing neural substrates can be turned on or turned off simply by activating different muscle groups in your body. What's more, not only do these body movements and expressions enhance your personal feelings of safety; they also modify how others feel when interacting with you.

In our next two chapters, we'll be making this a reality by exploring the key mechanism of change in RO DBT, social signaling, and teaching you specific skills to activate and signal social safety—all without having to think about it too much (or at least, not very much…tee hee)!

CHAPTER 4

Social Signaling Matters

Imagine you're out to lunch with a new coworker. During the meal, while smiling and nodding, they say, "Last night, I discovered that my partner was having an affair. Plus," they add, still smiling and nodding, "I found out we're now bankrupt because he spent all our money on this other person." Continuing to smile, they say, "So I decided to set fire to the house." And then, with a big smile and a singsong voice, they ask, "So how was your evening?"

What would you think or feel if you interacted with someone who behaved like this? Would you want to spend more or less time with them? Most people report the coworker's behavior as phony, odd, or off-putting and prefer not to spend more time with them. (BTW, if you haven't made the connection yet: this coworker's nonverbal signaling represents a prototypical example of one type of OC social signaling known as overly prosocial—albeit perhaps exaggerated to get the point across.) We chose this story to start the chapter off because it illustrates a core RO DBT principle underlying the key mechanism of change—specifically, when it comes to close social bonds, "it's not *what* you say, it's *how* you say it" that matters most. Smiling when you reveal to another person that your partner's having an affair, you're bankrupt, and you set fire to your house isn't the best way to win friends (at least in most people's books). In this chapter, we'll further explain the key mechanism of change in RO DBT and why social signaling matters (not necessarily in that order, tee hee).

For most OC people, interpersonal difficulties stem from this very core principle—that is, it's not *what* they say but *how* they say it. Displaying a flat face and using a monotonic voice when reporting you're happy or thrilled about something is confusing the same way that smiling when revealing distressing events feels phony: what you're saying is clearly at odds with how you're saying it. And most OC individuals tend to habitually inhibit or downplay expressions of emotion or mask emotions by displaying expressions unrelated to what they're feeling. What's expressed on the outside (publicly revealed) frequently does not reflect what's felt on the inside (privately experienced). And when your social signals are indirect, inhibited, or masked, it makes it hard for others to get to know you or trust what you say. Such habits to mask, downplay, or inhibit emotions also influence *what* you say—the words you choose to express yourself. You might end up habitually using words or phrases that are vague, indirect, obscure, or perplexing, which makes it harder for others to know what you're trying to say or send mixed messages, even when unintended.

Let's have some fun with mixed messages—and play the "What's The Real Meaning Behind This?" game. BTW, practice being a little flippant when you play (tee hee), because the "answers" are not the only ones possible.

What's The Real Meaning Behind This?

Here's how to play.

1. Cover up columns 2 and 3 with your hand or a piece of paper. No peeking (tee hee).
2. Now read the text in the first row under column 1, "What an OC Person Says."
3. Your job is to guess what's in column 2, "What They Actually Mean," and column 3, "What Other People Hear." Don't be too serious about it (tee hee), and again, no peeking!

1. What An OC Person Says	2. What They Actually Mean	3. What Other People Hear
"Hmmm."	"I don't agree."	"They're interested in what we're saying."
"Probably."	"No" or "Not likely."	"A very good chance."
"Yes, but…"	"No, and here's how you're wrong."	"They agree in principle, but they might have a few minor concerns."
"I was a bit disappointed."	"I was really annoyed" or "I was really distressed."	"It doesn't really matter."
"I'll try."	"I don't plan to do anything."	"They're committed to doing something different."

Well done! How successful were you at playing this game without getting too serious about your answers? The point here was to make a point (tee hee) about how words can contain hidden messages. Similarly, nonverbal signals that are ambiguous in nature, such as inhibited facial expressions, can also be used to conceal inner intentions or feelings. They often send mixed or off-putting messages, even when unintended or without awareness on the sender's part.

Ultimately, the words we choose to express ourselves and the ways we express ourselves matter greatly. They're not only subject to misinterpretation, but also the only means available for others to know who we are. For example, you might have a habit of furrowing your brow and frowning when you're concentrating or listening intently. Unfortunately, most people interpret frowns and furrowed brows as signs of disapproval or dislike, which can trigger reciprocal frowning from recipients and reduced desires for affiliation.

What social signaling habits do you have that might unintentionally send mixed messages?

____

____

____

____

____

____

To what extent do you purposefully use vague or indirect communication to avoid something, hide your inner experience, control others, or get what you want? What might your answers tell you about how you see other people?

____

____

____

____

____

In RO DBT we teach something called the *key mechanism of change*, the active ingredient for creating a life worth sharing and breaking free of emotional loneliness. The formula is this: Open Expression = Trust = Social Connectedness. But before we explain what we mean by this, let's consider the social downsides of an overly constrained, inhibited, or masked style of social signaling.

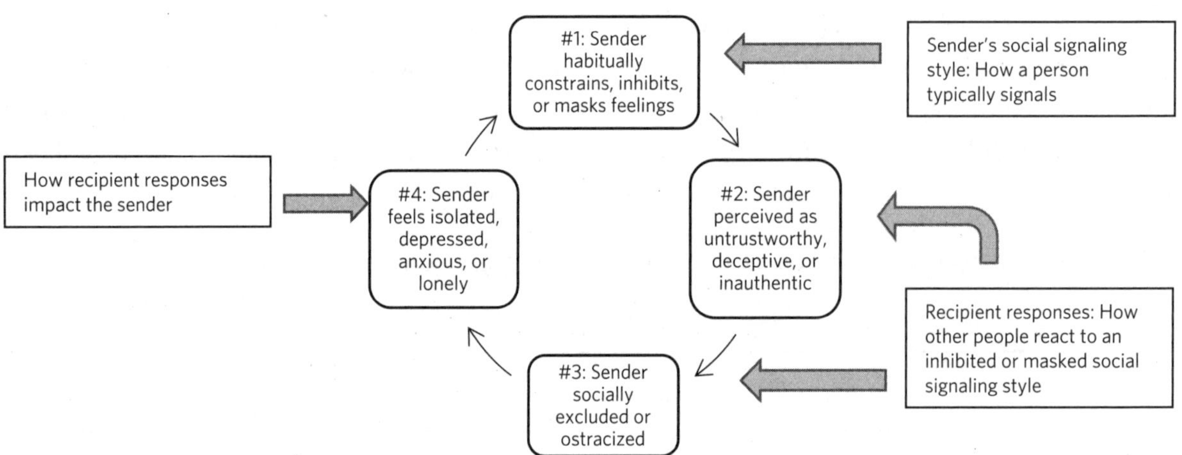

Figure 4.1. The Downsides of an Overly Constrained, Inhibited, or Masked Style of Social Signaling (adapted from Lynch, 2018a)

As you'll see from the top of the figure, habitually constraining, inhibiting, or masking feelings represents the modus operandi of OC social signaling. *Constrained and inhibited* refers to attempts you might make to suppress or downplay expressions of emotion, like flat facial expressions, monotonic voice tone, or low self-disclosure. *Masking* refers to attempts to display one emotion in order to cover up (or mask) the expression of another—pretending to be happy when feeling sad, smiling to hide anger, complimenting a rival to hide envy. Robust research shows that habitual inhibition, constraint, or masking of feelings leads to one's being perceived as untrustworthy, inauthentic, or stilted—and thus less likely to be invited into a tribe (e.g., Boone & Buck, 2003; English & John, 2013; Kernis & Goldman, 2006; Mauss et al., 2011). Interestingly, both inhibited, muted, and flat expressions *and* overly prosocial, insincere, and feigned expressions—map on to this research. Both styles rarely reveal or express vulnerable emotions, either publicly or privately, and both are a major factor in making social ostracism more likely (Lynch, 2018a). Yowsers!

The cycle of rejection associated with constrained, inhibited, and masked expressions is also self-perpetuating. As seen in figure 4.1, when a sender habitually constrains, inhibits, or masks their feelings (#1), recipients are more likely to perceive them as untrustworthy, deceptive, or inauthentic (#2) and socially exclude or ostracize them (#3)—which negatively impacts the emotional well-being of the sender, because our brains are hardwired to make us feel anxious, depressed, and unsafe when we're socially rejected (#4). And recall chapter 3: when we don't feel safe, defensive arousal and fight/flight responses dominate; our facial expressions become frozen, and we can only fake a smile—further impairing our ability to signal friendly intentions and leading to still further ostracization and isolation. In this way, the vicious cycle continues.

As Nicole notes, "When I first learned this, my initial reaction was 'But wait a minute—I AM trustworthy!' Upon reflection (and with a little help from my friends), I came to realize that my tendencies to flat facial expressions and holding my cards perpetually to my chest made others uneasy."

Thus, the major problem with an inhibited style of signaling is that it makes social ostracism more likely. And when we feel socially ostracized, our threat system goes through the roof! We might have fancy phones, great careers, clean houses, even social media followers, and an awesome shoe collection—but our primordial brains respond to social ostracization, perceived or real, as certain death; our ancestors wouldn't have survived very long without their tribe! Consequently, we're hardwired to be hypervigilant for possible signs of social exclusion. Research shows that we can quickly spot the angry face in a crowd of people, and angry faces hold our attention (Fox et al., 2000; Schupp et al., 2004). Indeed, we're constantly scanning others' facial expressions and vocalizations for signs of disapproval—that is, information about our social status, the extent to which our behavior is socially desirable, or the degree to which another person appears to like us.

What's more, you might think you're giving off *neutral* signals by inhibiting or limiting expressions of emotion, but end up transmitting ambiguous and inscrutable messages instead—and human brains read ambiguity as danger. For example, simply reducing or limiting the amount of eye contact during interactions has been shown to trigger negative feelings associated with being ignored or ostracized in recipients (Wirth, Sacco, Hugenberg, & Williams, 2010). Blank expressions are often interpreted as disapproving (Butler et al., 2003)—and similarly, a low frequency or conspicuous absence of expected or customary prosocial signals (smiling, affirmative nods) in situations that call for open expression (like a romantic date) are often interpreted to mean dislike, regardless of the sender's actual intentions. After all, back in our primordial caves, it was better to err on the side of caution to protect our basic survival—to assume any form of ambiguous signal a sign of disapproval or potential ostracism, and do something about it, rather than carry on as if nothing had happened.

Unfortunately, because OC people are motivated to constrain, downplay, or mask their expression of emotion, both positive and negative, they tend to believe that others operate similarly. Remember, according to RO DBT, we don't see the world as it is, we see it as we are. Thus, they may consider candid expressions of emotion untrustworthy, manipulative, deceptive, or even a sign of weakness. Take a second to process this: *To what extent do you consider candid expressions of emotion manipulative, deceptive, or a sign of weakness? Is there something here to learn?*

____

____

____

____

The good news is that there is a way to break out of this pattern.

Consider figure 4.2. Essentially, it shows that you can reverse the downward spiral of an inhibited social signaling style, simply by changing how you socially signal. But before we get carried away, let's examine why Open Expression = Trust = Social Connectedness is posited to work and the research behind it. Cool!

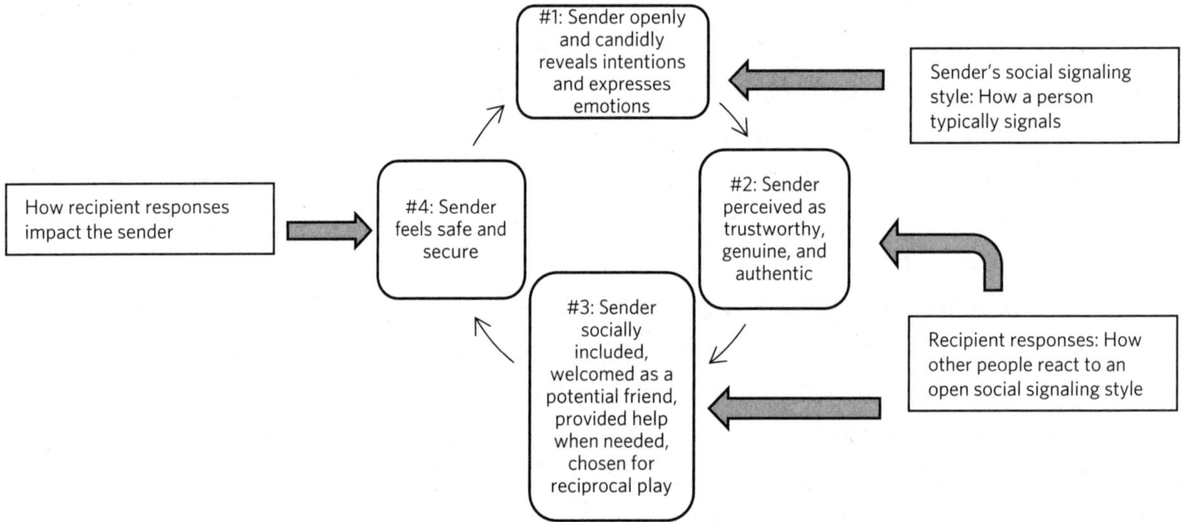

Figure 4.2. The Advantages of Open Expression and Candid Self-Disclosure (adapted from Lynch, 2018a)

First, believe it or not, compared to other animals, humans are hypercooperative. We're able to share resources, work together, and form strong bonds with genetically dissimilar others (non-kin) in a manner that's unparalleled in the animal world (Marean, 2015). What enables this is our highly sophisticated social signaling system, which allowed us a quick and safe means to evaluate and resolve conflict and manage potential collaborations (Lynch, 2018a). What's interesting is that we use other people's social signals to judge whether we trust them or would like to spend more time with them. Our brains can reliably detect the extent to which another person is likely to engage in reciprocal cooperative behaviors. For example, we can recognize another's friendly intentions through emotion-based touching, smiling, and their overall level of emotional expressivity (Boone & Buck, 2003; Brown & Moore, 2002; Brown et al., 2003; Hertenstein et al., 2006; Schug et al., 2010). And research shows that when we practice open expression and self-disclosure, we're more likely to be perceived as trustworthy, and as a result, become more socially connected (Boone & Buck, 2003; Kavanah et al., 2024; Mauss et al., 2011; Feinberg et al., 2011). We "drop our guard," so speak, leading to a positive cycle of safety and increased feelings of safety. Ultimately, revealing intentions and emotions to other members of our species was essential to create the type of strong social bonds that are essential for our survival and the cornerstone of human tribes (see box 4.1, "RO Fun Fact: Humans Are Expert Social Safety Detectors").

Box 4.1. RO Fun Fact: Humans Are Expert Social Safety Detectors

Our brains are hardwired to detect the extent to which another person is feeling genuinely relaxed versus tense, uncomfortable, or self-conscious during interactions. For example, research shows that we are adept at knowing whether a smile is genuine or phony and that we can accurately detect tension in the voice of a person, even over the telephone (Pittam & Scherer, 1993).

Research shows that exposure to a few minutes of nonverbal behavior, or even just a picture of the face, leads observers to form reliable impressions of a stranger's personality traits, socioeconomic status, and moral attributes like trustworthiness and altruism (Ambady & Rosenthal, 1992; Kaul & Schmidt, 1971; Kraus & Keltner, 2009).

Think about it. *Who would you prefer to spend time with? Someone who hides or rarely expresses inner intentions, thoughts, or emotions—or someone who's willing to openly reveal what they're experiencing inside when the situation calls for it?* As a species, we instinctively recognize the value openness brings to relationships. We tend to trust open-minded people because they're more likely to reveal than hide their feelings during conflict and they don't automatically assume that their way is the best, right, or only way. Open expression of emotion thus enhances intimacy, because it signals to others that you trust them (because you're revealing your inner self) and that you're trustworthy because you are not hiding anything. It's the essential glue needed to develop genuine intimacy with others.

The cycle outlined in figure 4.2 goes *opposite* to the downward spiral that occurs when someone habitually constrains, inhibits, or masks feelings. Specifically, when a sender openly and candidly reveals their intentions and expresses emotions (#1), recipients are more likely to perceive them as trustworthy, genuine, and authentic (#2) and then to socially include, welcome, help, or play with them (#3)—which positively impacts the sender's emotional well-being by increasing feelings of safety and security (#4). Recall from chapter 3 that when we feel safe, we naturally feel relaxed and socially engaged, our social safety system is on (PNS-VVC), our heart and breathing rates slow, we can effortlessly make eye contact, our laughter and smiles are genuine, we're better able to listen to others, and we're more likely to want to reach out and touch someone. And what's double-cool, for those compulsive strivers out there, is that you *don't have to try to feel safe*. You only need to learn how to *signal safety to others*—and presto, instant improved relationships! Before you can say *flipertyflumken* (a word we just made up), people seem happy to make your acquaintance or spend time with you. Like magic! And what's triple-cool: you won't have to do fancy calisthenics, meditate for hours, think happy thoughts, take acting lessons, or resolve past traumas to experience the benefits of prosocial signaling. The tools you need to signal safety to others are already hardwired into your basic programming. But to know how to take full advantage of these evolutionary gifts, you—like most people—will need a little training. And you'll get that training in our next chapter. So, hang in there—help is on its way!

Emotional Expression Is Always Context-Dependent

We're aware of imagining that some of you might be thinking, *Gosh, if I express myself, it'll* all *come out*—that loosening inhibitions will mean expressing *all* emotion, without any awareness or consideration of the environment you're in. As Nicole notes, "It reminds me of a meme I saw that said, 'If people could see what I'm thinking, I'd get punched out a lot.'" Fortunately, open expression *does not* mean simply expressing your feelings willy-nilly. Nor does it mean pretending that everything's okay, uncontrolled venting, or blaming others for your emotional reactions. It means revealing emotions in a way that acknowledges our responsibility in creating them.

Effective emotional expression is *always* context-dependent. A flat face is the most effective expression during a game of poker—but not so much during a first date. Conversely, sometimes, controlled expression is what's *needed* to be effective, avoid unnecessary damage, or live by one's values (Lynch, 2018b). For example, you might need to pretend to enjoy a meal you normally dislike when it was cooked in your honor, or to inhibit an urge to shout in an emotionally charged discussion with your adolescent child. Inhibiting an expression of emotion can also be an act of kindness—like suppressing a laugh when your friend yet again mispronounces a word they've struggled to learn—or necessary to achieve an important goal, like getting through passport control without delay. Effective expression accounts for the type of relationship—for example, when you're with a competitor, a new boss, or the police versus your best friend, spouse, or next-door neighbor.

The point is: to form long-lasting intimate bonds, we must reveal vulnerability, at least occasionally. Recall from chapter 1 that openly revealing our private feelings, doubts, concerns, or beliefs to another person transmits two powerful prosocial messages:

1. *We trust them*—because when we don't trust someone, we hide our true intentions and mask our feelings.
2. *We're the same as them*—since revealing vulnerability signals that we share a common bond of human fallibility (nobody's perfect; tee hee). Revealing vulnerability is thus the foundation of true friendship.

Okay! Now that we've learned a bit about OC social signaling and how it impacts relationships, let's hear from Elijah and Tula:

• *Elijah*

Nobody really knows this about me, but my outward appearance as an agreeable, upbeat, and caring person is mostly an act. Yet, maintaining this prosocial persona is exhausting—I feel like I'm always on stage, always performing. I obsessively rehearse or plan what I'll say or do during social interactions to make it look spontaneous and often practice laughing or smiling in the mirror. I've also developed strategies to avoid appearing anxious or awkward, like sitting rather than standing during interactions, asking questions about the other person's life to avoid talking about myself, or feigning interest or excitement about something to change an unwanted topic. People outside of my immediate family often describe me as a wonderful person who's always polite and caring—yet no one knows who I really am. Beneath my mask, I feel like a fraud. My outward behavior's often forced or feigned. I smile when distressed, compliment someone to hide dislike or envy, or express caring and concern when I don't feel any. After social events, my face often hurts from smiling so hard. When I feel like I can't keep going on like this, I remind myself that everyone's phony, just like me. But lately I've started to wonder if I'm fooling myself. Maybe my cynicism is just a story I tell myself to justify staying the same. The problem's that I'm unsure how to change.

• *Tula*

One of my goals is to start dating again, but I just don't seem to have the hang of it. I think it's partly because when I dated in the past and things would start to get more serious, disagreements would come up. Nothing big, but little irritations. And I like to think I'm hell on wheels at work, but I abhor conflict in my personal relationships. I remember one time I'd planned an elaborate weekend getaway with a person, Evan, that I'd been dating for a few months. They cancelled at the last minute because they had family coming to town. I was really annoyed! When Evan asked me if I was okay with the change in plans, I said, "Yes, that's fine" but with a flat-face and monotonic tone of voice. Then I told them I had to leave because I had an appointment (which wasn't exactly true). A few days later, I was still feeling annoyed. I decided to give Evan a taste of their own medicine—and sent them a text-message to tell them that I was busy with a new work project (which also wasn't exactly true), and wouldn't be available for another weekend getaway at this time. I never heard from them again. Part of me thinks it's proof they never really cared about me, and people can't be trusted. Another part wonders whether things would've turned out differently if I hadn't reacted the way I did. And what's sad is—I think I was really starting to like them.

Elijah and Tula's stories represent prototypical examples of the two most common OC social signaling styles and the underlying beliefs and consequences that maintain them. Elijah's tendencies to be excessively prosocial backfire; not only are they exhausting, but they make him feel like a fraud. Tula's tendencies to not be expressive or behave prosocially in situations that call for it are equally problematic. Although their social signaling styles are essentially opposite, both can damage relationships. Moreover, Elijah and Tula's superior capacities for self-control also makes it possible for them to influence others without being too obvious about it—even when they're under high stress. Still, when what's expressed on the outside frequently does not reflect what's felt on the inside, relationships suffer, because this ultimately makes it harder for others to know who Tula or Elijah really are and trust their intentions.

Now let's take a moment to reflect on your social signaling style—the behaviors you do and don't exhibit in the presence of others, whether they're verbal or nonverbal, deliberate or unconscious, or intentional or inadvertent—and how it may impact your connectedness with others.

Exercise: Your Social Signaling Style

This exercise is designed to *expand the list of social signaling habits that you started in chapter 2, and determine whether you lean more toward Elijah's or Tula's style of signaling.* In other words, when the going gets tough, do you try to appear *charming and nice* (Elijah) or *stoic and strong* (Tula)? So, pull out your list—and get ready to add to it. Use the questions below to facilitate your search for potential problematic social signals.

How do you typically express your emotions, thoughts, and inner experience when under stress or in conflict? *For example, when you're angry at someone, do you smile and pretend all is well, or go flat-faced and act indifferent? Do you sometimes walk away but make it appear like you're not?*

____

____

____

____

____

How do you typically express your emotions, thoughts, and inner experience when you're feeling happy or excited? *For example, to what extent do you join in with others when they smile or laugh? How often do you fake a laugh or smile to please others? Would your friends describe you as generally flat-faced or smiley? To what extent do you fake enthusiasm or excitement when around others?*

____

____

____

____

____

Which social signaling habits have others given you feedback about? Which social signaling habits have you noticed that you would like to change? *Examples include ways of speaking, rate of speech, tone of voice, pausing, talking over people, standing too close, never shaking hands, slouched posture, finger pointing, excessive nodding, looking down, lack of eye contact, staring, rarely laughing or smiling, pouting or going silent, ignoring questions, flat facial expressions, and more.*

____

____

____

____

____

Well done! How did it go? *Were you able to identify some new social signaling habits? Which questions did you struggle to answer or dislike the most? What might this tell you about your openness to change?*

And BTW, whenever you struggle knowing whether or not to change a social signaling habit, get in the habit (tee hee) of asking yourself these two clarifying questions to help you decide:

1. *Would I teach a child to signal or behave in a similar manner?*
2. *Am I proud of this social signal?*

Both questions help you determine if your social signaling habit is something *you value*. Recall from chapter 2 that *values* are the principles or standards that one considers important in life, and *goals* are how a given value is expressed or achieved. If you answer no to either of these clarifying questions, the social signaling habit is likely *not* something you value, because you wouldn't teach it to a child or aren't proud of it yourself. Changing that social signaling habit would be a good idea.

But whatever you do, don't start trying to fix the habits you've identified yet—remember, that's what perfectionists do (tee hee). Monitor them instead, recording your observation in your (hopefully) growing social signaling diary (like we did in chapter 2). To do this, pick one or two social signaling habits from those you identified above that occur frequently (e.g., daily). Then, for the next week, monitor their frequency, when and where they occur, and with whom, just as you did in chapter 2. And don't forget to record the apparent impact of the social signal on other people. For example, do people on the receiving end appear more engaged, interested, pleased, or attentive? Or do they go silent, look away, avoid eye contact, or change the topic? Again, don't feel like you need to do anything about what you observe. We'll be teaching you how to change problematic social signals in the very next chapter.

For now, simply be kind to yourself when identifying and monitoring your social signaling habits. Ultimately, there's no right or optimal way to socially signal, each of us has our own distinctive style of expression, and we all bring perceptual and regulatory biases with us wherever we go. Identifying personal social signaling habits isn't easy, because it requires a willingness to examine our actions—not just from our perspective, but from the perspective of those on the receiving end. (Yowsers!) But in this chapter, you've begun the work. And as you work through this and future chapters, that work will be rewarded!

Moving Forward

In summary, people cannot know who you are unless you reveal who you are. Plus, we trust what we see, not what is said. People inevitably prioritize nonverbal expressions over verbal ones as more truthful indicators of a person's inner state. In light of this, RO DBT uniquely prioritizes social signaling as the primary mechanism of change—the way to help you increase your closeness to others and your ability to achieve valued goals. In our next chapter, we provide specific instructions on how to change your social signaling to make it more prosocial and enhance your abilities to connect with others.

CHAPTER 5

Activating and Signaling Social Safety

As we learned in our last chapter, openness and cooperative intentions are evaluated less by our words than our actions (for example, facial affect, voice tone, rate of speech, eye contact, body posture, and gestures). Facial expressions are particularly powerful nonverbal social signals. We often closely examine others' facial expressions in interactions. Indeed, modern humans possess more facial muscles than any other animal species; it's estimated that we can make over ten thousand different facial expressions (wow!). Yet most people display only *one tenth of one percent* of the total number of expressions possible—that is, approximately one hundred out of the ten thousand possible. Yowsers! So, before we tell you more about what this chapter is about, you better get practicing—you have ninety-nine hundred more expressions to discover! Which BTW, also highlights the primary aim of this chapter—to expand your prosocial signaling repertoire to both activate and signal social safety. So, let's get started!

As we have been learning, many of the problems perfectionistic OC individuals struggle with stem from how they perceive novel, unexpected, or ambiguous stimuli (like an unfamiliar person) or react to feedback from others (like an unexpected email). According to the RO DBT model of emotions (Lynch, 2018a), our brains are evolutionarily hardwired to appraise ambiguous stimuli, like a blank facial expression or unfamiliar sound, at the sensory-receptor level, as a potential threat; the cost of not detecting a true threat stimulus, for our ancestors living in harsh environments, was too high to ignore. True enough, about all humans rate ambiguous stimuli as more unpleasant than unambiguous stimuli; they're also associated with longer reaction times (Hock & Krohne, 2004). We've also learned that OC biotemperamental predispositions for heightened threat sensitivity make it more likely for OC individuals, in particular, to see the potential for harm, in situations like walking into a party, over the potential for reward, triggering defensive arousal and urges to flee—often at a preconscious level. Feeling threatened impairs prosocial signaling: our face may go flat, and we might only fake a smile. Flat, constrained, rigid, and phony facial expressions are not only off-putting to others; they also communicate to the sender's brain that the threat is real—which exacerbates feelings of anxiety.

What's super interesting is that social signals also function to trigger similar neural substrates and emotions in the recipient of the signal as those being activated in the sender, via a process known as micromimicry. Robust research supports both the reality of micromimicry (Hess & Blairy, 2001; Moody et al., 2007; Vrana & Gross, 2004), and the fact that we both unconsciously adopt the postures, gestures, and mannerisms of our close companions and desire to spend more time with those who mimic us (Lakin & Chartrand, 2003; Lakin et al., 2003). The point is, mimicking the facial expressions of others triggers the same brain structures, mirror neurons, and physiological experience of the mimicked person (Montgomery & Haxby, 2008; Van der Gaag et al., 2007).

Micromimicry reflects the operation of the mirror neuron system, which is what leads you to micrograimace, in a matter of milliseconds, when you see another person suddenly grimace in pain—an act that triggers the same neurons in your brain that are firing in the other person's brain in response to their pain. Being able to viscerally feel what another person feels in this way likely lent our species an evolutionary advantage. It's the seed of empathy and altruism—what makes us, for instance, willing to risk serious injury, even death, to save someone we might hardly know. Unfortunately, micromimicry can also make it *harder* to feel empathy or connect with others—depending on what's being expressed. As we've learned, neutral, flat, and expressionless faces are frequently interpreted as hostile or disapproving, regardless of the sender's intentions, triggering automatic defensive arousal in the recipient (Butler et al., 2003). And when we're defensively aroused—when our SNS-mediated threat system is activated—our capacities to perceive others' behavior empathically are suppressed, making us less adept at reading the social signals of others (recall the RO DBT neuroregulatory model from chapter 2). Indeed, the flat face is such a powerful social signal that it's the one of the most frequently used facial expressions of villains in Hollywood movies (because they scare the heck out of us!). This is because the cost of *not* detecting a true disapproval signal, implying tribal banishment, was too high to ignore for our primordial ancestors. Consequently, we're constantly scanning the facial expressions and vocalizations of other people for signs of disapproval; we're biologically hardwired to interpret low-intensity, neutral, or ambiguous social signals as threatening or disapproving; and our modern brains still respond to such signals *as if* we're living in primordial times—making us fundamentally a socially anxious species. (Yowsers!)

The problem, for perfectionistic OC individuals, is that their innate, biotemperamental predispositions for heightened threat sensitivity *amplify* this evolved, inherent signal-detection bias. It makes it even more likely they'll perceive new, ambiguous, or unfamiliar situations as potentially dangerous—which reduces social safety (PNS-VVC) activation, and makes frozen or phony facial expressions that interfere with social connection more likely. This process can be exacerbated even further by family-cultural-environmental messages valuing constraint and control. As a result, they might exhibit a resting flat face in most situations, inadvertently making others less likely to want to spend time with them or trust their intentions, which further reinforces self-concepts of being an outsider or unlovable. Wow! The good news, and what this chapter's all about, is that: although you can't talk yourself out of biotemperamental predispositions, you can *minimize the negative effects of heightened threat sensitivity and overlearned habits for inhibited expressions by activating an area of the brain linked with social safety*. Super!

As we learned in chapter 3, activating our social safety system (PNS-VVC) changes how we feel inside and how we socially signal on the outside. For example, when we feel safe, we're less likely to display frozen facial expressions because we naturally feel more easygoing and able to express flexibly. Plus, via the processes associated with micromimicry, prosocial signaling from one person can positively impact others by activating social safety responses in them. This, in turn, makes it more likely for those others to feel increased trust and desire to spend more time with the sender, thereby increasing social connectedness. Essentially, by activating different muscle groups in our body that our brain naturally links to safety, we can change both how we feel *inside* and how we signal to others on the *outside*—which positively impacts our relationships.

This chapter will be teaching you *social signaling skills*—ones that have been shown to enhance social connectedness and are experienced universally, across cultures, as friendly and prosocial, because they're innate and biological, not learned. For example, regardless of culture, we raise our arms high, with our palms facing outward, when we celebrate success. Athletes who are blind and therefore have never seen another person's facial expressions or gestures display the same emotional facial expressions and gestures as athletes who aren't blind when they win or lose (Matsumoto & Willingham, 2009). The many universal or cross-cultural facial expressions, voice tones, and body movements that have been proposed and researched include smiling, frowning, laughing, staring, glaring, shrugging, pouting, wincing, blushing, bowing, gazing, winking, nodding, beckoning, and waving (see Russell et al., 2003 for a review). The basic idea: if you want to form a close social bond and stay in it, you must be able to signal that you care about someone other than yourself—and universal prosocial signals are a core means for achieving this.

With universal prosocial signals, you can stop ruminating or worrying about how to get along with people and let your body do the work instead. The exercises in this chapter are designed to teach you how. But if you really want to learn these new techniques, you can't just read about them—you need to practice them to fully experience their benefits. So, make a commitment, right now, to *do* rather than think about the exercises and practices outlined in this chapter (and all other chapters too), to viscerally discover their utility. But before we teach you *what to do*, let's first examine *what you don't want to do* when it comes to social signaling (tee hee).

What Not to Do

Robust research shows that revealing vulnerability or distress to another person enhances intimacy (e.g., Laurenceau et al., 1998) and is a marker of a trusting relationship. Yet, as we've been learning, most perfectionistic OC individuals strive hard to not reveal weakness or vulnerability in relationships. They tend to communicate their needs, wants, and desires indirectly and are experts in the "art of disclosing without disclosing." Consequently, it's not uncommon for an OC person to say "I'm fine" even when they're highly distressed or unhappy. Rather than directly answer a request for personal information, you might change the topic, answer a question with a question (for example, "What do you think?"), respond vaguely ("I'm not sure" or "Maybe" or "It depends"), report that you don't know (when you do), or provide long, rambling explanations that never get around to answering the question. Indirect and disguised social signals are powerful. They allow you to avoid disclosing personal information and to influence others without ever having to admit doing so. That is, they contain plausible deniability. If it's unclear what a person believes or feels, it becomes very difficult to criticize or hold them accountable. Figure 5.1 illustrates the scary power of the flat face when it comes to hiding intentions. Because when you don't show much—no one knows much.

Figure 5.1. When You Don't Show Much, No One Knows Much

Have you ever found yourself behaving this way, however inadvertently?

___

___

In addition, as noted earlier, flat facial expressions are powerful not only because of the absence of expression, but because they're often deployed in situations where prosocial emotional expression—like smiling or nodding affirmatively—is the norm, or expected: for instance, at parties, or on dates. Sustained flat facial expressions are likely to be interpreted as disapproval, dislike, or deceptive by most people. For example, even seasoned speakers find blank stares and expressionless faces in the audience disconcerting. See the box "Not So Fun Facts" for more examples of social signals that recipients are likely to interpret as social rejection—and, in case you're wondering, these strategies aren't recommended for use (tee hee). And don't forget: we've also learned that trying *too* hard to appear friendly can get you into trouble too. Excessive prosocial signaling and forced politeness, when it's context inappropriate, pervasive, or unresponsive to others' social-signals—like a frozen-wide, teeth-exposed smile, or an overly singsong voice—is also experienced as insincere, phony, or deceptive.

Box 5.1. Not-So-Fun Facts

If you want to make someone miserable...

- Never smile during greetings or interactions.
- Never laugh when they laugh—even if you find what they're saying funny.
- Don't shake hands or acknowledge them when they greet you—or look away and pretend not to notice them.
- Avoid eye contact. When you do look at them. put on your best flat face.
- Look bored, look away, and yawn whenever they speak—never give an affirmative nod.
- A little contemptuous smile never hurts. If you can throw in a disgusted eye roll, all the better. Or, start gagging.
- Keep those eyebrows down! Though, if you really don't like them, your eyebrows will be down anyway (so forget about this one).
- And last but not least—never admit to anything! (Tee hee.)

In summary, we're constantly social signaling around others via microexpressions and body movements, even when we're desperately trying not to (silence can be just as powerful as non-stop talking). Indirect and ambiguous signaling frequently leads to misunderstanding or distrust, regardless of your intentions, because it's hard to know what the true meaning or the sender's intentions are. Ambiguous signals harm social connection and, when they're used pervasively, result in social ostracism and feelings of loneliness. Conversely, open expression and vulnerable self-disclosure are received by most as a social safety signal. We tend to trust those who freely express their emotions, particularly when the situation calls for it.

Now, let's take a moment to reflect.

How frequently do you openly reveal inner experience or vulnerable emotions to another person?

____

____

____

To what extent are you proud of the way you communicate your emotions, intentions, and beliefs?

____

____

____

Would you encourage another person or a young child to behave similarly? What might your answer tell you about how you see yourself and your own social signaling style?

____

____

____

Okay, we've covered the basics on what not to do. Now, let's look at what you *should* do, when it comes to activating and signaling social safety and friendly intentions. Yippee!

What You Should Do

What you *should* do involves several specific expressions, like the eyebrow wag and the closed-mouth cooperative smile, plus some specific adjustments to voice tone, prosody, and more. We'll explore each one below.

The Eyebrow Wag

The eyebrow wag or eyebrow flash is a universal social acceptance signal involving a simultaneous upward movement of both eyebrows, most often accompanied by a genuine smile, kind or happy eyes, and melodic tone of voice. Eyebrow wags are nature's way of saying, "I like you" or "You are in my tribe." They manifest across cultures, often without conscious awareness, in a wide range of social situations, including greetings, flirting, offering approval, seeking confirmation, and thanking (Grammer et al., 1998). It's also conspicuously absent when we are greeted by someone who dislikes us or during interactions with rivals—though the lack of an eyebrow wag should not be assumed to be definitive proof of dislike: the other person might be in pain or distress, which turn off prosocial signaling; or they might only rarely eyebrow-wag with anyone, perhaps because they're also OC. Eyebrow wags not only signal cooperative intentions; they also activate the social safety system, in both sender and recipient, and thereby facilitate openness and receptivity to new information or critical feedback.

Take a look at illustration 5.1. Notice how the expression of concern and the eyebrow wag are nearly identical—except for the placement of the eyebrows. Switch back and forth from one picture to the other. Can you viscerally feel a difference between the two? Which expression feels more friendly, fun, or open? Which would you want to spend more time with?

Eyebrow Wag

Expression of Concern

Illustration 5.1. Using Eyebrow Wags to Signal Social Safety

Now, let's practice raising our eyebrows! Get your smartphone out, turn on the camera, set it to selfie mode, and record yourself while you practice. (You can also simply look into a mirror, of course.)

- Begin by making a flat face.
- Next, make an expression of concern, by furrowing your brow.
- Lastly, change your expression by raising your eyebrows.

Pay special attention to what it feels like inside as you move from one expression to another. Which expression feels more friendly and open? Repeat the process—a couple of times.

When you're done, watch the recording of yourself, and evaluate what it feels like to be on the receiving end of these social signals.

Finally, show your recording to a friend. Ask them: which expression feels more friendly, or which would they prefer to spend more time with?

You can also expand this exercise still further. Say to your friend, "It's really great to see you!"—first, with a concerned facial expression; then, with your eyebrows raised.

Finally, try these two expressions again—this time asking your friend the question, "Have you put the garbage out?"

Ask your friend which versions felt more friendly. And consider: did your voice tone change depending on which expression was used?

___

___

___

Most people report that saying "It's really great to see you!" or "Have you put the garbage out?" with their eyebrows down automatically changes their voice tone to one more flattened or monotonic. Recall from chapter 3 that when your eyebrows are raised, your social safety system is activated. Thus, when our social safety system is on, it's easier to exhibit a musical tone of voice, with our inflection going up at the end of sentence. This is because our social safety system contains nerves that govern the muscles in our body needed to communicate and form close social bonds (Porges, 2011). So, it can innervate our laryngeal and pharyngeal (or "voice box") muscles, allowing us to use a musical tone of voice to communicate warmth and friendliness to others. Thus, simply raising or lowering your eyebrows when speaking with someone can change not only how they perceive what is being said but literally *how* it's being said—whether we use a monotonic or musical tone of voice. But don't just take our word for it—we'll offer you some exercises to help you try it out and discover the proof for yourself!

The next time you're in a challenging situation or receiving feedback, rather than adopting an expression of concern or a flat face, practice raising your eyebrows (see illustration 5.1), both when you're speaking and when listening. This signals affection, interest, and openness while simultaneously making it more likely for you and the person you're speaking with to viscerally experience the interaction more positively. Sometimes simply raising your eyebrows while listening to someone is all that's needed to signal you're listening with an open mind and nondefensively.

Here are some more techniques to try. You might check them off as you try them over the next week or two.

- ☐ Mindfully observe what happens when you raise your eyebrows when interacting with others.
- ☐ Practice raising your eyebrows when being given critical feedback from someone. This signals openness on your part, and makes it more likely for you to be able to hear what's said (via social safety activation; see chapter 3).
- ☐ When you're unclear about something someone's said, request additional information with an easy manner by raising your eyebrows as you make the request.

- ☐ Use eyebrow wags when asking for help, e.g., at the pharmacy or the airport. (You might even find that you get upgraded on your flight—true story, tee hee!)
- ☐ Use eyebrow wags to change how you respond to events in private. For example, practice raising your eyebrows when thinking about a painful event or memory. Notice what happens in your body when you do so.

The Closed-Mouth Cooperative Smile

Smiles are powerful social signals. We emotionally respond to them within milliseconds, before conscious awareness is even possible (Williams et al., 2006). Across cultures, smiling signals social acceptance, friendly interpersonal intentions, happiness, and other positive emotions (Horstmann & Bauland, 2006; Lundqvist & Öhman, 2005; Parkinson, 2005). But not all smiles are the same, and not all reflect friendly intentions. Contemptuous smiles, for instance, signal disdain; envious smiles signal pleasure upon discovering a rival has failed. Plus, it's easy to overcorrect by smiling too much or too intensely. Most often this translates into "frozen" and nonresponsive, open-mouthed smiles, involving displays of the upper teeth that are held constant. Such smiles are quickly experienced as phony by both the sender and recipient. Plus, have you ever noticed how hard it is to genuinely smile with pleasure when you're feeling threatened or uptight? This is because your social safety system is switched off (or inhibited), and you can only fake an enjoyment smile. Or consider what happens when you're asked to smile for the camera, but the cameraperson fumbles, delaying the picture. Your candid smile of genuine pleasure might quickly fade into a frozen, polite smile that feels increasingly phony the longer you hold it. So, how does a person genuinely smile when feeling uptight?

The solution to the dilemma is the closed-mouth cooperative smile. This smile, contrary to other, consciously produced smiles, can be held static for relatively long periods of time *without* feeling contrived or phony. Plus, the closed-mouth smile is more likely to be experienced by both sender and the recipient as a genuine smile of pleasure, and thus trigger reciprocal smiling and social safety responses. For example, it is common for an automatic deep breath or sigh of contentment to arise almost immediately after engaging a closed-mouth cooperative smile, implying social safety (VVC) activation. The PNS-VVC regulates not only the social signaling muscles of our head and face, but also certain neuroinhibitory vagal fibers that deepen and slow breathing and lower our heart rate—both essential for signaling genuine warmth and calm friendliness during interactions.

A closed-mouth cooperative smile (see illustration 5.2; a photo of lead author Tom) involves turning both corners of the mouth upward and stretching the lips—but keeping the mouth closed so that the teeth are not exposed. It almost always is accompanied by direct eye contact, a slight narrowing of the eyes, and the crow's-feet wrinkles (or activation of the orbicularis oculi muscle) that characterize genuine smiles of pleasure. It signals genuine affection and friendly, open intentions—even when you may be

Illustration 5.2. The Closed-Mouth Cooperative Smile

feeling miserable inside. Your brain simply can't tell the difference. Social safety responses in yourself and in others can also, often, be enhanced when you pair the smile with an occasional eyebrow wag.

Let's practice smiling! Get your smartphone out, turn on the camera, set it to selfie mode, and record yourself making a closed-mouth cooperative smile (or use a mirror, at least for the first part of this exercise). See if you can match the expression in the photo above: make sure your mouth is closed when smiling, and your eyes slightly narrowed. Pro tip: if your smile feels too big, it might not be! Many OC folks tell us they're not used to smiling like this or perhaps ever. You might even experiment with making it bigger!

Take a slow, deep breath after you activate the smile. Then, compare your closed-mouth smile to a frozen open-mouthed smile with exposed teeth. Which feels and looks more genuine?

Now, ask a friend or family member to join you in your practice. Begin by asking the other person to talk about something they did that day for one to two minutes. While they talk, display a frozen open-mouthed smile with your teeth exposed. Keep that smile going the whole time they're speaking. Then, switch roles and have them hold a similar toothy, frozen smile while you talk about your day. Then discuss what it felt like for each of you—both when displaying the toothy grin and when on the receiving end.

Next, have the other person tell you about their plans for tomorrow—but this time, listen with a closed-mouth cooperative smile. Switch roles, and when you're both done, give each other feedback about how it felt, both when holding the smile and receiving it. Was it different than the experience you had with the frozen toothy smile? Which expression would you prefer to spend more time around?

From there, start practicing closed-mouth cooperative smiles—especially during challenging social interactions (e.g., when asking for help, requesting information, or listening to critical feedback). What impact do they have both on yourself and on the interaction?

The Big Three + 1

The Big Three + 1 combines eyebrow wags and closed-mouth smiles with two other universal social signals that communicate safety. If you're sitting down, start with the + 1. This involves leaning back in your chair, rather than sitting forward. It's a bit like slouching or relaxing on a big couch; it says to your brain, "I'm chilled out." (The + 1 can only be used when sitting, which is why it's separated from the other three.) Next, engage the Big Three by: (1) taking a slow deep breath (telling your brain "all is well"); (2) engaging a closed-mouth cooperative smile; and (3) raising your eyebrows. All three can be done at the same time, whether one is sitting, standing, or lying down.

The Big Three + 1 can be done anywhere, anyplace, and with anyone (see illustration 5.3). Let's practice! Get your smartphone out, turn on the camera, set it to selfie mode, and record yourself while you practice (or, again, use a mirror). See if you can match the expression in illustration 5.3, and try crossing your legs as you lean back. Then, compare this with sitting forward, with an expression of concern—a flat, expressionless face with slightly furrowed brow. Which looks and feels more chilled out?

Ask a friend or family member to join with you in your practice. Sit facing each other and, while maintaining eye contact, lean forward in your chair, displaying an expression of concern. After about thirty seconds, lean back and engage the Big Three + 1. Switch roles, and have them try each pose. Then, give each other feedback about how the practice went (e.g., did you remember to raise your eyebrows?) How did it feel to be on the receiving end of each expressive stance? Which felt more friendly, open, or receptive? Which felt more chilled out?

Some OC individuals report that they find the Big Three + 1 awkward or difficult when first learning it. This typically stems from lack of experience (e.g., with eyebrow wags), overlearned expressive habits (e.g., habitually displaying resting flat facial expressions), or rigid rules (e.g., "always sit up straight," "never show emotion"). The good news is that with a little practice, the Big Three + 1 can start to feel like a natural part of your expressive repertoire. It also activates our social safety system almost anywhere and anytime, however stressful the situation. When it's engaged, our brain-body reacts "as if all is well." So don't give up! Practice! Practice! Practice! For example, use the Big Three + 1 to slow down rather than speeding up

Illustration 5.3. The Big Three + 1

during challenging interactions, times of conflict, or when you find yourself compulsively feeling like you should work harder. It'll signal friendly safety to recipients even when you're feeling anything but safe inside. Repeat often and as needed.

Prosody and Voice Tone

Prosody refers to the nonverbal components of speech, such as rate (how fast or slowly you talk), pitch (the relative sound frequency—high or low), intonation (emerging pitch movements during speech), rhythm (how speech is organized into regular time intervals), and loudness (voice volume; see Reed, 2011). Rate of speech and tone of voice can tell us much about someone's current emotional state and the type of person they are (warm or cool, fearful or calm, dominant or submissive). For example, research shows that people can accurately detect tension in a person's voice (Pittam & Scherer, 1993), even over the telephone. One way we evaluate whether a person is trustworthy is whether what's said verbally matches how what's expressed nonverbally. Someone at a party who says "I'm having a great time" in a flat, monotonic voice is not likely to be believed. Nor is someone who says, with an upbeat tone of voice, "I'm having a great time!" when their house is burning down likely to be believed.

Research shows that folks who are depressed are more likely to use a flat, monotonic, and expressionless voice when speaking; to talk more slowly than others; and to exhibit longer pauses during conversations (e.g., Cannizzaro et al., 2004; Hoenig et al., 2014; Yang et al., 2013). Similarly, they may more likely end a sentence with a downward rather than upward inflection—which can signify a low mood, but also be interpreted as boredom or disinterest, making those on the receiving end less likely to affiliate. Unfortunately, OC biotemperamental heightened threat sensitivity makes a monotonic and expressionless voice more likely. In an effort to compensate for this, some develop an overly singsong or hypermelodic tone of voice that does not reflect inner experience (such as a happy singsong voice when feeling envious or resentful) or is context-inappropriate (such as a happy singsong voice when reporting that your partner's having an affair). Interestingly, empathic responses have been shown to be accompanied by prosodic matching; that is, the person responding mirrors the same voice qualities the speaker used (Couper-Kuhlen, 2012). In general, if you want to signal friendly intentions, match the voice tone of the person you are interacting with. If their voice tone is sad, so is yours; if their voice tone is excited, yours will be too. The most obvious exceptions to this "rule" are during times of conflict. Matching the voice tone of someone yelling in anger by yelling back typically escalates the conflict.

Fortunately, you can change overlearned vocal habits with a little practice. Try these strategies.

- ☐ If you tend towards an overly prosocial melodic or sing-song voice, practice matching your tone of voice to the topic being discussed, rather than always sounding "upbeat." For instance, if you're talking to someone about a major loss, use a sad or angry voice, not a happy or content one.

- ☐ If you lean toward a monotonic or flat voice tone, practice ending sentences with an upward inflection rather than a downward one. During times of conflict, practice signaling nondominance and doing the opposite of instinctive, monotonic, commanding voice tones. Raise your eyebrows (making a natural musical voice-tone more likely), and combine this with a quick shoulder shrug and *postural shrinkage*, moving your shoulders downward or collapsing them inwards (see figure 5.2 for illustrations of nondominance gestures).

Note the physical posture and raised eyebrows are essential; they help automatically change your monotonic voice tone from that of a command to an open-minded, friendly request or observation. Ultimately, to communicate emotions and intentions clearly, regardless of your vocalization style, it's important that your facial expressions, body postures, and voice tone match the emotion you wish to communicate! See box 5.2 for additional tips.

Box 5.2. Tips on Changing Voice Tone

1. Practice displaying differing emotions in your voice. Can you sound angry? Timid or meek? Silly or playful? To enhance effects, match your facial expression and body movements with the emotion in question.
2. Practice changing volume to capture listeners' attention, varying it to match your feelings or to communicate intentions. For example, when angry or wanting to get attention, raise your voice volume; when wanting to signal compassion or love, lower it—say to a whisper. Vary voice volume during interactions, too, to match what you wish to communicate.
3. Practice changing pace or rate of speech. When you want to communicate gravity, sadness, indifference, or seriousness, slow your rate of speech. If you want to communicate significance, excitement, or agitation, speed it up.
4. Practice pauses in speech to allow the other person time to respond, or for emphasis. Transitional pauses are short interruptions in speech that allow space for others to talk. Dramatic pauses set the mood or create suspense by prolonging the pause, and allow the listener time to digest what's said before you move on.

Signaling Openmindedness and Nondominance

Surveys show that most people dislike "know-it-alls"; conversely, most report liking people who are open-minded and we instinctively recognize the value openness brings to relationships. For example, open-minded people are more likely to reveal than hide their inner feelings during conflict, making them trustworthy. We want to spend time with them because they're humble; they're more likely to give others the benefit of the doubt in interactions and don't automatically assume that their way is the best, right, or only way. Essentially, openness is a powerful social safety signal because it acknowledges one's inherent potential for fallibility and signals your willingness to learn from what the world has to offer. Thus, RO DBT considers "openness" humility in action—a stance that reflects the precept "If I know anything, it's that I don't know everything, and neither does anyone else" (M. P. Lynch, 2004, p. 10).

Openness evolved in our species as a core means for establishing strong collaborative relationships; it also represents the cornerstone of all new learning. But that doesn't make it easy to do. Being open means you can no longer automatically assume your perspective is correct. Ouch! (Tee hee.) Practicing radical openness requires you to take responsibility for your choices and responses to the world—meaning you can no longer simply blame others, fall apart, expect the world to change, or get down on yourself upon discovering a painful truth. Bummer! (Tee hee.)

We'll talk more about what it means to practice radical openness in our next chapter. For now, know that simply allowing yourself to consider the possibility that your perspective may be wrong or that the feedback you're receiving may be correct or helpful, and then communicating this to another person, automatically sends a powerful message of friendship, openness, and equality (Lynch, 2018a). Signaling openness helps ensure that our cooperative intentions are perceived as intended, especially in times of potential conflict. It allows others the luxury of dropping their guard, too, because they can sense that you're open to their point of view. Crucially, openness does *not* mean approval, naively believing, mindlessly giving in, or resignation.

Nonverbally, openminded behavior is associated with expressions and gestures universally associated with friendliness, curiosity, and nondominance: eyebrow wags, smiling, openhanded gestures, shoulder shrugs, affirmative nods, a musical tone of voice, and taking turns during conversations—basically, all the things you've likely been practicing throughout this chapter! Furthermore, the most powerful signals of open-mindedness usually involve expressions of humility, nondominance, and appeasement.

- Research shows that *appeasement gestures*—like lowered gaze, blushing, and postural shrinkage—are essential when you're making an apology. People distrust expressions of guilt (such as saying, "I'm sorry") if they're unaccompanied by bodily displays of appeasement (Ferguson et al., 2007; Halmesvaara et al., 2020). Such nonverbal displays of appeasement signal that you value the relationship because you're viscerally distressed by the effect your actions have had, which makes it easier for the other person to trust you won't commit them again.

- *Nondominance signals* are essential when you want to encourage critical feedback or communicate that you aren't trying to manipulate or control the other person. They combine appeasement signals (e.g., slight bowing of head or shoulder shrug, openhanded gestures) with cooperative-friendly signals (e.g., warm smile, eyebrow wags, eye contact). Plus, since expressions of nondominance signal equality, humility, and respect, they're also extremely useful when you're making a difficult request, asking for help, confronting, or providing someone corrective feedback. (See figure 5.2.A for an example of the former, and figure 5.2.B for an example of the latter.)

Figure 5.2. Appearement and Nondominance Gestures

Many OC individuals (but not all) report finding it difficult to display nondominance and appeasement gestures—even when the situation clearly calls for it. Some report finding the very *thought* of displaying nondominance or appeasement revolting—recall the importance to most OC individuals of not appearing vulnerable. If you don't have much experience displaying signals of appeasement or nondominance, it'll likely feel a little awkward or phony when you first try them out. But the best way to get over this feeling and improve your social signaling is to practice, practice, and… practice some more. So, buckle up, because it's time to practice signaling humility, nondominance, and appeasement! (Yippee! Tee hee).

As before, get your smartphone out and record yourself during your practice (or use a mirror). Let's start with appeasement gestures—the ones essential for an apology to be received as genuine. When making an apology, since you've actually done some form of harm to another, like stepping on their toe, and regret doing so, it's important to combine appeasement gestures with expressions of concern. So, you wouldn't want to smile or display eyebrow wags; doing so would make your apology appear insincere.

- Record yourself saying "I'm sorry" with appeasement gestures and a concerned expression (e.g., slight bowing of head, slight shoulder shrug, openhanded gestures, furrowed brow, slight grimace of pain). Record yourself doing this several times. Notice which gestures you find most difficult or awkward to display; these are the ones you'll need to practice the most.
- Next, record yourself saying "I'm sorry" but *without* an appeasement gesture—for instance, with your shoulders back and chin up.
- Record yourself again saying "I'm sorry" with shoulders back, chin up—but now add a smile and eyebrow wag.

- Lastly, go back and watch all the recordings you made in this part of the exercise. Are you able to notice a difference between the apologies made with appeasement gestures and expressions of concern versus those without? Which feels most sincere?
- Practice using appeasement gestures in the real world, at times an apology is warranted.

Next, let's practice signaling nondominance (yowsers! Tee hee). These are the signals to use when you want to communicate equality with another, encourage or give feedback, communicate that you're not trying to manipulate or control another person, or ask for help. They combine appeasement signals like a slight bowing of head, slight shoulder shrug, or openhanded gestures with cooperative-friendly signals like a warm smile, eyebrow wags, and eye contact.

- Record yourself practicing displays of nondominance, and repeat them multiple times. Use figure 5.2 as your guide for what nondominance displays look like.
- When you're done, watch the recording of yourself and evaluate what it feels like to receive this social signal.
- Were there any gestures you found difficult or awkward to display? (Again, these are the ones to practice most.) For added fun, show your recordings to a friend. Ask them which expression feels more friendly or which they'd prefer to spend more time with.
- Start looking for opportunities in the real world where it'd be helpful for you to display nondominance, and try it out. Notice how they impact interactions. Record any observations below. And remember: it'll take time for these gestures to start becoming a natural part of your social signaling repertoire—and the interpersonal rewards you'll experience from using them will be well worth it. So, don't give up and keep practicing.

____

____

____

____

____

____

Silly Social Safety Signaling

We might've titled this section "How to Signal Safety by Not Being Serious," but we thought that sounded too serious to really convey the importance of being silly (tee hee). But—why would silliness be beneficial? Most adults work hard to avoid appearing silly in front of others. Most likely our avoidance stems from our deep-seated fear of being socially humiliated or ostracized. Still, many people also *enjoy* behaving in a silly manner, particularly when around friends. In fact, some even make a living out of it, like clowns or comedians! Regardless of age, silly behavior around another person—especially when they have less social power than you—is an act of kindness, and a powerful signal of nondominance, equality, and friendship. It signals, to anyone lucky enough to be present, that (1) we are the same as them, (2) we trust them, and (3) they're in our tribe. Think of how often we make funny faces or use silly voices when talking to young children. It's because we recognize acting silly with kids helps them feel safe and lets them really explore, learn, and grow.

And as any parent knows, the best silly behavior stems from the heart and is as much fun for the sender as it is for the recipient. The problem, for those of us who are no longer children, is that having fun while being silly can be hard to do. But even cranky adults can learn to enjoy being silly—it's all about giving yourself permission, throwing yourself into the deep end, and then practicing, again and again. And for those of you squirming (and we know you're out there; tee hee), know that you only need be silly for a second or two for it to create beneficial social bonding effects. Moreover, you need only be silly around those with whom you wish to establish or maintain a close social bond. Indeed, most people reserve silly behavior for family, friends, young children, and others they feel safe with and strong affection towards. But it also works with people you don't know very well! (Yowsers!) So, what does a silly social signal look like?

Silly behavior—like friendly jokes, teasing, or play—always involves some form of exaggerated yet prosocial signal. What makes it fun and exciting is how boldly it tends to violate societal norms and expectations—ideally spontaneously, without much premeditation. For example, if you're reading this book in a room occupied by your family or friends, simply getting up and walking backwards while saying "beep boop bop bope," like a stiff robot, will likely elicit smiles and giggles—and convey to those observing that you're in a playful mood and mean them no harm. It's also unexpected and violates social norms; you don't usually behave like a robot, and walking backwards isn't a socially sanctioned means of mobility. Finally, it's non-threatening, because it doesn't involve feedback or *require* a response from the person observing. In other words, silliness is meant to be socially bonding, not challenging.

Importantly, being silly doesn't mean silly all the time—that would be silly (tee hee). Some situations—like attending a funeral, stating an important opinion, or soothing a friend's pain—call for solemnity, seriousness, or gravity. Also, how another person will respond to your silly behavior depends on many factors, like how well they know you, the extent they see you as a friend, or their current mood. But regardless of how it's expressed, or what you feel or think inside, silly behavior, deployed at the right time, always gets its prosocial message across—even when you might feel like you're being seen as "a total wacko and out of your mind" (tee hee). (The only exception to this is when another person strongly dislikes you, or genuinely wishes you harm. In these situations, which we'll discuss further in chapter 9, other strategies are needed.) And none of these caveats should stop you from acting silly, especially when among friends or with people you wish to develop a closer relationship with. Engaging in silly social signaling with another person makes it clear to them that you mean them no harm, lightens up tense social interactions, and models both the importance of not always following the rules and the fact it's healthy to not take life or oneself too seriously.

> **Tom reflects:** *One of my uncles (Uncle Peter) has a habit of appearing to fall asleep whenever a family discussion was about something he was bored with or if the discussion became too heated—and if it continued, he would eventually begin to snore (often quite loudly). Everyone knew he was fake sleeping—but usually someone would nudge him to "wake" him up. Whereupon he would suddenly sit up and with an exaggerated yawn and sleepy voice and cheesy grin say something like "Did I miss something?" Although not everyone found it particularly funny in the moment (especially if they were involved in the heated discussion), his loony behavior always seemed to lighten things up. And his antics and self-effacing humor are what makes him so approachable and fun to be around!*

The story above highlights how you don't have to be funny or make the other person laugh to achieve social bonding benefits from a silly social signal. But you might be wondering, especially if you're not used to silly social signaling, what to do *after* a silly social act. How will others take it? How should you respond?

As you might guess, it depends, in part on the context you're in and the relationship you have with those on the receiving end. If the other person laughs or joins in by being silly themselves, then you most often won't need to do anything afterwards; your signal of social safety appears to have worked as intended. However, as a rule of thumb, *if your silly behavior is not reciprocated in any form* (e.g., by a slight smile or chuckle), it helps to *shrug your shoulders and say with a smile: "Oops, just trying to lighten things up."* This can also be combined with a brief explanation of your odd behavior, if they continue to be nonresponsive (to make it clear that you are trying to be funny not challenging). For example, say you decide to try out the silly robot move described earlier. If nobody reacts, shrug your shoulders and say with a smile "Oops, just trying to lighten things up." And if they continue to be nonreactive or appear confused, you might explain your actions further, by saying something like, "I'm reading a book about the importance of being silly, and I thought I'd try an example of what a silly social signal might look like. So, did it seem silly enough to you?" *(Big smile.)* Like any new skill you learn, silly social signaling is likely to feel awkward at first—especially if you don't have much experience with it. So, practice, practice, and practice some more.

Let's take a moment to reflect about silliness. Record your answers to the questions below in the spaces provided.

When I hear the word "silly," what type of thoughts, emotions, or images arise?

____

____

____

Have I ever been given feedback that I work too hard or that I need to relax? Would being silly help with that?

____

____

____

How often do I find myself laughing, chuckling, or giggling without trying? How often am I silly? Who am I silly around? When was the last time I was silly?

____

____

____

Do I ever feel like an impostor when telling someone a joke or a funny story? What do I fear might happen if I were silly around my friends, family, or children? To what extent do I believe being silly is a silly thing to do (tee hee)?

____

____

____

____

____

Now, let's practice! We'll use a blend of two silly social signals that take only seconds to do but universally signal safety, humor, and nondominance. Super!

The "Oh, My Gosh!" silly social signal. In many ways, silliness is intentionally revealing vulnerability to another person for the benefit of the relationship. The "Oh, My Gosh!" silly social signal is one means of doing this, while keeping things light. It involves a blend of two nondominant expressions that together signal openness, transparency, humorous vulnerability, shared experience, and friendly intentions. It also involves not hiding how you feel—especially in situations that involve feeling surprised, "caught-out," or like you've done something wrong when you actually haven't. For example, after tasting an unexpectedly spicy morsel of food, you might openly show your astonishment, rather than hiding it.

For most people—and especially if you lean OC—feeling surprised, caught out, or like you're doing something wrong is often experienced as shameful, even when that's unwarranted. What is great about the "Oh, My Gosh!" signal is that it helps you "go opposite" to *unwarranted* shame or embarrassment. Openly revealing vulnerability with humor tells your brain that there's nothing to be ashamed of, whereas trying to hide it tells your brain that you must've done something wrong. Plus, since we're all fallible, recipients of this signal experience social safety too, since revealing vulnerability to another human being essentially says, "I'm the same as you." It signals that "we're all in this together" and celebrates our shared potential for fallibility. The reality is all humans react similarly to certain types of stimuli. For example, we all "duck down" when encountering a looming object; *not* ducking would be atypical behavior. Thus, not showing distress after making a mistake, or hiding astonishment or surprise after encountering something unexpected, are also atypical for most humans—suggesting that the sender is special or different from others. What's nice about the "Oh, My Gosh!" is that it allows one to express vulnerability without getting too heavy about it.

So, how do you do it? As you'll see in illustration 5.4, it most often begins with a brief "Oops" expression involving an open, round mouth, wide-open eyes, and raised eyebrows, followed immediately by a cheesy "appeasement grin" involving raised eyebrows and a slight shoulder shrug accompanied by a wide-open smile, with teeth showing. It usually triggers shared laughter, smiling, nodding, and giggling from recipients. You can use it to signal openness and shared vulnerability after making a minor mistake (like mispronouncing a word), when you want to signal that the topic you're about to discuss may be anxiety producing (but don't want to make a big deal out of it), or when you want to signal that reacting anxiously would be normal response (e.g., we all feel anxious when encountering the unknown). What's cool is that the "Oh My Gosh!" signal doesn't need to be long-lasting or extreme to make its point—it takes only seconds.

So, let's practice the "Oh, My Gosh!" (Yippee!) As before, get your smartphone out and record yourself during your practice, or use a mirror.

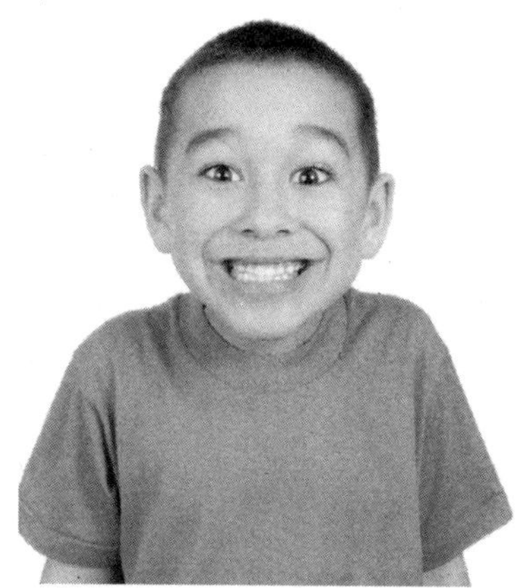

"Appeasement Grin"

Illustration 5.4. The "Oh My Gosh!" Silly Social Signal

- Let's start with the "Oops." Use illustration 5.4 to guide you. Form your lips into a tight but open circle (as though saying "Oh!"), and raise your eyebrows, with your eyes wide open, in an expression of astonishment. It can help to say "Oops" aloud when you're first practicing.
- Now, try it again. Only this time, follow the "Oops" expression with an appeasement grin, raising your eyebrows and giving a slight shoulder shrug and a cheesy grin (a wide, open-mouth smile with teeth showing).
- Repeat the process a couple of times.
- When you're done, watch the recording and evaluate what it feels like to be on the receiving end of this social signal. Were there any gestures or expressions you found difficult or awkward to display? (Again, these are the ones to practice most.)
- For added fun, show your recordings to a friend. Ask them which expression feels more friendly or which they'd prefer to spend more time with.
- Finally, start looking for opportunities in the real world where it would be helpful for you to display nondominance—and start trying out what you have learned. Notice how they impact interactions. Record any observations below.

Like any new skill you learn, signaling the "Oh My Gosh!" is likely to feel awkward at first—especially if you don't have much experience with it. But, since we know most OC folks tend to be overly serious, performance-focused, and hyperperfectionistic, learning how to signal a little levity may come very useful.

Movement, Speed, and Flow

The social signaling skills we have taught in this chapter represent only a subset of the total possible. (Remember from the start of the chapter how many facial muscles humans possess!) The advantage of learning universal prosocial signals is that you can use them to override overlearned OC tendencies for indirect and ambiguous signaling that's subject to misinterpretation by recipients by interspersing prosocial signals into your conversations. And what's double cool is that it doesn't take long to get the prosocial message across; you can often do it in just milliseconds.

But is it possible to have too much of a good thing?

Yes! Just like chocolate cake, prosocial signaling is great in small doses, but too much, and it can lose its appeal. Excessive prosocial signaling is just as off-putting as none at all. Ultimately, what's important to remember is that easygoing interactions involve a movement, speed, and flow that adjusts according to the situation you're in and the responses of those you're interacting with. For example, when leaning back in your chair in the Big Three + 1, don't forget to lean forward occasionally too, varying the gesture so it remains natural to those receiving it. When we're among friends, we naturally sit forward, sit back, gesture expansively when making a point, smile, frown, look concerned, or take a sip of our tea—often without thinking about it. Sitting still or in one position for a long period of time—that is, being forced with your performance of a gesture like the Big Three + 1—inevitably starts to feel odd, not only to those receiving your social signal but to you as the sender. In fact, frozen expressions, postures, or gestures feel phony because they actually send a message to the brain that danger may be present, not safety. Consider when a rabbit sees a fox: the first thing it does is freeze all body movement, to make it less likely to be seen; the freezing is an expression of its felt sense of threat. Real people, in real-life friendly exchanges, do not sit still, always smile, or keep their eyebrows raised the entire time—unless they're doing some major drugs! Don't take our word for it: go to a park, crowded restaurant, or shopping mall and notice the gestures, facial expressions, and movements people use when interacting with each other. We unconsciously adopt the postures, gestures, and mannerisms of our close friends, and we desire to spend time with those who mimic us (Lakin & Chartrand, 2003; Lakin, Jefferis, Cheng, & Chartrand, 2003). For example, when our friend laughs, we laugh with them; when they take a sip of water, we take one too. When we distrust someone, by contrast, we don't mimic or match their social signals; instead we automatically tighten our gestures and body movements, look away or blankly stare when they speak, don't laugh at their jokes or smile when they do, and so on. Observe which postures, gestures, and facial expressions result in people moving closer together, and which result in people moving away, averting their gaze, or breaking contact.

Universal prosocial signals are also often expressed as blends. For example, we might signal noncritical appreciation or warmth by slowing our pace or rate of speech and slightly lowering our volume of voice (which mimics how we speak to those we love in our most intimate moments; Lynch, 2018a), combined with a warm closed-mouth smile, an eyebrow wag, and affirmative nodding. Note some prosocial signals can be held longer than others. For example, the closed-mouth cooperative smile can be held for relatively long periods of time (say, a minute) without your feeling or looking awkward—especially when you're listening to another person who is speaking to you. And you can enhance it still further by adding a prolonged eyebrow wag. Again, don't take our word for it; try it out yourself! Next time you're in a conversation involving feedback from another person, raise your eyebrows and engage a closed-mouth smile for five to twenty seconds or so when the other person is speaking. Experiment with differing durations, too, and notice how it impacts your feelings about the other person or the interaction itself. But whatever you do, don't forget that the core idea: make sure you're *interspersing* your conversations with *occasional* prosocial signals, ones that change over the course of the conversation in response to the signaling of the person you are interacting with. So, sit back or sit forward, frown or smile, but whatever you do, make it real.

The last section of this chapter pulls it all together by linking the social signaling you've been practicing to valued goals.

Linking Social Signaling to Valued Goals

A core premise of RO DBT is that our individual experience of well-being is highly dependent on the extent to which we feel socially connected or part of a tribe. And so, an overarching goal of RO DBT is *creating a life worth sharing*, through the practice of radically open living. Radically open living means learning how to flexibly adapt your behavior to everchanging circumstances in order to achieve goals or live according to your values, in a manner that accounts for the needs of others. For OC folks, this can mean learning how

- to not always play by (or enforce!) the rules,
- to not always base decisions on winning or achievement,
- to let go of compulsive striving or obsessive self-improvement, and
- to learn how to celebrate ineffective moments as opportunities for growth.

Another way to create a life worth sharing is to practice social signaling according to your values. For example:

- If your valued goal is an improved relationship with someone, you might try signaling interest rather than boredom.
- If your valued goal in a given moment is to be taken seriously, you might signal gravity and confidence—looking the other person in the eye, speaking calmly but firmly, keeping your shoulders back and chin up.
- If your goal is to establish a close social bond, signal friendliness, with eyebrow wags, warm smiles, openhanded gestures, a musical tone of voice, nodding, taking turns in conversation, or gently touching them on the arm.
- If your valued goal is to be honest and forthright, express what you're feeling inside on the outside, when the situation calls for it. When sad after a loss, cry. When uncertain about something, shrug. When you like what you hear, nod to affirm it. When praised, smile warmly and express thanks.
- If your valued goal is to be fair-minded, signal openness. When listening to feedback, use an eyebrow wag. If you're sitting, lean back in your chair. Slow the pace of conversation by taking a deep breath. Take turns, and allow the other person time to respond. Validate others' experience by matching their expression, rather than staying calm or flat. Use openhanded gestures, maintain a musical tone of voice, and signal nondominance by shrugging when you're uncertain.
- If your valued goal is to not be arrogant, signal humility. Maintain eye contact, bow your head slightly and shrug your shoulders, and use openhanded gestures and a compassionate voice tone.

Now, to end the chapter, let's take a look at how Elijah used the skills outlined in this chapter in his life.

• *Elijah*

Since I've been learning some RO DBT skills, I've started to recognize how some of my overcontrolled perfectionistic tendencies aren't all that helpful—especially in my relationship. I think part of what gets in my way with my partner is that I'm always trying to be the "nice guy" with everyone, but when I come home, I can be a little, well, not so nice. It's hard work to be polite and upbeat all the time while keeping everything running smoothly. Most people don't appreciate the amount of self-sacrifice it takes. The one place I do expect appreciation is at home—and I hate it when my partner doesn't show appreciation for my sacrifices. I mean, not that we've ever discussed it—and I don't ask for appreciation, because I don't believe I should have to ask for it at home. Suffice it to say, it's also one of the issues we're most likely to argue about.

What really brought it home to me was when I decided to "help" my partner out by rearranging their desk in their home office—it's always such a mess. So, one morning before work, while they were still asleep, I got out the vacuum, duster, trash bags, glass cleaner, furniture polish, sponge, mop, and a bucket. I took everything off the desktop first. There were layers of old papers, books, discarded tissues, and other trash all piled up on top. I threw out anything that looked useless, and then put everything else in a couple of big boxes that I thought I'd sort out later. I then organized their bookshelves alphabetically (don't ask me why they've never done this before) and returned any loose books to their rightful places on the shelves. I then cleaned their desk and computer and vacuumed and polished every available wood surface. It took more time than I'd expected, but I went to work with a sense of accomplishment, all while my partner blithely slept on.

That evening, I was late getting home, because I was forced to make a special trip to the only store that sells the special French furniture polish I like, to replace what I had used that day, plus another side trip for some lip balm. I was exhausted and hungry when I finally arrived home. That quickly turned into annoyance—my partner, rather than showing any appreciation for me cleaning up, started to tell me about how they'd had to cancel a talk they were supposed to give at their bird club earlier that day, because they couldn't locate the lecture notes they'd carefully placed on top of their desk the night before. "That's too bad, dear," I said—I remember my teeth were gritted—and then I told them I wasn't hungry and was going to bed "to read." My partner then asked, "What's wrong?" I replied, "Nothing, I'm fine," with a forced smile—and I started to turn away. But I could see their look of concern, and the hand they'd extended towards me. It was at that moment that I realized I had an opportunity to change how things went by changing how I was responding. I remembered that one of my valued goals is to practice being more open and vulnerable with my partner—including admitting to feelings or behavior I'm not proud of, that could damage our relationship—rather than hiding or pretending everything's okay.

So, I took a deep breath, eyebrow-wagged, and said, "It's kind of embarrassing to admit this. But I just realized I'm pouting—and that's not how I want to behave when it comes to our relationship. I told you I was going to bed because I wanted to punish you for not showing any appreciation for how I rearranged your desk today. So, you were right to ask me 'What's wrong?' because there actually was something wrong. I also realize you never asked me to rearrange your desk—I just did it. And although I thought you'd be delighted, I never stopped to consider that you might not have wanted things reorganized." I paused, and then using an appeasement gesture and an expression of concern, I said,

> *"So, not only do I apologize for my standoffish behavior—I'm also really sorry that my need for neatness interfered with your lecture today. Next time, I'll ask before I clean." Then I smiled, warmly. And my partner responded warmly back! They thanked me for being so honest. Pretty soon we were both laughing about how things don't always work out as planned. What could have been a disaster turned into a moment of intimacy, and a very nice dinner too!*

Elijah's story illustrates what's possible when you bring RO DBT social signaling skills into your life. He chose to be more candid and honest about his feelings, rather than pretending he was fine and walking away. Openly acknowledging desires to punish his partner, admitting to behavior he was embarrassed about, and then apologizing for any harm done—all are powerful prosocial and intimacy enhancing signals. They signal that you trust the other person, because we don't reveal vulnerability to people we distrust. And they allow the other person to drop their guard, because you're taking responsibility for how you may have contributed to a problem without falling apart, which makes it more likely they'll respond similarly. With his warm smile, Elijah was able to extend his apology further without getting too heavy-handed about it. This served to signal to his partner that Elijah was sincere, and not harshly blaming himself for his mistake, either. Taking responsibility for how you may have contributed to a problem, and openly revealing your feelings and desires to those you wish to be close to, have enormous benefits. Not just for the relationships, but also for you—because when you start living by your values and true feelings, integrity and self-respect flourish.

Moving Forward

In our next chapter, we'll move to radical openness and self-enquiry skills. It's an important part of our journey together, one we hope will be both exciting and challenging! But before we go there, we encourage you to commit to practicing the social signaling skills you learned in this chapter and monitoring their impact on your relationships. Use the worksheet below to monitor your progress and record what you learn. And have fun!

Worksheet 5.1. Activating and Signaling Social Safety

Social Signaling Skill	Days Practiced	Impact on Relationships
Eyebrow Wags	☐ Monday ☐ Tuesday ☐ Wednesday ☐ Thursday ☐ Friday ☐ Saturday ☐ Sunday	
Closed-Mouth Cooperative Smiles	☐ Monday ☐ Tuesday ☐ Wednesday ☐ Thursday ☐ Friday ☐ Saturday ☐ Sunday	
Big Three + 1	☐ Monday ☐ Tuesday ☐ Wednesday ☐ Thursday ☐ Friday ☐ Saturday ☐ Sunday	
Changing Voice-Tone	☐ Monday ☐ Tuesday ☐ Wednesday ☐ Thursday ☐ Friday ☐ Saturday ☐ Sunday	

Social Signaling Skill	Days Practiced	Impact on Relationships
Nondominance and Appeasement Gestures	☐ Monday ☐ Tuesday ☐ Wednesday ☐ Thursday ☐ Friday ☐ Saturday ☐ Sunday	
Playful & Silly Signals ("Oh My Gosh!," "Oops!," cheesy appeasement grin)	☐ Monday ☐ Tuesday ☐ Wednesday ☐ Thursday ☐ Friday ☐ Saturday ☐ Sunday	
Movement, Speed, and Flow	☐ Monday ☐ Tuesday ☐ Wednesday ☐ Thursday ☐ Friday ☐ Saturday ☐ Sunday	
Signaled According to My Valued Goals	☐ Monday ☐ Tuesday ☐ Wednesday ☐ Thursday ☐ Friday ☐ Saturday ☐ Sunday	

Social Signaling Skill	Days Practiced	Impact on Relationships
Other Social Signaling Skills Practiced	☐ Monday ☐ Tuesday ☐ Wednesday ☐ Thursday ☐ Friday ☐ Saturday ☐ Sunday	

CHAPTER 6

Radical Openness and Self-Enquiry

Thus far, we've discussed a lot about how OC brains are wired, how they respond to the world, and what keeps them stuck. Plus, in our last chapter we learned how to activate and signal social safety and considered how openness and open-mindedness might be useful. But you might've noticed that we haven't said much explicitly about "radical openness"—which seems fairly important considering it is the "RO" in RO DBT (yowsers!). *For example, what does radical openness mean? Why should I care about it? How will it help me?* This chapter aims to answer these questions—and to encourage you to cultivate a personal practice of radical openness and self-enquiry.

Let's begin with some core precepts. For example, radical openness assumes that we don't—we can't—know reality just as it is. We all bring perceptual and regulatory biases—the beliefs and habits shaped by our "nature" and "nurture"—with us into every moment. These biases often interfere with our ability to be open and learn from new or disconfirming information. And, perhaps more importantly, they can negatively impact our relationships. One example of a perceptual bias that can powerfully and negatively impact relationships is known as the 'fundamental attribution error' (Ross et al., 1977). *Attribution errors* affect how we determine who or what is responsible for having caused an event. Often, we tend to judge others' behavior as revealing something fundamental about their character or personality; we blame them. Our own behavior, by contrast, is the result of circumstances or contexts beyond our control; we don't blame ourselves.

What's amazing is that our perceptual biases are so much a part of us that we often don't even recognize them as biases; it's a bit like asking a fish to notice the water they are swimming in. For example, expectations about someone change how we behave, or socially signal, when we're around them. For instance, you've heard that a new person attending a meeting is unfriendly, so you don't bother to introduce yourself. This impacts *their* behavior—they opt not to speak to you—which reinforces your original expectations of them as unfriendly, in a self-fulfilling prophecy. Essentially, your expectations about *what will happen* ("They'll be cold to me") can influence *what does happen* (you behave in ways that make it likelier they'll behave coldly). Before you know it, you've got a new enemy at work—and in this particular case, your hostility would be directed towards someone you've never actually met. Yowsers!

But biases aren't just about expectations—they also have to do with what you attend to. For example, have you ever noticed that we're more likely to pay attention to things that confirm our beliefs and ignore or dismiss anything that doesn't? Social psychologists call this phenomenon a 'confirmation bias'. Examples include searching for proof that your belief is true, interpreting evidence that supports your view favorably, recalling only selective information that supports your view, or believing that views held by most people are always right (see figure 6.1, "Who Me, Biased?"). This cartoon demonstrates how perceptual biases can influence not only personal responses but also others' well-being (yowsers!).

We all do this sort of thing sometimes. And for those of us with high threat sensitivity (like OC folks), it can become a habitual way of responding that can impair relationships because it is predisposes us to see the potential for harm in unexpected, novel, or ambiguous situations rather than the potential for reward (or safety). When pervasive, it can result in an angst-ridden, lonely existence.

Figure 6.1. "Who Me, Biased?"

Take a moment to consider the following questions.

When you're confronted with a different point of view about something important, how do you typically respond?

What is your favourite strategy to avoid hearing a different perspective or opinions you don't agree with? Do you walk away, change the topic, talk over, pretend to listen, act bored? Or something else? *How open do you feel to considering the possibility that your beliefs and perceptions about the world or other people may sometimes be wrong or biased?*

What expectations or beliefs do you strongly hold about yourself, the world, or other people? For example, a belief that others will work as hard as you will, that the world should be stable or orderly, or in your ability to overcome any obstacle or solve any problem. *How might these expectations or beliefs impact your relationships?*

Let's hear from Tula:

A friend of mine who knows that I spend a lot of time alone often makes suggestions for how I can broaden my circle of friends. Whenever she says stuff like this, I usually act bored and try to change the topic. But inside I'm angry, because she doesn't understand what it is like to be a social outsider. And I feel envious because she makes building friendships look so easy. So, I feel justified ignoring her advice, because her attempts to be helpful prove that she doesn't really know me.

Tula's recollection helps demonstrate the ways we can work to avoid feedback or novelty, justify our actions, interpret events so as to stay closed to new perspectives, or reject suggestions or corrective feedback. However, knowing when we're operating from a state of closed-mindedness can be extremely difficult. For example, have you ever been convinced you were open in the heat of the moment, only to realize later that you weren't? And sometimes, our perspective "feels so right" that it "feels wrong" to question it. Yet, as a species, we uniquely value fairness (Shaw & Olson, 2012). For example, unlike most species, humans do not automatically side with their allies or kin (DeScioli & Kurzban, 2009) and most people desire to be perceived by peers as fair-minded. Openness and fair-mindedness are valued because they enhance social connectedness and signal social safety to others: essentially, "I will take your needs into account." Yet, we're not always fair or impartial, and our perceptual biases can trick us into believing otherwise. For example, one way to maintain an illusion of impartiality is to always consider *our opinions as statements of fact* and *statements from others as opinions.*

> **Tom reflects:** I have come to realize that when I find myself trying to convince others (or myself) that I am open, most often I am not.
>
> (Lynch, 2018a, p. 186)

How does closed-mindedness manifest in your life? For example, during a heated discussion do you

- frequently repeat, justify, or reexplain yourself or your point of view,
- avoid eye contact or look down,
- speak with a commanding, sarcastic, or monotonic tone of voice, or
- repeatedly interrupt, change the topic, speak faster or louder, or talk over the other person?

How do you behave when you're not open? Use the spaces below to record your answers.

____

____

____

____

____

____

____

RO DBT posits that there's a way to loosen the grip of closed-minded thinking and behaving. It involves the creation of a *temporary state of self-doubt* in which we recognize that *we don't see things as they are, but as we are*—because it's impossible for us to rid ourselves of our personal backgrounds or the biogenetic predispositions that bias our perceptions (Lynch, 2018a). According to RO DBT, healthy self-doubt requires balancing *trusting versus distrusting* oneself. Essentially, the question is, *to what extent can I trust my personal perceptions at any given moment to accurately reflect reality?*

> One secret of healthy living is the cultivation of healthy self-doubt.
>
> (Lynch, 2018a, p.184)

Of course, in absolute terms, the answer to this question is: perhaps never. But the synthesis for this dilemma, from a RO DBT point of view, involves learning to *listen openly to criticism or feedback*, without immediate denial (or agreement), and *developing a willingness to experience new things with an open heart, without losing track of one's values.* Ultimately, openness and receptivity to new experiences, alongside flexible control and intimacy and connectedness, are the building blocks of psychological health according to RO DBT (see chapter 1). Radical openness also holds that we often learn the most from those areas of life that most challenge us. In radical openness, we don't assume the world needs to change so we can feel better. We set an intention to explore those areas of our lives that are difficult, painful, or disturbing. We practice willingness to surrender our preconceptions about how the world "should be" to adapt to the everchanging environments in which we find ourselves. And, at its most extreme, we actively seek out the things we might wish to avoid, in order to learn.

Now let's dig a little deeper by considering what radical openness is and is not (adapted from Lynch, 2018b, p. 62):

Radical Openness Is	Radical Openness Is Not
• Being open to new information or disconfirming feedback in order to learn. • Learning to celebrate self-discovery: freedom from being stuck. • Rewarding—it often involves trying out novel ways of behaving that may help us cope more effectively. • Courageous—it alerts us to areas of our life that may need to change. • Capable of enhancing relationships—it models humility and readiness to learn from what the world has to offer. • A process of purposeful self-enquiry and willingness to acknowledge one's fallibility, with an intention to change (if needed). It can be both painful and liberating. • A way to challenge our perceptions of reality based on assumptions that we all have perceptual and regulatory biases, and thus, *we don't see things as they are—we see things as we are.* • Being *open* to learning new things, which involves a willingness to consider that there are many ways to get to the same place. • About taking responsibility for our personal reactions and emotions—without falling apart or automatically blaming others or the world. • Meant to help us adapt to an ever- changing environment, rather than being stuck rigidly responding to situations in ways that don't actually serve us.	• Approval, naively believing, or mindlessly giving in • Assuming one already knows the answer • Something that can solely be understood intellectually—it requires direct and repeated practice • Rejecting the past • Expecting good things to happen • Always changing • Being rigid about being open

Nicole notes that, as someone who leans toward OC, the concept of practicing radical openness initially ran counter to every fiber of her being! Her biotemperament was one that craved certainty, predictability, symmetry, and perfection. But over time, as her practice of radical openness grew, so did her relationships.

So, how do you go about developing a practice of radical openness? By practicing a skill, we call Flexible Mind DEFinitely. (We played around with calling it Flexible Mind *DEFiantly* but decided that would be too silly, even for us, tee hee.) The first three letters of DEFinitely are capitalized because they form an acronym or memory aid, with each capitalized letter representing a different skill. So, let's DEFinitely get going! (Sorry, we couldn't resist saying that. 😊)

Flexible Mind DEFinitely

D: Acknowledge current-moment Distress (or unwanted emotion). The first letter in this skill is brought to you by the *letter D*, which stands for *distress* (or any unwanted emotion). The reason we start with acknowledging distress is because distress usually means that our SNS defensive-arousal system has been activated, making us automatically less open, because our brain has already "decided," usually without conscious awareness, that the situation we're in is threatening (rather than safe or rewarding). Thus, current-moment distress can often alert us to our biases and areas in our lives where we may need to change or grow. In fact, often, our most powerful moments of self-growth occur when we attend to what we don't want to know, admit, or change about ourselves. Acknowledging distress and unwanted emotions helps you make contact with your personal unknown (the place you may need to grow), a process known in RO DBT as *finding your edge*. Your *edge* almost always pertains to actions, thoughts, feelings, images, or sensations that are associated with things you want to avoid, are embarrassed about, or don't want to admit to. Importantly, your edge does not have to be about big issues or emotions for learning to occur. Our reactions to minor events (like feeling upset about someone yawning while you're speaking) can teach us as much as more dramatic ones (like arguing with your partner).

That said, it's important to note that painful emotional reactions are not always "edges." Personal unknowns or edges are an *atypical response* to an event—meaning, it's not how most people would have responded in similar circumstances. For example, feeling anxiety when a bomb goes off or when you're unexpectedly asked by your teacher to take over the class lecture would be normal responses, not necessarily your personal unknown. So, how can you know for certain if your reaction to an event was normal or atypical? There's no perfect way (sorry), but one helpful way is to examine the extent you find yourself brooding or ruminating about the event after it was over. Feeling anxious when asked to take over teaching a class is how most people would respond, but not being able to stop thinking about how wrong it was to be asked in the first place is atypical (and possibly your edge). The point is: you can expect life to provide you with plenty of opportunities to practice finding your particular edges (😊).

In that spirit, right now, take a moment to recall an event that occurred in the past week where you felt distress or an unwanted emotion that may have signified you were at your edge. For example, look for a time when you felt challenged, criticized, or invalidated, or instances where things did not go as expected, planned, or predicted; or small grievances, like annoyance at someone tailgating you on the highway or not saying "Thank you." It could even be about something you have recently read in this book!

Describe the distressing event in the spaces below. *What happened and who were you with?*

____

____

____

____

From there, with your distressing experience in mind, ask yourself:

1. *Was I in a novel or uncertain situation?*

   ____

2. *Did I feel invalidated, misunderstood, or criticized?*

   ____

3. *Were my expectations or beliefs about the world, other people or myself being challenged? Did I feel a need to defend myself or desire to attack the other person?*

   ____

   ____

   ____

4. *How was my reaction to the event atypical or different from how others may have responded in similar circumstances?*

   ____

   ____

   ____

5. *What emotions did I feel? What thoughts did I have? What sensations did I feel? For example, tension, annoyance, fear, numbness?*

___

___

___

6. *Did I brood or ruminate about the event or situation afterwards? Did I find myself thinking about the event at times I should've been attending to other matters?*

___

___

___

With this, you've done the first step of the skill, which is to *acknowledge* that distress or unwanted emotion was coming your way that could be your edge. This brings us to the second step in Flexible Mind DEFinitely.

E: Practice self-Enquiry. After acknowledging distress—locating a possible edge—you'll practice self-enquiry to learn from your distress, rather than automatically denying, avoiding, distracting, regulating, or accepting it. Self-enquiry is healthy self-doubt in action; it begins by asking yourself, in challenging situations, *"Is there something here for me to learn?"* rather than automatically assuming your perspective is correct, defending yourself, or trying to emotionally down-regulate. In self-enquiry, we recognize that in order to learn anything new, we must first acknowledge our mistake or lack of knowledge. It's particularly useful whenever we find ourselves strongly rejecting, defending against, or feigning agreement with events or feedback that we find challenging or unexpected. It's integrity in action, because it recognizes that our personal well-being is highly dependent on others, and there's no escape from our tribal responsibilities or prior commitments. In fact, a core RO DBT principle is that our perceptual and regulatory biases mean we simply can't achieve this degree of self-awareness in isolation. We need others to point out what we can't see ourselves.

> If you value integrity: start training yourself to face yourself.

Importantly, self-enquiry is not ruminating about a problem, because it's not looking to solve the problem, avoid discomfort, or come up with a better way to justify our perspective. The main idea when asking "Is there something here for me to learn?" is to locate a probing question, image, or word that brings you closer to your personal unknown (or edge)—rather than quickly find an answer. Quick answers to self-enquiry dilemmas usually function to regulate, and most often reflect old learning or desires to avoid uncertainty. This is why it's important to keep your self-enquiry practices short (e.g., five minutes in duration). Longer practices can sometimes be secretly motived by desires to find a quick solution or force insight. Short and frequent (e.g., daily) practices, using the same question or a new question that's emerged from the previous day, are usually more effective. Allow yourself time to discover what you might need to learn, over a period of days, rather than quickly searching for a way to confirm your worldview, explain things away, or regulate. Indeed, a self-enquiry practice might eventually lead you to the conclusion that there's actually nothing to learn from the situation you were working with or that being closed was actually what was needed at that particular time.

Practicing Self-Enquiry

The good news is that self-enquiry can be used both during (in the heat of the moment) and after a challenging event. To use self-enquiry in the heat of the moment, follow these steps.

1. During challenging or emotionally charged social interactions, such as:
    a. When you're feeling misunderstood, invalidated, annoyed, tense, numb, stubborn, resistant, or superior, or
    b. When your social signaling suddenly changes—e.g., you find you become less talkative, suddenly avert your gaze, or stop smiling
2. Rather than looking for how you can prove your point of view: *consider the possibility that you are at your edge.*
    a. Silently ask yourself, *Is there something here for me to learn?*
3. Then, quickly turn your mind back to fully participating in the interaction.
    a. To maximize open-minded listening, whenever you find you're feeling less receptive, repeat the question: *Is there something here for me to learn?*
    b. Notice what happens in your body each time you ask the question. Does your breathing slow or your body feel more relaxed? Do your facial expressions or body posture change?
4. Be suspicious of quick answers.
    a. Quick answers often represent desires to control, avoid, or defend oneself (masquerading as insight).
    b. Quick answers also block further self-enquiry, because the "answer" removes the dilemma by making the unknown known again.
5. After the interaction, examine your experience.
    a. Ask: *What was my edge?* Or, *What question do I need to ask myself to bring me closer to my personal unknown?*
    b. Use this question, image, or word to facilitate further self-enquiry.

(For a handout of these steps, visit http://www.newharbinger.com/50782.)

When practicing self-enquiry *after the event*, find a place where you can be alone for five minutes and bring with you some paper and a pen, or come back to this workbook. Begin the practice by looking for a question, image, or word that brings you closer to your edge. A good self-enquiry question is one reflecting genuine curiosity—one we don't already believe we know the answer to. Perhaps the best self-enquiry question is the one you dislike the most (tee hee)! You can also use one of the questions below.

- *What is it that I don't want to admit to or think about?*
- *How have I contributed to the problem?*
- *What is my edge trying to tell me?*
- *If my dark side could speak, what would it say?*

Record verbatim, without editing, whatever thoughts, emotions, images, memories, or sensations that arise during the practice. Notice and record any new edges that emerge. After about five minutes, stop the practice.

____

____

____

____

____

____

____

____

____

____

____

____

Allow yourself three to four days of repeated practice for each edge, and then *let it go.* There's no need to keep focusing on the same event—if nothing useful arises, then so be it. Trying to dig deeper is trying to force new learning to occur. It's ruminating in disguise and most often motivated by perfectionistic tendencies to find a solution. And don't worry: if the edge you were exploring is an important one, it'll show up again in your life in some other way. You can afford to let go of it now. Instead, look for global patterns in your practices, and notice how questions and your approach to them evolve over time. For example, during practices:

- *Do you tend to justify, defend, or explain yourself?*
- *Do you tend to lose focus easily, daydream, launch into long stories, go numb, or desire to give up?*
- *Do you tend to blame yourself or others for your problems?*

Answers to these questions often lead to a new area of self-growth—a new line of self-enquiry. Regardless, the overall aim of a self-enquiry practice is new learning—and so, after three to four days of repeated practice around the same issue, some sort of answer is likely to appear. And that's okay. Just remember: every answer that emerges from self-enquiry, however seemingly profound, wise, or discerning it may appear, is still subject to error (tee hee).

Importantly, self-enquiry is intended to allow space for new learning to emerge, don't be surprised when it doesn't—even after four days of repeated five-minute practices. The idea is to have a light touch, rather than trying to force new insights or work harder. Allow yourself the grace and freedom of not always having to have an answer, and recognize that you can always return to a certain question again—say, when circumstances change, or if bodily tension keeps reemerging around the same issue. In our experience, most of the time, something useful *does* emerge from repeated self-enquiry practice about a particular edge. The idea is to keep your practices short but frequent, and record observations in your self-enquiry journal. And who knows—you might be pleasantly surprised by what you discover! (Tee hee.)

Here are additional self-enquiry questions you may find helpful (Lynch, 2018b, p. 63).

- *Is it possible that my bodily tension means that I am not fully open to what is happening right now? If yes, what am I avoiding? Is there something here to learn?*
- *Am I talking more quickly or immediately responding to the other person's feedback or questions? Am I holding my breath or breathing more quickly? Has my heart rate changed? If yes or maybe, what might this mean? What's driving me to respond so quickly?*
- *Do I find myself wanting to automatically explain or defend myself, or to discount what's happening or the other person's point of view? If yes or maybe, is this a sign that I may not be truly open? What is it that I might need to learn?*

- *Am I saying to myself "I know I'm right" no matter what they say or how things seem? Or do I feel like shutting down, quitting, or giving up? If yes or maybe, what might this mean? Is there something here to learn?*
- *Do I believe that further self-examination is unnecessary because I have already worked out the problem, know the answer, or completed the necessary self-work about the issue being discussed? If yes or maybe, is it possible that I'm not willing to truly examine my personal responses?*
- *Am I finding it hard to engage in self-enquiry? If yes or maybe, what might this tell me about myself or the situation I am in? Is there something here to learn?*

You might've noticed that most self-enquiry questions do not begin with "why." Why? Mainly because asking why encourages explanations of reasons believed to underlie the existence or occurrence of an edge; they don't challenge its existence and its underlying assumptions. Answers to why questions often end up sounding like old stories we've told ourselves (often for years) or justifications for our behavior that keep us stuck in old patterns rather than leading to something new or encouraging change. After all, most people who lean toward OC are fixers and problem solvers; and crave the why. But what is more important is actually the "what"—as in, "What is it that I need to learn about myself or about this situation?"

Imagine this scenario. Your friend has agreed to come to coffee, but is twenty minutes late. You're a punctual person and expect the same of others. You might be noticing an irritation grow or find yourself ruminating on how your friend is always late. Or you might think something like, "They need to get their priorities straight." If you don't do self-enquiry with these thoughts and feelings as they arise, your friend might find you tense and distant when they arrive—just twenty minutes late, because a full bus simply blew past them. But if you turn toward the irritation or rumination you feel and ask yourself, *Is there something here that could be learned?* you might end up much more open when your friend does arrive. You could also ask other self-enquiry questions: *Am I automatically blaming another person or my environment for my emotional reactions?* Or, *Where did I ever get this idea that the world should conform to my schedule?* Or, *Is this tension telling me I am not open to being flexible at this very moment?*

Making Self-Enquiry Part of Daily Life

To cultivate healthy self-doubt as a capacity, it's helpful to practice daily (without being too rigid about it; tee hee). Again, one way to ensure this happens and track your progress over time is to start a self-enquiry journal. If you've ever kept a journal or diary, this might be a natural extension for you. However, the kind of journal we're talking about here isn't a narrative of events, but a leaning into an edge, as described in the DEF skill. Generally, you'll record the images, thoughts, emotions, and sensations that emerge during a solo five-minute practice after a challenging event. You wouldn't pull out your journal in the heat of the moment ("Excuse me, I'm recognizing an edge—let me practice some self-enquiry so I can flexibly respond"). Instead, you'd sit down to practice at the next best opportunity. Your journal can also be used to record insights, thoughts, questions, or potential edges that spontaneously arise as you go about your day that you wish to save for a future self-enquiry practice.

Let's take a peek at Tula's journal to understand how it works.

- *Tuesday*

My friend Yonas stopped by today when I was in the middle of doing some chores. I've told him repeatedly to call before stopping by, but he tells me that his schedule is too sporadic to predict that (he works as an internet repairer) and that internet/phone connectivity is usually offline in the areas he's sent to make repairs. I felt myself getting hot, and annoyed that his unexpected visit meant that he would see my house before I had a chance to tidy up. And true enough, when he arrived and glanced around, he winked and said, "Wow, really lowering the standard around here!" Although RO DBT skills had taught me about friendly teasing, at the moment I was—what? Embarrassed? Angry? Well, maybe both. But the thought that gets me closer to my edge is something like, How dare he comment on a work in progress! *So, what feels more like an edge? The teasing? Or the "how dare he"? "How dare he" seems like an old story—it regulates me a bit, so maybe it is about being teased. Hmmm. So, what is it that I need to learn? Hmmm. I'm not sure. Nothing is showing up. Wait…something just popped up—*Is there a part of me that is afraid to show my real life to my friends? *That seems close—but I don't feel I'm fully at my edge. Wait… something else has arisen:* Is it possible that being offended by teasing is one of the ways I block intimacy? *Ouch. I don't seem to like that question. So, it looks like a good one. But it's been about five minutes now—I need to stop my practice for today. Ugh. I will look at this some more tomorrow.*

Did you notice that Tula first described the challenging event and how she reacted to it, without justifying, explaining, or defending herself? Plus, she recorded verbatim whatever arose in her mind during the practice—without editing, say to make wording more coherent or appear wiser. For example, she allowed herself to record her confusion about emotions that were experienced (anger or embarrassment?). Importantly, her overall focus wasn't on finding a solution for her distress, but finding and deepening her understanding of her edge. This included noticing which question, thought, emotion, image, or sensation brought her more closely to it. Here, it was a question she didn't particularly like: *Is it possible that being offended by teasing is one of the ways I block intimacy?* She then stopped the practice. *Gasp!* Stopping a practice abruptly like this can feel strange or difficult for people who lean toward OC; their intolerance of uncertainty makes them more likely to seek quick answers and then fix problems right away in order to prevent future ones from occurring. Self-enquiry goes opposite to these tendencies. In it, you give yourself the grace of uncertainty and adopt a stance of open curiosity, with the overall aim of personal growth. Thus, Tula puts the journal away until tomorrow—where she'll use the question she ended with to kick-start her practice. So, let's look at what happened then.

- *Wednesday*

Okay, so the question was "Is it possible that being offended by teasing is one of the ways I block intimacy?" I have an urge to say no and be done with this. Looking further in, however, I notice some sadness coming up. It brings a memory of when I was little and felt like such an outsider at school. Everyone seemed to know how to joke and tease each other. They made it look easy. But, when I tried to tease or join in, they looked offended or something. And I thought to hell with this. What's coming up now? Anger. No one taught me how to tease. In fact, as far as I can remember, no one in my family ever teased or joked with each other. But where did I ever get the idea that it was someone's job to teach me how to tease? Is it possible that my resentment about not being taught how to tease allows me to feel that my avoidance of teasing is justified? I feel some tears welling up. Hmmm. What is it I need to learn? What makes teasing feel so dangerous? Wait, I think the question that gets me closer to my edge is: Do I trust my friends enough to let them tease me? *Hmmm. Wait, maybe a step closer…* Is my resistance to teasing more about me not trusting myself to know how to respond? *Ouch, that last one hurt. I think I should stop here. I'm worried that I'll fall back into trying to solve things too much. Tomorrow, I'll begin my practice with this last question.*

Tula continued this self-enquiry on teasing for another two days. The idea is to limit your practices to three to four days for each edge—and then move to another, with the understanding that you might return to a particular edge later. This keeps your practices from getting too heavy. Remember, OC folks tend to be too serious about life; be careful not to turn your self-enquiry practices into another burden. And if you're worried about finding another edge, don't bother—there usually is one waiting for you just around the corner (tee hee)!

> When you start asking "What do I need to learn?" instead of "What did I do wrong?" when things don't go your way, perfection no longer exists as the metric by which you judge success.

Tula's self-enquiry journal also highlights some other broad principles. First, the entries were short because the practices were short (approximately five minutes). Second, note she consistently ended a practice when she noticed desires to solve the problem or get a quick fix. Recall that most people who lean toward OC *love* to fix things! And thank goodness, as this has helped our species survive. But, as we've been learning throughout this book, too much fixing is not only exhausting; it often leads to more problems. Self-enquiry helps us practice letting go of compulsive fixing, by temporarily embracing uncertainty, and then letting it go—knowing that you can always return to it the next day. For Tula, her brief but repeated practices of self-enquiry about the same edge—on teasing—ultimately became an important step in her journey to learn how to not always take life so seriously and playfully interact, joke, and enjoy both teasing and being teased by her friends. Wow!

Thus, if you haven't done so already, we encourage you to start a RO self-enquiry journal. Importantly, self-enquiry is a personal journey. It's for you alone; neither your journal entries nor the insights, emotions, thoughts, or new learning that emerge during a practice need to be shared with anyone (even your therapist). That said, it can be fun and socially bonding to share your experiences from self-enquiry practices with, say, a like-minded friend. So, don't keep it a total secret—you may be pleasantly surprised by what happens when you reveal your inner experience, doubts, and fears to a person you want to be closer to! And in our opinion—and as you'll see in chapters to come—the risk is worth it.

Okay, phew! We have now completed the E in DEFinitely. But before we move on, let's practice what we've learned.

- To begin, recall the edge you hope to work with (which you discovered when practicing the D in DEFinitely).
- From there, do a self-enquiry exercise, in your journal or the space below, using the skills from the E in DEFinitely as your guide. Briefly describe the events that elicited the edge you're working with, and then ask, *What is it that I might need to learn?* Use the questions offered in this chapter, or others that emerge, to deepen your practice, recording what arises—without editing what you write. Remember that the goal of self-enquiry is not to find a good answer but to find a good question and then allow an answer—if there is one—to be discovered over time. Be suspicious of quick answers; often they are old stories disguised as insight.
- Keep your practices short. Allow about five minutes, and then stop when time is up (regardless of where you are). You don't want to be *too* rigid about this, of course—but try to stay within this time frame.
- After you've completed the practice, plan for a follow-up self-enquiry practice, ideally the next day. Start that practice off using the question, image, or word most closely aligned with your edge from the previous day.
- And after four days—you're done! At least, until the next edge arises (tee hee).

If you find yourself resisting self-enquiry, or unable to locate your edge, use the questions below to explore your resistance.

- *What might my resistance be trying to tell me?*
- *Is it possible that I'm numbing out or shutting down in order to avoid taking responsibility or make important changes?*
- *What does my resistance tell me about myself or my willingness to engage in learning this new skill?*
- *What am I resisting? Is there something important for me to acknowledge or recognize about myself or the current moment?*

Let's also review a few reminders about what self-enquiry is NOT.

- The goal of self-enquiry is to find a good question (or image, memory, or thought) that gets you to your edge, NOT to find a good answer.
- Self-enquiry is NOT ruminating about a problem, because it's not looking to solve the problem or avoid discomfort.
- Self-enquiry does NOT mean that truth does not exist, or that we should never trust our intuitions. Instead, it means allowing ourselves to not always assume we're right, so we can stay open to all possibilities.
- Self-enquiry does NOT mean getting down on oneself. Yet it can be painful, at least temporarily, because it often requires surrendering long-held convictions or cherished beliefs.
- Self-enquiry is NOT expecting the world to change or blaming others.

Well done! We're ready for the final step in Flexible-Mind DEFinitely!

F: Flexibly respond with humility. Flexibly responding is doing what's needed in the moment, and adjusting one's behavior to changing circumstances in whatever way is needed for optimal performance—in a manner that accounts for the needs of others and how our behavior may affect them. Interestingly, flexible responding may only really matter when we are around others. When you're alone—say, stranded on a desert island—it probably doesn't really matter whether you insist on doing the dishes "my way," dutifully wake at 6 a.m. every day, eat the last doughnut, rearrange the furniture, yell, cry, work until 2 a.m., talk to yourself—or fart aloud, for that matter (tee hee)—because no one's around to be impacted by your behavior. For our primordial ancestors, members of the tribe unwilling to be flexible in how they met personal needs (e.g., peeing upstream of the tribe's fresh water supply), prioritized their needs over others (e.g., ate their fill before sharing with others), or appeared unconcerned or unaware of how their behavior might harm others (e.g., falling asleep on guard duty) were likely to be ostracized or banned from their tribe, making personal survival less likely. Which is why RO DBT considers emotional well-being a social process, and probably why we care so much about the opinions of others.

Indeed, the emphasis on accounting for others' needs in the achievement of personal well-being is what differentiates RO DBT from most other treatments. In RO DBT, individual well-being is inseparable from the feelings and responses of the larger group or community. This is informed by observations and research showing that our personal happiness is highly dependent on other people and the extent we feel part of a tribe. Robust research shows that when we feel connected, we feel less agitated, less anxious, less depressed, and less hostile. Yet, accounting for the needs of others while trying to flexibly respond to changing circumstances is challenging to do! Mainly because it may require temporarily foregoing the fulfillment of personal needs, when a situation calls for it—for the benefit of another, to maintain an important relationship, or to contribute to the tribe—and ideally without *always* expecting something in return (which, BTW, is the foundation of a true friendship). Yowsers!

But that doesn't mean that flexible responding means giving up on ever meeting one's personal needs, mindlessly capitulating, or simply giving in to the needs of another. Again, we're *taking the needs of others into account while taking care of ourselves*. We're finding a balance between personal needs and the needs of others in order to live most effectively and create a life worth sharing (with others). Similarly, flexible responding is humility in action, yet it can boast with the best of them, when boasting is needed—for example, to ensure that hard work is recognized—and it can also mean being arrogant with the arrogant, for example to stand up against injustice to protect others. It means being receptive to disconfirming feedback *without* simply giving up or automatically abandoning one's prior convictions. When you're OC, this may translate into temporarily letting go of rigid rule-governed behavior, urges to fix, desires for order and structure, or desires to appear calm or in control. You might not complete a task on time, break a rule, reveal a vulnerability, or allow yourself to be late for an appointment, so as to avoid damaging an important relationship, validate another's perspective, or help someone achieve a valued goal.

In addition, flexible responding takes context into account in deciding how one should behave—especially when it comes to emotional expression. For example, sometimes inhibiting an expression of emotion is necessary—whether for survival (e.g., when captured in war), to protect oneself or one's tribe (e.g., not letting an opponent know you're afraid), or as an act of kindness (e.g., a mother suppressing tears when telling her young son he's been diagnosed with cancer). However, sometimes appearing too controlled, too self-possessed, or too accepting in circumstances that call for open and uninhibited expression of emotions (e.g., discovering your best friend has just won the lottery, or praising a child for a job well done) can send the wrong message. Effective expression is flexible because it accounts for the type of relationship you're in (e.g., with a competitor, a new boss, or the police, versus with your best friend, partner, or next-door neighbor) and the appropriateness of expression in a given context (e.g., getting through passport control, a business meeting, a high-stakes poker game, or going out on a first date). Thus, effective flexible responding when around other people involves three transacting elements (see figure 6.2):

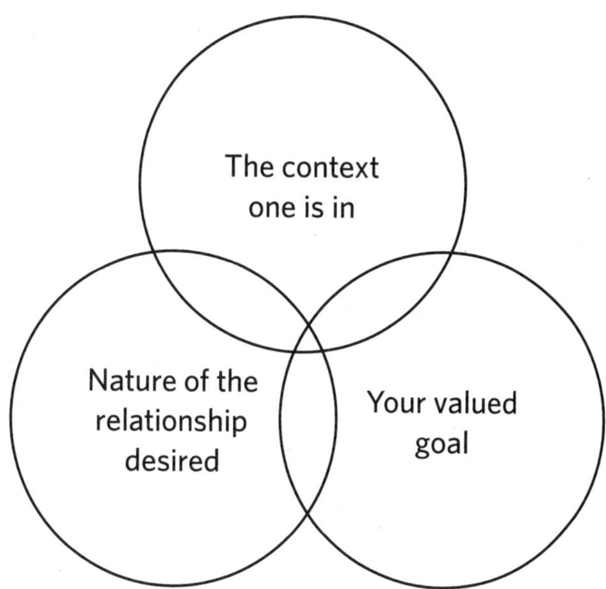

Figure 6.2. Flexible Responding Involves Three Transacting Elements

As you'll see, you can use your valued goals to guide how and what you express (socially signal) to achieve the type of relationships you desire.

To do this,

- Start by reflecting on the level of intimacy you would like to have with the other person.
- Then, match your nonverbal signaling to your valued goals. Ask: *To what extent does my social signaling reflect my valued goals?* For example, is there any chance that your tendencies for flattened facial expressions and monotonic voice tones go against your valued goal of showing interest in other people? If you find yourself struggling to answer, consider asking a friend the same question and see if their response helps you decide.
- If you decide that your social signaling may be problematic, then ask: *What do I need to do differently? What social signals do I need to learn to display in order to more fully live by my valued goal?* For example, if your valued goal is to be seen as confident but not arrogant, you might signal openness and humility when stating opinions by maintaining eye contact, using openhanded gestures,

and speaking calmly, with shoulders back, interspersed with occasional shoulder shrugs (see "Linking Social Signaling to Valued Goals" in chapter 5 for more examples).

Essentially, your valued goals help guide you how to behave. For example, you might wish to tell a lie or bend the truth in order to win an argument, but upon reflection, recognize that doing so would go against a valued goal you have for honesty and integrity. That would make lying a less likely outcome—which is likely to benefit your relationships while simultaneously enhancing your self-esteem; we all feel good when we're acting in line with our values. (Yowsers!)

Identifying your valued goals for different relationships also helps you flexibly modify your social signaling depending on the situation you're in. For example, for a parent whose valued goal is to maintain frequent contact with their young adult son living away from home, flexible responding may involve making their initial response to their son's calls home an expression of warmth and interest rather than worry and concern—even when it's 2 a.m., or when they themselves have had a bad day. *The point is, you don't have to feel good on the inside to signal friendly intentions or live according to your values on the outside.* That's why flexible social signaling is also such a powerful tool in the pursuit of wellbeing. It provides benefits for both the sender and the recipient—with an improved relationship the most likely outcome.

Now let's put the F in DEF into practice! To begin, recall the edge you identified when practicing the D in DEFnitely above, as well as the outcomes from the self-enquiry work you did when practicing the E skills in DEFinitely. If the edge you chose earlier did not involve another person, then think of another edge or challenging event that did involve another person or other people. If possible, pick an edge concerning someone with whom you desire a close relationship, like a friend, spouse, or family member. Now, with this event in mind, ask: *To what extent does (or did) my social signaling reflect my valued goals?* Use the additional questions below to help deepen your search for how best to flexibly respond.

- *What type of relationship and level of intimacy do I want with this other person (or persons)?*
- *How do I want to be perceived by the other person?*
- *How has my social signaling impacted the relationship?*
- *What emotion do I wish to express?*
- *Does the emotion I wish to express fit my valued goals?*
- *To what extent did the consequences of my social signaling achieve my original intentions?*
- *To what extent am I proud of how I socially signaled?*

Write your reflections in the space provided.

____

____

____

____

____

____

Next, using your reflections above as a guide, practice flexible responding. Ask:

- *What do I need to do differently?*
- *What social signals do I need to learn to display in order for me to more fully live by my valued goal?*
- *What might I need to change about my social signaling to achieve the type of relationship I desire with this person or adjust to the changing circumstances?* (Be specific. Describe the nonverbal features that may need to be present to ensure your message is received as intended—e.g., changes in voice tone, rate of speech, eye contact, head nodding, smiling, appeasement and nondominance gestures, eyebrow wags, or the Big Three + 1. See chapter 6 for other ideas.)

Use the additional questions below to help deepen your search for how to best flexibly respond.

- *Do I need to practice signaling my intentions or emotions more directly to this other person?*
- *To what extent do I need to take into account contextual factors? For example, will the interaction occur at work or at home?*
- *To what extent do I need to ensure that I am responsive to what the other person's signals? For example, displaying sadness when they reveal a loss, laughing or smiling when they laugh or smile.*

Record your answers to any one of these questions below. And don't forget to record specifically both *what* you might need to say and *how* you might need to say it to flexibly respond and meet your relationship goals.

Now, take what you came up with above and put it into practice in the real world! And afterwards, evaluate how it went using the following questions as a guide.

- *Did your practice of flexible responding appear to change how the other person behaved during the interaction?*
- *If so, how did it manifest? Did the interaction go as you might have hoped or expected? If not, then what is it you might need to learn?*
- *Do you feel closer or further away from them after the interaction? What might this tell you?*
- *Is there a part of you purposefully trying to make this difficult? For yourself? For the other person? What might this mean? What is it that you need to learn?*

Yippee! And phew! You've now successfully completed the DEF skills in DEFinitely! Well done—most DEFinitely! (Sorry, we couldn't resist saying that…again. 😊)

Moving Forward

OK, now that we're all radically open and raring to go—oh wait, radical openness needs to be practiced over and over (sorry 😊). So, do be sure to continue practicing the skills you've learned in this chapter, especially in moments you've hit an edge or your overcontrol tendencies have kicked into overdrive.

Having said that, we're ready for the next step in our journey: learning how to learn from feedback. (Yikes!)

CHAPTER 7

Learning from Feedback (Yikes!)

As we learned in chapter 6, radical openness asserts that we often learn the most from those areas of life we find most challenging. Interestingly, what we often find most challenging is feedback from other people. In fact, most people dislike corrective feedback, often strongly. It can be painful to be on the receiving end because it can imply that we've done something wrong, or feel like rejection. Research shows that social rejection triggers the same areas of the brain that are triggered when we experience physical pain (Eisenberger & Lieberman, 2004). Corrective feedback also highlights those areas in our life that may need to change, and change is difficult.

But it's also a primary means to acquire vast amounts of knowledge and skill that would be impossible to acquire on our own. Imagine trying to design a rocket capable of flying to the moon without any assistance or prior knowledge of physics, mathematics, or aerospace engineering. Even if you had access to all the necessary textbooks, it's unlikely you'd feel very confident about your design or the calculations you used to determine mass ratios, launch trajectories, or exhaust velocities without feedback from an experienced rocket scientist. In fact, the capacity to benefit from the tribe's collective wisdom, without having to experience everything yourself, may be a defining feature of the human species.

You may agree with this, and yet, if you experience maladaptive perfectionism, you're equally likely to believe you must never make mistakes and always be right. Such beliefs make it hard to be open to feedback, because being open means you can no longer automatically assume your perspective is right. A seemingly unsolvable dilemma can emerge: if you must always be right, receiving feedback often means you're wrong, and made a mistake; yet, receiving corrective feedback is also often the only way to grow. Yikes!

This chapter will provide you with skills to help resolve this dilemma, derived from two fundamental RO DBT precepts (Lynch, 2018a):

1. *We don't know everything; therefore, we will make mistakes.*

2. *In order to learn from our mistakes, we must attend to our errors.*

To begin this journey, let's start out with a story. Cool!

The Story of Oog-Ahh (Sometimes a Cow Is Not a Cow)

(Adapted from Lynch, 2018b, p. 408)

Once upon a time, long ago, in a Stone Age hunter-gatherer community called "Tribe Roc," lived a tenacious tribal member known as Oog-Ahh (meaning "little one with strong will"). From a young age, Oog-Ahh dreamed of being a great hunter. Unfortunately, fate seemed to not be on his side. Over the years, Oog-Ahh became increasingly near-sighted—a fact he tried to avoid admitting; sometimes even to himself, after smacking into a tree.

His poor eyesight soon became a liability on hunting expeditions. And things only got worse, when he mistook the Tribal Chief's foot for a groundhog, accidentally spearing him in the toe. Despite these setbacks, Oog-Ahh persevered.

One day he and his fellow tribe members were out hunting and gathering, as was their way, when suddenly Oog-Ahh froze and pointed excitedly, saying, "Oooga booga buggy tooga!" ("I see a cow!") "Nup, Oog-Ahh," the other members replied, "buggy booga teartooga toc!" ("No, Oog-Ahh, it's a tiger— run away!")

Oog-Ahh faced a dilemma— should he believe his own eyes or his tribe's? Standing firm might prove his worth as a hunter and mean cow for dinner for everyone! But then, listening to his friends might prevent him from being dinner. Ultimately, Oog-Ahh chose to eat his pride and ran away with his tribe as fast as he could—as low growls were heard from behind.

Everyone was happy! Oog-Ahh was able to live another day, and the tribe was able to benefit from his excellent mushroom-picking abilities the following morning. And over the years, Oog-Ahh's retelling of his infamous encounter with a man-eating cow, with gleeful self- effacing caricature, became a source of tribal legend and delight for the weans (or "children," as we now know them). Thus, Oog-Ahh's openness to feedback made his dreams of becoming a legend come true.

The moral of this story is that Oog-Ahh's willingness to openly listen to critical feedback was not a mistake. To survive, Oog-Ahh had to be open to receiving feedback that challenged his perceptions—specifically, that his cow was not a cow, but a tiger instead. Equally importantly, the tribe had to be willing to provide Oog-Ahh with critical feedback to save him and tolerate a potential temper tantrum (Oog-Ahh was sometimes a little scary, because he liked to carry around a big stick). The point is: giving and receiving feedback is best when it's a two-way street. Revealing our opinions, beliefs, and observations to others (e.g., "Hey, I see a cow… Let's go check it out") provides them an opportunity to give us feedback (e.g., "Yep, that's a cow," or "No, that's a tiger!"). It also granted our species a huge evolutionary advantage; individual survival and success no longer depended solely on personal perceptions or trial-and-error learning. This helps explain why we're so concerned about the opinions of others—and why we ought to practice being open to feedback—and be like Oog-Ahh (tee hee).

Feedback: The Good, The Bad, and The Ugly

The good news about feedback is that not only is it the quickest and most efficient way to acquire new knowledge, but it's part of our social glue. It helps us understand our role, function, and status in our tribe or community. Back in our cave-dwelling days, feedback allowed us to know if we were really pulling our weight in the tribe. Feedback can be direct (e.g., "I would like you to listen more effectively") or indirect (e.g. a social signal from another person such as a frown, yawn, or smile).

But if feedback is such a basic part of the human interchange, why do most of us dread it so much? Well, the bad news about feedback is that it can be painful to receive. If you lean toward OC, again, you may hear feedback as criticism or a reminder that you're not perfect. Plus, as we've been learning, being open to feedback requires a person to drop their perspective (at least temporarily) in order to absorb a new one. And who wants to do that—especially when you know you're right? (Right?) Moreover, being open to another person's perspective also necessitates a willingness to trust the good intentions of the person we are interacting with, or to believe in the correctness of the source of collective wisdom (such as a written document or a tribal elder's memory). The worry is: *What if the source of my new learning is wrong or intentionally deceptive?* Oh, my! But most of us can also recall a time when we initially rebuffed feedback only to learn later that it was actually helpful (a.k.a., eating humble pie).

Finally, there's the ugly about feedback. Say your neighbor decides that to become a rock star, they must learn how to play the electric guitar, and ear-splitting howling, screeching sounds start emanating from their downstairs apartment every day and most of the night. Ouch, talk about "feedback"—that hurts the ears just thinking about it! Unfortunately, this chapter won't be teaching you how to appreciate amplified acoustic feedback beloved by guitarists (tee hee); nor will it address how to give neighbors feedback about noise, specifically. We'll be learning how to *give* feedback in a later chapter (chapter 9). Here, we'll learn *how to be receptive to feedback from others.* The basic idea is that before you start giving others feedback, it helps to know how to take feedback from others yourself. Importantly, being receptive to feedback doesn't necessarily mean accepting it as truth—so, part of our work working with feedback will be determining whether to accept or decline it too. Let's get going!

Not All Feedback is the Same

Again, believe it or not, our personal well-being and sense of self are highly dependent on feedback from our fellow tribal members. Innately, most of us recognize that simply looking in the mirror and telling ourselves that we're lovable, competent, or good doesn't really get the job done. We depend on our fellow tribal members to verify our worthiness by providing us feedback. Interestingly, feedback from others, or interpersonal feedback, can be placed into two broad classes, as feedback that targets (1) performance and achievement of goals, or (2) participation and social connection.

Performance-based feedback is about how you're behaving (e.g., thinking, feeling, speaking, working, or functioning) compared to others in achieving goals or meeting societal expectations and norms. It can be verbal, or nonverbal (e.g., a harsh glare directed towards someone laughing during a funeral). And it usually matters most to the person on the receiving end, when it pertains to the achievement of goals relevant to their personal well-being. But how people respond to performance-based feedback varies widely. For example, as we have been learning, perfectionistic OC folks hold high standards about performance and are hyperconcerned about making mistakes. Consequently, most of them prioritize performance-based feedback over participation-based feedback targeting social connectedness. If this describes you, you're likely to strongly dislike any form of attention that makes you feel evaluated, examined, appraised, or criticized—making performance-based feedback your nemesis (and something you may not want to admit or reveal to others).

In contrast, *participation-based feedback* is not about achieving goals or behaving in accordance with societal norms, but about engagement and participation in community and intimate relationships. Tribal bonds and intimate relationships depend on reciprocal exchanges and participation from all members to be successful. For example, you might receive requests to participate in community efforts, like participating in the maintenance of a community garden, that are about joining with others for the benefit of the entire tribe. Requests for participation from close friends, family, or partners, on the other hand, often involve intimacy bids or requests for greater closeness: bids like "tell me more about yourself," or "let's spend more time together."

Interestingly, when OC individuals participate with others, it's often done out of a sense of social obligation, not anticipatory reward. Ask an OC person, "Why did you go to the party?" and you are likely to hear something like, "Because it was the right thing to do" rather than "Because I thought it would be fun." Maybe you've even said this to someone yourself at some point! And because OC folks value prediction and control, they're more likely to prefer participating in structured social events that involve a set agenda, clearly defined goals, or preassigned roles—like business meetings, classes, town hall meetings, or a choir rehearsal. They're more likely to turn down, avoid, or find excuses to not attend unstructured—and thus unpredictable—social events requiring spontaneity, joining with others, or sharing inner experiences, like picnics, parties, or romantic dinners. And BTW, it's usually not because they don't desire to be close to others. Often, it's more about not knowing *how* to get close to someone.

Take a second to think about how this may manifest in your own life. Have you struggled recently with participation-based feedback? And—have the skills you've learned so far shown you some ways to begin opening up?

____

____

____

____

Performance- and participation-based feedback can also be about things you've done "right," not just what you need to improve. Perhaps unsurprisingly, perfectionistic OC people may find praise just as difficult as harsh criticism. They may believe that *only outstanding performance* is worthy of reward, that praise means more will be expected from them, or that they're being manipulated. As a result, they're more likely than others to automatically ignore or downplay the praise, change the topic, or imply they don't deserve it.

Fortunately, if this describes you, change is possible. But first, let's explore some of the *ways we wiggle our way away* from feedback first. (BTW, we thought about making "Ways We Wiggle Our Way Away" into a song, but lucky for you, our editors put a stop to it.)

How Do You Typically Take Feedback?

For people who lean toward OC, there are two common patterns that have been identified, referred to in RO DBT as Fixed Mind and Fatalistic Mind (Lynch, 2018b). Fixed Mind involves vigorous resistance and energetic opposition to unwanted feedback. It's like the captain of a ship who, despite repeated warnings of icebergs ahead, refuses to slow down or change course. Essentially, change is unnecessary, because "I already know the answer." When we're in Fixed Mind, we feel justified condemning, rejecting, or denying other points of view and indignant about being challenged. We don't need to listen to other perspectives; we already know what's right, correct, or the best way to proceed, or we may believe that our perspective is the only logical, obvious, or possible one to have. In Fixed Mind, we often nonverbally signal disdain, superiority, or dominance towards a person delivering unwanted feedback, with moves like crossed arms, finger pointing, frowning or scowling; standing with our hands on hips, shoulders back, and chin raised upward; or speaking with a commanding or dismissive tone of voice, interrupting, or talking over others. Finally, when in Fixed Mind, we may try to convince ourselves (and others) that our stubborn refusal to listen to feedback is morally justifiable and necessary to protect ourselves or the weak, correct a greater wrong, or retain our self-respect.

In many ways, Fixed Mind is arrogance in action. Feeling indignant about feedback we dislike proves that we care about our convictions. Refusal to consider other perspectives can become a badge of honor, and public condemnation of anyone who disagrees or questions our beliefs can be or feel like an act of courage. It sometimes gets rewarded, too. For example, stubborn refusal to back down can win admirers; repeatedly insisting an opinion is a fact can wear down the opposition; rigidly staying on course can win a race.

That said, insisting things be done *your* way or refusing to consider other perspectives ultimately comes with a cost. It damages relationships and makes new learning less likely (yowsers!). So: *What reinforces your Fixed Mind? What does it get you? What does it allow you to avoid?*

____

____

____

____

Think back to a recent argument with someone. To what extent were you confident that your point of view was right, and the other person's was wrong? Is it possible this is a sign you were in Fixed Mind?

____

____

____

____

Again, Fixed Mind isn't always "bad," as in maladaptive. Sometimes we need it to protect ourselves or others, prevent harm, or maintain our self-respect. But be careful if you start feeling self-righteous about it. Moreover, having a strong preference does not always mean that someone's operating from Fixed Mind. Sometimes a person simply doesn't like the taste of watermelon. The test is whether they're willing to reexamine their preference (e.g., to avoid watermelon) as circumstances change over time (e.g., say you're stranded on a desert island and watermelons are the only thing available to eat).

Fatalistic Mind is the dialectical opposite of Fixed Mind. Imagine that the ship captain, after hitting an iceberg, retreats to their cabin, locks the door, and sulks, ignoring pleas for help from the crew or passengers or dismissing them as pointless. Fatalistic Mind says: Change is unnecessary because change is impossible—making abandonment of duty, giving up, or shutting down feel like appropriate responses.

Rather than directly resisting unwanted feedback, Fatalistic Mind emotionally distances itself from the person providing the feedback. Discontent or dislike about unwanted feedback is signaled indirectly, through behaviors like pouting, sulking, moping, frowning, pursed lips, downcast eyes and lack of eye contact, slouched posture, sighing, crying, moaning, slowed speech, delayed responses or long pauses when queried, or a gloomy, flat, or monotonic voice tone.

As you might guess, Fatalistic Mind isn't something most people aspire to. It signals doom and gloom and a general unwillingness to seek solutions, collaborate with others, or participate in community. "I've tried everything there is to try. So, why bother?" Since Fatalistic Mind's negative attitude isn't particularly admirable, we often need to justify its existence, both to ourselves and others—for example, by self-righteously claiming the "right" to fall apart because you've been the victim of unfair circumstances or uncaring others. Or you might imply you're being forced to agree or comply with unwanted feedback by powerful others. We may contend that being overwhelmed, defeated, or beaten down is a normal or appropriate response to bullying or unfair coercion—and that passive resistance is the only way to fight back. Sneakiness, underhandedness, and deceitfulness can thus become righteous acts of courage.

Consider: Learning to cope with not getting what you want and taking responsibility for how you may have contributed to a problem—without falling apart or expecting others to solve it for you—is a core developmental task and a sign of maturity.

Essentially, rather than directly resist unwanted feedback (like Fixed Mind), Fatalistic Mind pouts about it. Of course, it's also true most adults see pouting as a generally immature way of coping, because it refuses to acknowledge a basic truth about life: "You can't always get what you want." When you pout about receiving unwanted feedback, you're signaling that it's unfair or wrong for others to say anything that might upset you, tell you something you don't want to hear, disagree with you, correct your performance, or expect you to behave responsibly, like other members of your community are. Think about it: Would you encourage a young child to pout when they don't get what they want, or stop trying at the first sign of trouble? If not, then you're not likely to be proud of your behavior when you're in Fatalistic Mind either.

Again, Fatalistic Mind signals discontent without admitting to it. It indirectly expresses disagreement and passively resists—making it hard to challenge and easy to deny, because the way it's expressed has plausible deniability. For example, *"Who, me angry? That's a laugh." "I'm not being quiet to punish you, I just don't feel like talking right now." "No, really, I'm fine. Let's do it your way."*

Even though we're often not proud of Fatalistic Mind, it does get rewarded or reinforced at least occasionally. Appearing devastated or wounded by feedback may elicit protective responses or sympathy from observers, who may try to soothe, reassure, or defend us. It may also lead people to simply stop giving you feedback or avoid difficult topics when around you. *What reinforces your Fatalistic Mind? What does it get you? What does it allow you to avoid?*

____

____

____

Ultimately, both Fixed and Fatalistic Mind damage relationships; they both rigidly assume their perspective correct and their responses righteous. A Fixed Mind, for instance, is convinced it already knows the answer and is willing to fight to prove its point. A Fatalistic Mind is equally convinced of the correctness of its perspective—in this case, that it's unfair for the world or other people to expect them to change or tell them things they don't want to hear; it'll fall apart, give up, or shut down to prove it (and then blame you).

Sometimes people flip from Fixed Mind (fighting or resisting change) to Fatalistic Mind (shutting down or giving up). For example, when Fixed Mind's stubborn insistence fails to win the argument or get you what you want, you might flip to Fatalistic Mind and pretend to agree while inwardly vowing never to change. The main point is that both Fixed Mind and Fatalistic Mind often share similar functions or motivations—for example, a desire to control, win, or prove one's correct—which are expressed in different ways. But when we operate exclusively from either perspective, we make new learning difficult, and we damage relationships by refusing to listen to alternative ideas or feedback suggesting change. Yowsers!

But here's the good news. Both Fatalistic and Fixed Mind are choices, *not* givens. For example, no one can force you to pout or sulk; nor is pouting the only response possible when you don't get what you want. You can *choose* a different way of responding: a different path. But to choose a different path—you must first know the path you are on. Specifically, are you in Fixed Mind and actively resisting feedback, or are you in Fatalistic Mind and passively resisting feedback? Use the "Fixed-Fatalistic Quick Self-Check," below, to facilitate this process.

The Fixed-Fatalistic Quick Self-Check

Think of a recent time when you were given feedback you didn't like, didn't want to hear, or disagreed with. It could be feedback from a teacher, coach, boss, or work colleague pertaining to your performance (e.g., that you need to take a break), or feedback from a partner or friend pertaining to the relationship (e.g., how you express your emotions). Ideally, the feedback should have occurred in the past week. To score your Self-Check, just count the number of boxes you tick in each column. The column with the most boxes indicates which state of mind you were most likely operating from. If you don't check any of the boxes in either column, it suggests that you are responding to the feedback with an open mind. *And for added fun, reveal your score to a friend!*

☐ **F—Frustrated:** Feeling irritated, stubborn, opinionated, resistant, argumentative, frustrated, anxious, nervous, angry, numb, frozen, or empty. ☐ **A—Arrogant:** Thinking that it is wrong for others to question your point of view, feeling offended, indignant, self-righteous, or grandiose, convinced you are right or certain that the other person is wrong. ☐ **D—Defensive:** Quickly explaining or defending yourself, talking fast, interrupting, or talking over someone, dismissing, refuting, or ignoring feedback.	☐ **U—Unappreciated:** Feeling unappreciated, misunderstood, sorry for yourself, like a victim, entitled to special treatment, helpless, non-responsive, or shutdown. ☐ **P—Pessimistic:** Feeling pessimistic about change or that change is impossible ("Why bother?"), thinking that others must change first, or hoping problems will magically disappear. ☐ **P—Pretending:** Pretending to go along or that everything is okay ("I'm fine with your feedback") while secretly harboring resentment or frustration, making false promises or faking agreement to get what you want or stop unwanted feedback. ☐ **P—Pouting:** Being non-responsive, going quiet, sulking, falling apart, procrastinating, or giving up to punish someone for not agreeing with you, not giving you what you want, or suggesting you need to change.
☐ FIXED	☐ FATALISTIC

(Psst: did you notice the acronym formed in the Self-Check? "FAD UPPP"? Tee hee!)

Again, we don't always react to feedback from Fixed or Fatalistic Mind. Ideally, we respond open-mindedly—from Flexible Mind. But being open to feedback doesn't mean automatically accepting it as accurate or true. Regardless of your score on the FAD UPPP—Fixed, Fatalistic, or Flexible—you'll still need to practice some additional skills to know whether to accept or decline the feedback which is the next step in our journey. In RO DBT we refer to these skills as Flexible Mind ADOPTS (yes, another acronym, oh my!).

As you work through the next section, use the same event you chose for the FAD UPPP exercise above as a template for practicing your ADOPTS skills. This will help you put the acronym to work right away. So, let's get going!

Flexible Mind ADOPTS

A: Acknowledge that unwanted feedback is occurring.

If you don't notice that you're receiving unwelcome feedback, you can't learn from it. Unwelcome feedback can be verbal, nonverbal, or situational. It may be expressed indirectly (for example, when someone honks at you when your car drifts into their lane).

Did someone suggest that you do something differently? If so, then it's probably feedback. For example, "You never listen to me" is feedback to listen more!

When feeling criticized, relabel it as "feedback." Relabeling suggestions or comments you dislike as "feedback" accurately describes what's happening without making judgments about the sender's intentions—for instance, that they're purposefully trying to put you down or make you feel miserable—and that opens up the possibility for new learning to occur.

Let's hear from Tula.

My friend Yonas gave me some unwelcome feedback yesterday. He told me that he felt like I was not putting much energy into our friendship, despite my claiming it's important and my declarations about working hard to live by my valued goals and improve my relationships with others.

When you think about the event you chose for this exercise, what was your unwelcome feedback? Was it expressed directly or indirectly?

____

____

____

____

____

____

____

____

D: Determine if you are in Fixed or Fatalistic Mind and describe your emotions, sensations, thoughts, and actions.

To be more open to feedback, it helps to know if you're closed. In a challenging situation, use the Fixed-Fatalistic Quick Self-Check to discover whether you're (1) in *Fixed Mind and actively resisting feedback* or (2) in *Fatalistic Mind and passively resisting feedback.*

Describe the emotions, sensations, thoughts, and actions that occur in response to the feedback. Feedback that's unwelcome is almost always experienced as threatening—which activates our defensive arousal system (see chapter 3). Pay attention to your internal sensations and thoughts. For example, you may notice tension or some negative thoughts about the person giving you feedback; you may feel misunderstood, or consider the feedback unfair. Use the questions below to facilitate this process.

- *Am I talking more quickly—immediately jumping to respond to the other person's feedback or questions?*
- *Do I feel a strong desire to explain myself?*
- *Am I holding my breath or breathing more quickly? Has my heart rate changed?*
- *Am I feeling numb or emotionally shut down?*

Identify unhelpful rumination. Ruminating, brooding, worrying, or stewing about feedback is often a sign of resistance to it. For example, when we ruminate, we're usually not trying to learn; we're trying to find a solution that allows us to stay the same (e.g., to prove to ourselves that we're right and they're wrong!) or feel in control again (e.g., planning a way to dismiss the feedback). It represents an attempt to justify our way of thinking or avoid uncertainty. Use the questions below to determine if you're engaging in unhelpful rumination.

- *Do I find myself brooding or ruminating about the feedback more than is typical for me? For example, am I finding it difficult to sleep?*
- *Do I find myself thinking about the feedback during times when I should be attending to other matters (e.g., time with a loved one, a much-needed break, or an important work project)?*
- *To what extent is my rumination about trying to find a way to discount the feedback or the other person's perspective?*

Let's hear how Tula responded to Yonas's feedback about not putting much energy into their friendship.

> *My first thought was, oh for gawd's sake, can't he see I am trying? Nothing is good enough! And, as usual with feedback from people I care about, I felt flushed and agitated.*

Recall the event you chose for this exercise. *What did you discover using the FAD UPPP? What emotions, sensations, thoughts, and actions occurred—both during and after the event? To what extent did you ruminate afterwards? What might your answers tell you about your openness to the feedback?* Record your answers below.

____

____

____

____

____

____

____

O: Open to the new information by adopting a physical stance of openness and fully listening to the feedback.

Do this using the following skills.

- **Remember, tension in the body means it's time to practice being open.** Receiving unwanted feedback or requests can feel threatening, and create tension in your body (in seconds). Again, when we feel threatened, our threat system is activated (chapter 3), making it harder to hear what another person is saying, take in information, or think objectively. Assuming you want to be receptive (at least to some extent) to the feedback you're receiving, you can actually use this body tension as an "early warning system" to alert you to the possibility you're being closed, and practice skills to stay open instead. What's double cool is that you don't need to know what specific emotion you're feeling (e.g., fear, anger, disgust, shame etc.) to know how to respond. All you need remember is that tension in the body means it's time to practice being open, and then use the skills outlined below to facilitate this.

- **Nonverbally signal openness.** For instance, engage the Big Three + 1 by leaning back in your chair (if sitting), taking a deep breath, and closed-mouth smiling, with an eyebrow wag, while listening to what they have to say. Allow the other person time to speak, and use head nods to signal you are listening.

- **Let go of insisting that you're right, without automatically assuming that you're wrong.** Use the following statements to loosen the grip of Fixed or Fatalistic Mind.
  - *There may be something to learn from this feedback.*
  - *There may be some truth in what is being said.*
  - *The feedback isn't saying that I'm totally wrong in all situations.*
  - *Perhaps my resistance to this feedback is a sign that I'm in Fixed Mind. I can use this feedback to learn more about myself.*
  - *I'm working at being more open to the world. I can use this experience as an opportunity to practice openness.*
- **Let go of justifying, explaining, or rebutting.** Remember, being open and listening to feedback doesn't mean that you must agree with the other person's point of view. The goal is to nondefensively attend to what's happening in the moment.
- **Use your discomfort as a reminder to look for the "kernel of truth" that may be embedded within the feedback. Practice Flexible Mind DEFintely (chapter 6).** Practice self-enquiry in the heat of the moment, before you decide how to respond, by asking yourself, *Is there something here for me to learn?* (chapter 6).
- **Continue to loosen the grip of Fixed and Fatalistic Mind: openly admit to its existence by outing yourself, first to yourself, then to others.** For example, you might start by silently saying, *I'm in Fatalistic (or Fixed) Mind right now, and this is not how I want to live.* This can be hard to do because it means acknowledging that you're not coping as effectively as you might like; that you're being stubborn, rigid, or arrogant (Fixed Mind) or passively resistant and sneaky (Fatalistic Mind). The good news is that outing yourself is one of the most powerful tools at your disposal for effective, open living. It signals a willingness to take responsibility for your actions and emotions without falling apart or blaming others. Recall from chapter 5 when Elijah openly revealed to his partner that he knew he'd been pouting, and that wasn't how he wanted to behave. That honesty had a real prosocial benefit! Other examples of outing oneself to others include:
  - "Although it's hard to admit this, I don't think I have fully heard everything you've said because I've been so busy rehearsing what I want to say. I think I'm in Fixed Mind—and that's not how I want to live."
  - "Although a part of me doesn't want to admit this, I think I'm not being very open or fair with you right now."
  - "Rather than pretend everything is okay—as I might normally do— I'd like to let you know that I think I'm struggling with being open right now."

- **Keep it short.** When outing yourself about Fixed or Fatalistic Mind, you don't need to be long-winded. Sometimes all you need to say is "I'd like to let you know that I think I'm struggling with being open right now," and then move on.
- **Keep it light.** Outing oneself about being closed-minded is best delivered with a little chuckle (tee hee). For example, use the "Oh, My Gosh!" or the "Oops" combined with an appeasement gesture, from chapter 5, to make it clear you can laugh at your own foibles or reveal mistakes, without getting too heavy-handed about it.
- **Don't assume that outing oneself to another person will get you what you want.** And make it clear that you're not implying the other person is doing something wrong, should change what they are doing, or respond similarly by outing themselves too. Notice any judgmental thoughts that might arise based on the other person's responses, and celebrate unwanted or unexpected reactions by the other person as opportunities for self-enquiry.
- **Admit to the other person when your Fixed or Fatalistic Mind may have damaged the relationship.** And apologize, if an apology is warranted. For example:
    - "It's hard to admit this…but I think you should know that the reason I've been so quiet lately is because I wanted to punish you for not giving me what I want. I value our time together and our relationship. So, I apologize for my standoffish behavior earlier. It's not how I want to live."
- **But don't overapologize.** Openly admitting you may be operating from Fixed or Fatalistic Mind is already an act of contrition (a form of apology). Anything else—e.g., lengthy self-criticism and apologies—can make the person outing themselves feel in the "one-down" position: like they've done something wrong, or it's all their fault. Outing oneself and openly revealing vulnerability is nothing to be ashamed of. It's something to be celebrated, because it models humility and willingness to learn from the world, and is a core part of a healthy relationship.
- **Avoid common pitfalls by becoming familiar with what outing yourself is NOT.** Outing yourself is NOT:
    - Telling others they're in Fixed or Fatalistic Mind (e.g., "I know I might be talking from Fixed Mind, but I think you're in Fixed Mind too")
    - Getting the other person to practice outing themselves (e.g., "Now that I've told you about my Fixed Mind, it's only fair you tell me about yours")
    - Giving feedback, stating opinions, venting emotions, making judgments, or telling others how they feel or should feel (e.g., "I don't think you're listening to me"; "In my opinion, you're selfish")

- Telling someone about their social signaling (e.g., "I don't know if you're aware of this, but you look like you're pouting")
- Telling someone what to do (e.g., "I think you need to practice being more understanding")
- Defending oneself (e.g., "I'm doing this for you—it's not easy")
- Mindlessly letting go of your point of view (e.g., "I no longer think I deserve an opinion on this")

- **After outing yourself, ask for a restart of the interaction.** Take advantage of increased feelings of connectedness that normally occur after a person openly reveals vulnerability to another. For example:
  - "Now that I've told you that I don't think I've really been listening with an open mind, maybe we could start again. Would you mind repeating what you just said, and this time I'm going to see if I can listen more openly?" *(Eyebrow wag, closed-mouth cooperative smile.)*
- **Don't give up if the other person doesn't appear to respond as desired.** Remember: the point of outing oneself about Fixed or Fatalistic Mind is not to resolve a disagreement. Give the other person time to adjust to your disclosure. Don't assume a lack of reciprocal sharing on their part means that they don't desire a closer relationship with you; the other person may struggle with being vulnerable too. And, as noted earlier, Fixed and Fatalistic Mind commonly occur during emotionally charged disputes. Often, both sides of the dispute are operating from some form of one or the other. And ultimately, outing oneself about being in Fixed or Fatalistic Mind helps loosen up rigid responding *for the person who is outing themselves.* There is no guarantee on the response of the recipient, nor is securing a particular response the point. But the good news: when you out yourself with an easy manner, it's often received well. The recipient is less likely to experience your disclosure as a criticism or a disguised demand—and more likely to respond similarly and openly in return.
- **Take a short break when you find yourself stuck in Fixed or Fatalistic Mind coping.** For example:
  - "I'm not sure I'm coping as best I can right now. So, if it's okay with you, I'd like to take a break and spend some time apart, so I can think about how I'm responding. Perhaps we could meet up again tomorrow?"
- **Remember, if you miss an opportunity to out yourself in the moment, you can always out yourself later.** Revealing vulnerability to a person you want a closer relationship with works anywhere and anytime. It's never too late!
- **The simple act of admitting to yourself and others that you're closed-minded automatically makes it harder for you to keep being so.** Why? Because you've now gone "on record" (made

public) that you're behaving in a manner that you're not proud of or that goes against your values—making it harder to pretend otherwise and continue behaving poorly. To operate from Fixed or Fatalistic Mind, you must convince yourself that you *are not* operating from Fixed or Fatalistic Mind (tee hee).

- **Express appreciation for the feedback by saying "Thank you."** This signals openness to the person giving you the feedback. For this to work as intended, it helps to really mean it when you say it. Also, remember: expressing appreciation for feedback doesn't mean accepting or agreeing with it. It simply means you're open to hearing the other person's point of view and appreciate them for sharing it with you. Deciding to accept or decline feedback is a different set of skills that we'll be teaching you later in this chapter (so, keep reading, tee hee). In the heat of the moment, it often helps to express appreciation for the feedback yet slow down the process of deciding how you will respond to it, for example by saying, "Thanks for the feedback—but I'd like to take a moment to think about what you've just said before I respond."
- **When expressing appreciation for feedback, remember: it's not what you say, it's how you say it that matters most.** Recall, a person can say the words "thank you" sarcastically, dismissively, or disdainfully, and thus communicate the exact opposite of appreciation. To signal noncritical appreciation and warmth, get in the habit of saying "thanks for the feedback" with an affirmative head nod, eyebrows raised, and a closed-mouth cooperative smile—slowing down the pace of your speech, and slightly lowering your voice volume. Let's practice.
    - Get your smartphone out, turn on the camera, set it to selfie mode, and record yourself expressing appreciation for feedback using the phrases below.
        - "Thanks for the feedback."
        - "Thank you."
        - "I appreciate you telling me how you feel."
        - "Thanks for letting me know."
        - "Thanks for the feedback—but I'd like to take a moment to think about what you've just said before I respond."
    - Remember the idea is to practice saying these phrases with a warm closed-mouth smile, an eyebrow wag, an affirmative head nod, a slower rate of speech, and lower voice volume.
    - Experiment with differing combinations. For example, try taking a slow deep breath, after raising your eyebrows and smiling, just before you say the phrase. Then, try saying the phrases without any of the prosocial signals (e.g., with a furrowed brow, a frown, or a monotonic or sarcastic tone of voice). Notice how it changes the message being sent—despite your using the exact same words.

- As a bonus, when you practice the last phrase in the list, combine prosocial signals of appreciation with nondominance signals. For example, try slightly shrugging your shoulders.
- Show your recordings to a friend or family member. *Which phrase and combination of nonverbal signals feels and looks more genuine?* Record what you discover below.

____

____

____

____

Now, recall the event you chose for this exercise. *Which of the skills under the O in ADOPTS do you think might have helped you be more open to the feedback you received? Which skills do you think might have helped you signal that openness to the other person?* Record your answers below.

____

____

____

____

____

Remember, if the person giving you the feedback is a friend or someone you desire a closer relationship with—you can always out yourself or apologize about being closed-minded. Even after the event has passed (whether weeks, months, or years! Yowsers!). Now that you've identified the skills that you could use now, even though the event has already occurred, make a commitment to use them. Record what happens afterwards, either in the spaces below or in your RO self-enquiry journal.

____

____

____

____

Before we move to our next step in ADOPTS, let's see Tula's experience being open to feedback. (Recall the feedback from her friend Yonas that Tula was not putting much energy into their friendship.)

> *Immediately after thinking "Oh for gawd's sake, can't he see I am trying? Nothing is good enough!" I felt my body tense, my back stiffen, and my jaws and fists clench. Fortunately, I remembered that bodily tension means it's time to practice openness. So, I did a quick FAD UPPP and realized I was probably in Fixed Mind because I was feeling argumentative, indignant, and defensive. I reminded myself that Fixed Mind was not how I wanted to live. Rather than immediately defend myself, like I normally would, I did the Big Three + 1. I leaned back in my chair, raised my eyebrows, engaged a closed-mouth smile, and took a slow deep breath. Right away I felt my body relax, my jaws unclench, and my hands open. I then reminded myself that there may be some truth in what Yonas said. This isn't the only time I've heard it. And I could feel some tears welling up, because at the end of the day, I do want to be a good friend and not disappoint the people I care about by thinking only about me and my needs. So, I raised my eyebrows and took another slow deep breath, and said, "Yonas, you might be surprised to hear me say this, but I want to thank you for telling me about this." I then smiled warmly, and watched as Yonas returned my smile.*

P: Pinpoint what the feedback is suggesting should change.

- **Before you can know whether to accept or decline feedback, you must clarify what the feedback is suggesting should change—***ideally with the person providing the feedback.*
- **Silently ask yourself: What, specifically, are they suggesting that I do differently?** What might this new behavior look like?
- **Unfortunately, many people aren't great at giving clear feedback or making requests, which can make it hard for those on the receiving end to know what the feedback is about.** For example, it's common for people to make several points about different issues at the same time, use vague or unclear language, struggle being direct, or be unsure what exactly they want someone to do. Fortunately, there's a fairly easy way out of this (😊).
- **To achieve clarity-bliss: simply repeat back or summarize what you think you heard—and then, with open curiosity, ask the other person if your summary was correct.**
- **If the other person confirms your summary (e.g., by saying, "Yep, you got it" or "That's correct") that's great; it means you've successfully pinpointed what the feedback is, making you ready for the next step in ADOPTS.** Remember the goal of pinpointing is to accurately determine what the feedback is from the perspective of the person giving it—not to tell them what it should be, or how they could have done a better job delivering it.

- ➤ **If you want to give them feedback about how they gave you feedback, save it for later in the conversation,** after you've completed all the steps in ADOPTS. And spoiler alert: We still have 2.5 steps remaining (Yowsers!). Plus, remember, ADOPTS is about how to take feedback (effectively), *not* about *giving* feedback to others (a skillset that's yet to come!).

- **Most of the time, however, expect to have your initial summary of the feedback corrected, added to, or rephrased.** When this occurs, simply incorporate clarifications into an updated summary that you repeat back to them, and ask them to verify its accuracy or provide any additional clarifications. And don't despair when this happens: understanding perspectives that differ from our own is not an easy task. Keep listening and summarizing and with an easy manner, and don't be surprised if it takes two to three back-and-forth exchanges before everyone is in agreement. It often does!

Let's practice pinpointing using worksheet 7.1. Here's an example, centered on a conversation between Tula and her friend Yonas.

The Feedback (What I Think I Heard)	My Pinpoint (What I Summarized or Repeated Back to Them)	Their Response or Correction (What They Said About My Summary)
"Although you say you care about our relationship, you aren't putting much energy into it."	"When you say I'm not putting energy into our relationship, are you saying that you want me to spend more time with you and less time at work?"	"What I meant by 'energy' isn't so much about the amount of time we spend together. It's more about how we spend our time when we're together. Sometimes I think you're bored by me or not really paying attention. Like at lunch today—you kept checking your phone. I start to think you'd rather be somewhere else, and then I pull out my phone too. Before long, we're both staring at our little boxes like strangers waiting for a bus. I think turning off our phones when we're together might be a way for both of us to put more energy back into our relationship. Does that make sense?"

As you'll see, the worksheet has three columns. The first is labeled "The Feedback (What I Think I Heard)." The key thing to keep in mind is the emphasis on "think," because what we "think" we hear someone say may not actually *be* what they said (a topic we'll discuss further in chapter 8). We all have our perceptual biases; our memories are inevitably faulty; and it's as much about *how* a thing was said as *what* was said: again, a person could say, "You did a great job" in a way that sounds like they mean the exact opposite. Thus, RO DBT contends that the most accurate assessment of another person's feedback isn't what we "know" they said, but what we believe we heard or thought we heard. This use of language is purposeful, because when you acknowledge that *what you think you heard* is still subject to interpretation, it goes a long way towards breaking up Fixed Mind's rigid insistence on being *right* or knowing the capital-T Truth and making you open to alternative points of view.

The second column is labeled "My Pinpoint (What I Summarized or Repeated Back to Them)." Notice that what Tula summarized back was not the same as what she thought she heard. This doesn't mean it couldn't be—but most of the time, we don't always summarize exactly what we thought we heard. Our summaries reflect our perceptions (and biases).

Finally, the third column is labeled "Their Response or Correction (What They Said About My Summary)." Notice that Tula's pinpoint needed clarification from Yonas for the feedback to be understood. This is extremely common; see it as a good thing! Ultimately, until the person giving the feedback confirms your pinpointing is accurate, you need to keep reflecting back what you think you hear—likely multiple times. BTW, you may have noticed that Yonas's response to Tula's pinpoint was fairly lengthy. This too is highly common, so don't be surprised—keep working until the other person confirms you've got it right (but not perfect, tee hee).

Importantly, notice that without using her pinpointing skills to seek clarification, Tula may never have discovered what Yonas really meant when he used the word "energy." Initially she assumed it was about the *amount of time* they spent together. It was only after Yonas clarified Tula's first attempt at pinpointing that she learned it was about Yonas feeling that Tula was bored or not listening when Tula checked her phone for messages during their conversations. A key concept here is that you can never know for certain what another person thinks, feels, or intends unless they openly reveal it to you. So, don't assume you know. Get into the habit of asking for clarification whenever a message is ambiguous, unclear, or indirect.

BTW, it is also important to recognize that sometimes even if you repeat back the exact same thing the other person has said (at least as far as you can tell), they may still correct what you repeat back. Bonkers! Don't get cranky when this happens; remember, your aim is to understand what they are asking you to do differently—not to prove who is the better listener. Celebrate corrections of your attempts at pinpointing as refinements or editorial comments that will in the long run enhance your understanding. Kinda cool.

OK, now that we've seen how to use the worksheet, try using it yourself! You might practice using the example you chose earlier, in the O section of ADOPTS—returning to a prior discussion involving feedback from a friend, even after the event that incited it has passed, to conduct it more productively this time. (Again, there's no statute of limitations on revisiting such conversations—and doing so, particularly if your initial response to their feedback wasn't particularly open-minded or clarity-inducing, can be a good way to keep relationships healthy!) Or you can use it for scenarios involving feedback going forward, to practice pinpointing what the feedback suggests should change and adjusting based on responses and corrections. Regardless of what you decide to do, get in the habit of pinpointing feedback, and use this worksheet to guide your practice.

Worksheet 7.1. Pinpointing Feedback

The Feedback (What I Think I Heard)	**My Pinpoint** (What I Summarized or Repeated Back to Them)	**Their Response or Correction** (What They Said About My Summary)

HALT, STOP, CEASE AND DESIST!

We interrupt this skill for an important announcement! And we're making a big deal out of it—not because we like attention (though sometimes we do, tee hee), but because we need your attention! As it is now time to complete the .5 in the 2.5 steps left in ADOPTS! And it is a big deal, because the .5 step in ADOPTS is perhaps the most important skill of all in ADOPTS. Yowsers! Why? Because once you've pinpointed what the feedback is about, before you do anything else, you must decide whether to accept or decline the feedback. Fortunately, we've developed an effective and easy way to go about deciding, using a checklist that's been clinically tested over many years. So, before we move to the next letter in ADOPTS, let's practice using this checklist. You might try doing so with the example you used to practice pinpointing, to discover whether it's best to accept or decline the feedback you were given. Sound cool? We hope so—because that's where we're heading next.

Deciding Whether to Accept or Decline Feedback

After you've pinpointed what the feedback you received is about, use the following twelve questions to help determine whether to *accept* or *decline* it (adapted from Lynch 2018b, pp. 457–461, and available for download at http://www.newharbinger.com/50782).

Question	Yes	No
1. **Does the person have more experience than I do in this area?** **Note: This refers to whether the person providing the feedback has greater expertise or experience directly in the area the feedback is about. For example, if the feedback was about building your own personal computer, does the person giving you feedback know more than you about building computers?		
2. **Will accepting the feedback help maintain my relationship with the person giving me feedback?** **Note: In general, accepting feedback from someone we're in an existing relationship with usually helps maintain or improve a relationship, making the answer an easy YES. However, sometimes we're not in a relationship (of any kind) with the person giving us feedback (e.g., a taxi driver insinuating that the tip they were given was inadequate), or sometimes whether one accepts or declines feedback just isn't pertinent to improving or maintaining the existing relationship (e.g., the person providing the feedback genuinely doesn't care whether it's accepted or declined).		
3. **Will accepting the advice help me maintain or improve other important relationships?** **Note: Question 3 pertains to the impact accepting or declining the feedback may have on relationships outside of the one with the person providing the feedback. It's designed to help distinguish between feedback that may have relatively limited social consequences and feedback that may have broader social consequences. For example, your spouse might tell you that they wish you didn't always change the topic whenever the topic in question involves emotions. If your avoidance of emotional topics has generalized to other relationships—the answer would be YES.		

Question	Yes	No
4. Am I discounting the feedback to purposefully displease or punish the person? **Note: Intentionally discounting feedback to punish or upset the person giving it—is not only a good sign that you're closed to hearing the feedback, but also suggests that there might be something important to learn embedded within it.		
5. If necessary, am I capable of making the changes that are being suggested? **Note: This question is normally easy to answer. It simply refers to whether or not the recipient of the feedback is actually able to make the suggested changes. For example, if you're told your car is old and ugly, and you've pinpointed and confirmed that the feedback means "Please buy a new car," you'd only provide a YES answer if you had enough money to actually buy a new car. (Otherwise, the answer must be NO.)		
6. Will accepting the feedback help me steer clear of significant problems (e.g., financial loss, employment difficulties, problems with the law)? **Note: This is important because sometimes the feedback we're given may be linked to potentially significant consequences that are primarily nonrelational in nature.		
7. Was the person providing the feedback using a calm and easy manner? **Note: This question is answered NO only when the behavior displayed by the person providing the feedback is clearly emotional in nature (that is, an objective observer would agree that the feedback was emotionally based).		
8. Does the feedback refer to the actual situation I'm in, as opposed to the past or future? **Note: Feedback that doesn't pertain to the actual situation you're in is usually less relevant or helpful. For example, feedback about a speech you made ten years ago is likely less relevant than feedback about a speech you made last week.		
9. Am I in a long-term, caring relationship with this person? **Note: Feedback received from those who we live with or come into frequent contact with, over years, like family members or long-term friends, is more likely to truly reflect our strengths and weaknesses.		
10. Is the feedback I'm being given something that I've heard from others before? **Note: Feedback delivered from multiple independent sources is more likely to be accurate or important to consider.		
11. Am I tense or frustrated about this feedback? **Note: Feeling tense or frustrated about feedback suggests that we're threatened and defensively aroused, making us less open to feedback and more resistant to change. It can also be a sign that the feedback is worth listening to.		
12. Am I saying to myself, I know I am right, no matter what the other person says or how things seem? **Note: Since no one knows everything, rigidly insisting that your view or belief is right (at least for most matters) is a sign of closed-minded thinking.		

Scoring: Simply total up the number of YES responses, and then use the nifty scoring guidelines below to decide how to respond.

11 to 12 YES responses: Accept the feedback or request as reasonable, accurate, or effective, no matter what.

9 to 10 YES responses: Accept the feedback or request as likely reasonable, accurate, or effective.

7 to 8 YES responses: Accept the feedback or request as possibly reasonable, accurate, or effective, but continue to evaluate its utility.

5 to 6 YES responses: Accept the feedback or the request, but very tentatively.

3 to 4 YES responses: Politely decline the feedback or request, but remain open to alternative explanations.

1 to 2 YES responses: Firmly decline the feedback or request.

If you decide to decline the feedback or the request, you'll want to think through whether you should reveal this decision to the person providing the feedback. If it's significant feedback in a significant relationship, then it's probably important to discuss your decision with the other person. If it's less significant feedback or comes from someone with whom you have a more distant relationship, you may decide to simply move on.

Now, let's see what happened when Tula used the scale to consider the feedback she'd gotten from Yonas—a request to stop checking her phone during conversations and actively listen and pay attention instead.

1. Does the person have more experience than I do in this area? *I answered this as a NO. We both have about the same amount of experience when it comes to listening, paying attention to others, or not checking messages on our phone.*

2. Will accepting the feedback help maintain my relationship with the person giving me feedback? *This was an easy YES.*

3. Will accepting the advice help me maintain or improve other important relationships? *I realize now that I also check my phone during conversations with my family and meetings at work. No one's specifically pointed this out, but I don't want people to think I'm not interested in what they're saying. So, I answered this question—YES.*

4. Am I discounting the feedback to purposefully displease or punish the person? *In the past I would've probably pouted or gone quiet to punish Yonas—but this time I used skills. So, the answer is NO.*

5. If necessary, am I capable of making the changes that are being suggested? *Since I know now what he meant by "energy" and the changes he requested, this became easy to answer, as a YES.*

6. Will accepting the feedback help me steer clear of significant problems (for example, financial loss, employment difficulties, problems with the law)? *I answered this NO.*
7. Was the person providing the feedback using a calm and easy manner? *Yonas might've been anxious when he gave me this feedback, but his manner wasn't agitated or angry and he was polite. So, I answered YES.*
8. Does the feedback refer to the actual situation I am in, as opposed to the past or future? *I answered YES, because the feedback was about something that's going on currently.*
9. Am I in a long-term, caring relationship with this person? *The answer is YES, I have known Yonas for going on ten years.*
10. Is the feedback I am being given something that I have heard from others before? *The answer is YES. I've heard this type of feedback from others in the past—that I look bored or like I'm not paying attention.*
11. Am I tense or frustrated about this feedback? *I certainly was initially, so I decided to answer YES.*
12. Am I saying to myself, I know I am right, no matter what the other person says or how things seem? *I decided to answer this question NO, because after I found out what he meant by "energy," I saw the truth in the feedback.*

Tula continues:

When I counted the number of YESes, the total was eight. According to the scoring guidelines, seven to eight YES responses means you should accept the feedback or request as possibly reasonable, accurate, or effective, but continue to evaluate its utility. This makes sense to me—but I think my score should really be a nine, because now that I've had a chance to reflect on it, I think the feedback was on the mark.

Which brings us to the next step in Flexible Mind ADOPTS:

T: Try out the new behavior, once you've decided to accept the feedback.

Note: Only *after* determining that the feedback should be accepted should you actually attempt or try out the suggested change. (Makes sense, eh?)

- **Commit yourself to participate fully in the new behavior or change, without judgment.** The most important step, when learning from corrective feedback, is to actually try out the suggestion, while not giving yourself a hard time about the situation or the outcome, whatever it happens to be. This means practicing the new behavior repeatedly before you decide it doesn't work.

- **Remember, the goal of ADOPTS is to practice being open, not to practice being perfect.** New learning requires a willingness not to always have an answer.
- **Don't excessively rehearse the suggested change before trying it out.** (That's what perfectionists do! Tee hee.) For example, outside of formal lectures or speeches, rehearsing what you'll say beforehand often backfires—you stop listening to the other person, because you're too busy trying to remember your lines. Oops!
- **Compulsive planning or rehearsal may feel like wisdom, but may often function as avoidance in disguise.** For example, you might tell yourself, "I just need to read one more article, and then I'll be ready to try out the suggested change." Yeah—only one?
- **Remember, "There's nobody here but us chickens!" We're all scared when we try something new, but we're also scared when we don't.** Not trying out a suggested change you've decided is worthy may help you avoid feelings of anxiety in the short-term, but in the long-term it harms self-respect and our ability to fulfill our valued goals. When we take on the things we fear the most and learn from them, we grow stronger, and better able to live lives we value.
- **Expect to make some mistakes when you try out the newly suggested changes.** Learning new things usually involves making a mistake; otherwise, you'd already know how to do them! Feeling awkward when you're trying something new means you're learning, not that you're failing or doing something wrong.
- **Use self-enquiry when you find yourself ruminating or hesitant about making a suggested change.** For example, ask yourself the following questions:
    - *Will trying out this new behavior get me closer or farther away from my valued goals? What are my expectations or predictions of what might happen if I tried out the new behavior? Is there something here to learn?*
    - *What might my rumination be telling me about my expectations or beliefs about myself, others, or the world? Is my rumination about finding a way or plausible reason to avoid making the suggested change? Is it focused on how things should've been rather than how things could be? What might my answers tell me?*
    - *Am I ruminating to prove to myself or others that I cannot change? What am I trying to avoid? What do I fear will happen if I made the suggested change? What is it that I need to learn?*

Let's hear from Tula.

The commitment I made was to myself, but also to the people I want to be close to. My plan is to start making changes right away. For starters, less phone checking—and more head nodding and eye contact to show I'm listening.

Now it's your turn. How many YES boxes did you check for your own example? If your score was five or higher, what changes are you planning on making? How will you signal that you're committed to trying out the suggested changes to the person who gave you the feedback?

____

____

____

____

____

S: Self-soothe and reward yourself for trying out the new behavior.

Since celebrating success doesn't always come easy for people with perfectionistic OC…

- **Reward yourself for your willingness to practice being open, rather than assuming it's not a big deal. Being open is hard work!** Better yet—get in the habit of rewarding yourself every time you do something new or different, whether you feel like you deserve a reward or not. It's the willingness to try or practice that matters most, not the outcome! Learn to celebrate openness to feedback as a strength, not a weakness.
- **After an ADOPTS practice, or after trying out a suggested change, notice what went well and how you benefited.** *How did your practice of openness impact your relationship with the person giving you feedback? With others?*
- **Experiment with novel rewards rather than the same old reward over and over again.** For example, don't just allow yourself an extra cup of tea; make the reward more salient by doing something that's both novel and pleasurable. (Dare we say decadent? Yowsers!) For example, if you never allow yourself a long, hot bath because that would be a waste of water, reward yourself with one after using ADOPTS. (You can even add some aromatic candles for maximum decadence… Tee hee.)
- **Practice expressing gratitude to those who are willing to give you feedback—especially when they're friends.** Why? Because giving feedback can be just as hard as receiving it, and yet we need others to point out our blindspots in order to grow (see chapter 9). Receiving corrective feedback from a friend is a "gift of truth"—it can lead you to live more fully by your values and allow you to grow in ways that would be impossible without it. What's more, research shows that

people who express gratitude are more likely to report less anger, loneliness, and depression, and greater relationship satisfaction (Breen et al., 2010).

- **Lastly, remember that if you lean toward perfectionistic OC, you likely believe that rewards must be earned.** When it comes to ADOPTS, you can celebrate with impunity, because practicing ADOPTS is not for the faint of heart! It's hard work, and you deserve validation for doing it.

Now, let's hear what Tula did to self-soothe:

I confess when I first thought about rewards, my mind went totally blank! It's just not something I'm very used to—thinking about social stuff as something to reward myself for, or thinking about ways to reward myself for much at all. But I put down my pen, leaned back in my chair, raised my eyebrows (they'd been furrowed), engaged a closed-mouth smile (I had been frowning), and took a slow deep breath. I paused and thought, "What can I do that would feel good but also different? Maybe it's time to practice a little decadence, even, hmm?" I remembered that Yonas had been talking about wanting to visit a new ice-cream shop, and I do love ice cream. So, I picked up the phone and before you know it, I was sharing a double chocolate fudge sundae with all the fixings, without a phone in sight—with my friend, Yonas. Amazing!

What about you? Even if you're the kind of person who cringes at the term "self-soothe," consider for a moment how you might reward yourself after practicing ADOPTS, being more open, or living by your values. *To self-soothe or reward myself, I might try the following things:*

____

____

____

____

____

Moving Forward

Ultimately, being open to feedback is freeing, because we no longer need to defend our point of view as the only correct one possible. It acknowledges a basic truth in life, that the only thing we can probably know for certain is that we don't know everything, and neither does anyone else (M. P. Lynch, 2004). What's more, being open to feedback and requests for participation is critical for effective living and creating a life worth sharing. In this chapter, we've learned not only how to be more open to feedback but also how to decide when to accept it as helpful or let it pass. Learning to be open to feedback means you'll be more likely to learn more and also enhance your relationships at the same time. So, keep practicing! The end result is well worth it.

As promised, soon, we'll explore the opposite side of the feedback coin: how to give feedback (effectively) to the people we care about the most (chapter 9). But before you can give feedback to friends, you need to know how to make friends, and keep them. So, get ready to learn how to socially connect (or refine what you already know about it)—because our very next chapter is all about this! Yahoo!

CHAPTER 8

The Art of Social Connection (Or, How to Make Friends and Keep Them)

Friendship, like love, is a gift that must be given willingly. You cannot force someone to love you or become a friend. Chances are if you're working through this book, part of you recognizes that your maladaptive perfectionism has gotten in the way of relationships. It may be that you have exacting standards, or perhaps you're loath to let people know the "real" you—you know the expression, "warts and all." Or perhaps you never quite learned the skills needed to enhance social connectedness; after all, you can't buy your friends off the internet (well, at least as far as we know). Plus, for OC folks, making a friend can feel like losing control; interpersonal interactions are unpredictable, because you can never know for certain how the other person will respond. In this chapter, we'll dive into some cool ways you can enhance social connectedness with others, and learn to chill out a bit more as a result. Now, some part of you might be thinking, *Social connectedness and chilling out go together?* Recall what we've been discussing throughout this book: being in a tribe allows us to feel safe. So, let's take a closer look at how to go about achieving this.

You Can't Force a Friendship; Friends Choose Each Other

We like people who like us—*and*, to be liked, we must put ourselves out there (and take the risk of being disliked). Sitting at home waiting for our knight in shining armor or our beautiful princess to sweep us away works well in the movies, but not in real life. But finding and maintaining a genuinely intimate and mutually caring relationship with another person can be hard work! In this section, we'll look at ways to break that intimidating task down.

First, just as it's important to know the qualifications of a job you want to apply for, it is equally important to know the qualities of a friendship. So, take a moment and brainstorm (no censoring!) what you imagine are qualities of a genuine friendship:

- ☐ ____________________
- ☐ ____________________
- ☐ ____________________
- ☐ ____________________
- ☐ ____________________
- ☐ ____________________

If you struggled with this exercise on any level, that's okay. As a society, we don't talk enough about building or maintaining healthy relationships and friendships (or their healthy termination). One of the marvelous things about RO DBT is that we have a list of qualities that characterize genuine friendship. Here are just a few. (And BTW, these qualities are also applicable to your romantic and family relationships too!)

- You feel safe when you're together.
- You trust each other.
- You're willing to make sacrifices for each other, without always expecting something in return.
- You don't try to force change on each other.
- You're kind to one another.
- You'll apologize, if you happen to be unkind, and strive to repair damage.
- You're both open to feedback, even when it hurts.
- You give each other the benefit of the doubt.
- Neither person "keeps score" regarding favors, effort, or perceived slights.
- You're able to tease each other.
- You share successes and failures with each other.
- You validate each other.

Let's take a deeper look into the last item on the list, validation. By definition, *validation* involves communicating understanding and acceptance of another's feelings, thoughts, desires, actions, or experience (Fruzzetti & Worrall, 2010; Linehan, 1993). Being validated or understood by another person essentially says, "You're part of my tribe." It feels good because it confirms our sense of self-worth and signals that our perceptions and responses to the world are reasonable, understandable, or accurate. Healthy relationships depend on mutual and frequent validation. *Consider: when you feel understood, what does it feel like? Where do you experience it in your body?*

____

____

____

Importantly, when we try to validate someone, the person we're communicating with is the only true judge of our success. If they don't perceive your communication as validating, then, by definition, it was not validating. Thus, good intentions don't matter; what matters is whether the other person actually experienced our social signals as validating (Lynch, 2018b). Also note that what's validating to one person may be experienced as invalidating by another—one size doesn't fit all.

How frequently do you communicate understanding and acceptance to other people? To what extent do you feel understood and accepted by others in your life? What might your answers tell you about yourself or your relationships? Is there something here to learn?

____

____

____

For many perfectionistic OC folks, control, competency, and high performance were the expected norms of the culture, family, or community they grew up in. This can lead to beliefs that only outstanding performance is worthy of validation or appreciation. In contexts that prioritize performance over relationships, we may also be criticized for desires for validation (e.g., "You don't need to be 'understood'—you need to get back to your studies"). Plus, when being correct or winning is more important than being liked, we might struggle to understand the value of trying to understand another person's perspective, or consider validation unnecessary, unimportant, or something only weak people require. If this is the case for you, you may have relatively little personal experience in being validated or validating others. Of course, problems occur in relationships when people feel misunderstood. So, if there's a part of you that desires to improve your relationships or to form and maintain close social bonds, *you must be able to signal that you care about someone other than yourself*—and validation is a core means of achieving this. In fact, it requires us to understand the other person *and* to communicate this understanding back to them.

The good news is that validation is an interpersonal skill that gets better with practice. Plus, RO DBT has seven levels of validation, with specific skills at each level (Lynch, 2018b). BTW, for those strivers out there (tee hee): higher levels of validation are not necessarily better than lower levels. What's experienced as most validating and which level works best varies considerably depending on the context in which it's delivered. So, let's take a deeper look. Drum roll, please!

Level 1: Being Attentive: "You Are a Worthy Tribe Member"

This level requires you to *nonverbally* signal to the other person that you're attending to them. Examples include:

- Using affirmative head nods (signaling that you like them and are interested)
- Using eyebrow wags and a warm smile (signaling friendliness and cooperation)
- Turning one's body toward the other person (signaling interest)
- Using a prolonged shoulder shrug with openhanded gestures (signaling nondominance and openness)
- Keeping eye contact (signaling, in at least most cultures, interest, care or concern)

As you read through these non-verbal signals, ask yourself: *How often do I use these nonverbal prosocial signals in my everyday interactions? Are there certain times or relationships where I need to use them more? For example, do I need to put my phone down when my child comes home from school to talk about dinosaurs again? Could I use more head nods at the weekly work meeting?*

____

____

____

____

____

Level 2: Reflecting Back: "We're in the Same Tribe"

This level includes both Level 1 (being attentive) and reflecting back or simply repeating back to the other person what we heard them say, with humility. As you'll recall from chapter 7, sometimes we repeat what we heard, not what was actually said (those pesky worldviews!). But all is not lost, as true engagement means trying again! Let's take a look at an example (adapted from Lynch, 2018b, p. 399):

Person A: *(reflecting back what they believe was said)* So sometimes you listen to people and you don't like it.

Person B: *(correcting the feedback)* It's not that I don't like it. It's that listening doesn't matter to me that much—I do it because it makes them feel better.

Person A: *(attempting reflection)* Okay, so what I'm hearing is that it fits your values to help others, but you don't necessarily find it pleasurable to listen to them. Is that right?

Person B: *(agreeing)* Yes, I feel duty-bound to listen to others. I may not be enjoying it, but it makes them feel better, and that's what matters.

Again, when you reflect back what you believe you heard the other person say—a validating move—your reflection may not always be accurate. So it's important to be open to feedback that suggests this, and to be willing to be corrected until your reflection *is* perceived as accurate. Thus, when you don't get it right the first time—simply try again. Again, working to reflect back what you think someone's said, and being willing to adjust following further corrective feedback, are validating in themselves; they signal openness and a desire to know the other person for who they really are, not what we might want them to be.

Level 3: Empathic Mind Reading: "Welcome Home!"

An *empathic mind read* is usually needed when a person we're interacting with is struggling to communicate, express themselves, articulate a thought, describe a sensation, or label an emotional experience, or when they appear to be shutting down or withdrawing from the conversation. Empathic mind reading shares features with Level 2 validation (reflecting back). Both involve a dynamic process whereby one person communicates their understanding to another person and the other person then signals in return whether these observations were perceived as accurate. When a mind read is accurate, it's validating to the recipient because it helps restore their sense of control and can generate new insight about ourselves or the world for both parties. It's an act of kindness—when it's delivered with humility, and a willingness to accept that our attempt at mind reading may not be accurate or agreed to by the other person.

Importantly, a successful mind read does not mean approval of what the other person is saying or arguing. One can understand what another's saying and still disagree. What's more, an effective mind read always starts with some form of preamble or qualifier that signals to the other person that we're about to make a guess about what they may be feeling or thinking inside, because they're struggling to articulate it for themselves, while simultaneously signaling that what we're about to say may not be accurate, and we're open to correction.

There are several ways of going about this. Below are our top three favorite preambles:

1. **"I'm aware of imagining that you are..."** Using this phrase at your start of an empathic mind read signals to the other person that whatever you're about to say next will be a guess, not a statement of truth or fact. Recall, we can only know for certain what another person is feeling or thinking inside if they directly reveal it to us; anything else is just in our imagination. So, begin with this phrase, and then complete the sentence with whatever you imagine the other person might be thinking, feeling, or wanting. The phrase is a great way to encourage candid disclosure, and to take responsibility for your perceptions while signaling a desire for mutual understanding. For example, if you think someone's annoyed with you, instead of telling them they're annoyed, you might say, "I'm aware of imagining that you're feeling annoyed with me." Or "I'm aware of imagining that you don't agree with me." Or "I'm aware of imagining that you don't want to talk about this."

2. **"If I were in your shoes, I might be..."** Trying to put yourself in someone else's shoes and attempting to see the world from their perspective is the foundation of empathy, and validating for the person on the receiving end because it signals a desire to know their worldview. Begin your empathetic mind read with this phrase, then complete the sentence with what you're imagining the other person may be experiencing. Importantly, notice that the words "I might be" *qualify* your remark, as a guess or possibility, not a fact or the truth.

3. **"Maybe, you are..."** or **"Is it possible you might be..."** are also helpful ways of beginning an empathic mind read. Both phrases include qualifiers (i.e., "maybe" and "is it possible you might be") to signal the possibility we might be wrong. And remember: inevitably, sometimes, you'll get it wrong—but it doesn't matter. You're signaling that you're trying to understand the other person's point of view—and the important thing is to try again.

Level 4: "Based on Your History..."

Level 4 is all about communicating to another person that their experience is understandable based on what's happened to them in the past, or because of their biology or temperament. In fact, we've been using Level 4 throughout this book, when we say things like "Based on your history with perfectionism, it makes sense that trying some of this stuff might feel hard." Level 4 essentially tells the other person: *your behavior makes sense, and others with a similar history or biology would likely respond similarly.* For example, imagine you're going out for a late-night dinner with a friend who'd recently been mugged in a dark alley. As you're walking to the restaurant, you realize it's located down a dark and narrow street. Your friend freezes and says, "I'm feeling very anxious suddenly—I'm not sure it's safe to walk down this street." A Level 4 validation would be saying something like, "It makes sense you feel anxious—you were recently mugged down a dark alley that probably looked a lot like this street."

Importantly, seeing someone's behavior as understandable given their history or biotemperament doesn't mean we *must* approve or accept their response or consider it normal or appropriate. The point is to validate their feelings, even if we don't necessarily approve of what they feel or do. What's double cool is that you can use Level 4 to validate and give corrective feedback at the same time: e.g., "It makes sense you feel anxious—you were recently mugged down a dark alley that probably looked a lot like this street. But you're with me now, and there are other people around." (Spoiler alert: our next chapter is all about how to give feedback to friends—and still keep them as friends. So, keep reading—tee hee!)

Level 5: Normalizing: "You Never Left the Tribe"

This level essentially lets people know that others in the tribe would've responded similarly in similar circumstances (e.g., "Your behavior is not only understandable—it's how most people would respond, if they were in the same situation as you"). It communicates to the other person that they're still "one of us" even if they're harshly judging their own reactions. What's interesting is that, despite our claiming earlier that higher levels of validation were not necessarily better, Level 5 validation (normalizing) is almost always experienced as more validating than Level 4 (based on your history)—*if* (and this is a big "if") the Level 5 validation is actually true; if most other people would indeed respond similarly in the same situation.

To show you how this works, let's go back to the last example. Level 4 validation said, "It makes sense you feel anxious—you were recently mugged down a dark alley that probably looked a lot like this street." Level 5 validation would go something like this: "I think your anxiety makes sense, because dark narrow streets late at night are creepy for most everyone—including me. So, before we proceed, let's call the restaurant and confirm we're heading in the right direction." Can you feel a difference between the two different levels of validation? Did one feel more validating? Most people report finding the Level 5 validation more validating because it implies that our behaviour is normal (i.e., shared by most other people). But don't try to force a Level 5 validation when it doesn't make sense. For instance, being afraid to go to school is understandable (especially for someone who has experienced multiple traumas at school), but you couldn't validate it as "normal," because most people don't find schools inherently scary.

Level 6: Signaling Trust: "I Believe in You"

Broadly speaking, validation is an effective anti-shaming antidote. In addition, Level 6 validation is an *anti-fragilizing* antidote, as it signals to the other person that we trust their competence and capacity to do the right thing. It also treats the other person as we would like to be treated. It's not about offering solutions, but rather extending our faith that others can solve their own stuff without outside interference—even if that solution might not be what we would've chosen. If Level 6 could speak, it would say, "I trust you to do the right thing," "I believe in your competence," or "I have faith in your ability to follow through with prior commitments" (Lynch, 2018b). Put another way, it's behaving "as if" someone is capable because you know that they are. Sometimes it means having greater confidence in the other person than they do in themselves. (Think of how many times you've ever texted a friend, "You got this!")

Level 7: Reciprocity: "We Are the Same"

We cannot emphasize enough how powerful reciprocity is in relationships. When we match the nonverbal signals of our friends, it sends a powerful message that we care and share in their ups and downs. Imagine picking up a friend from a job interview and she comes skipping to the car door with a big smile on her face, announcing, "I got my dream job!" Do you look at her flat-faced and say curtly, "I told you you'd get it. I'm going to be late picking up the kids—get in." We hope not! Instead, we hope you'd match your friend's delighted smile, extend a hug or high-five, or even do a little dance together on the sidewalk. And reciprocity is not just about celebration. If a friend came to you and told you his beloved dog died, reciprocity would mean showing him a sad face, not just saying the right words with a flat face (e.g., "I am sad for you," without emotion). Matching their nonverbal display of emotion viscerally communicates to your friends that you feel their pain or joy.

Take a moment to reflect. *How often do you reciprocate during interactions (e.g., laugh or smile when a friend does)? Are there certain emotional states you find more difficult to reciprocate (e.g. celebrating someone's success, expressions of grief, loss, or fear)? If you struggle with reciprocity, what might be keeping you from joining with others? Is there something here to learn?*

____

____

____

____

____

Mutual validation is just one of the many qualities of a genuine friendship (see Lynch, 2018b, pp. 426–427 for a more fulsome list). And not just the Disney version of friendship! We need our friends to validate us, and we also need them to tell us what they really think or feel—even when it might be distressing to hear. For example, if you're out to lunch with a friend and wanting to impress the good-looking server, you better hope your friend tells you to pick out the spinach stuck in your teeth before you flash your beautiful smile in their direction! Sometimes kindness, too, means telling a good friend a painful truth (i.e., invalidating them) to help them achieve their valued goals. Yet we fear invalidation. Why? One reason is that we fear the social exclusion we sense may result. The other is that invalidation can be painful—it often highlights the very place we need to learn from the most, but may be secretly hoping to avoid. Indeed, research shows that invalidation, relative to validation, exacerbates negative mood and increases defensive physiological arousal (Shenk & Fruzzetti, 2011; Linton & Shaw, 2011), whereas feeling validated is associated with feelings of safety (Greville-Harris et al., 2016).

But here's the tricky part—sometimes we *need* to be invalidated, and not just to achieve valued goals but in order to learn, or even survive. That is, when our behavior is ineffective and we don't know it—or we don't want to know it—we need someone in our tribe to kindly point out our error. For example, hopefully you'd be willing to invalidate a friend who thinks it's safe to drink and drive! And, as we learned in chapter 7, being open to critical feedback provided a huge evolutionary advantage to our species, because our individual survival no longer depended solely on our personal perceptions. Thus, from an RO DBT perspective, the discomfort we might experience when we're invalidated is a reminder to practice self-enquiry. Essentially, learn to start asking *What do I need to learn?* instead of *How can I prove I'm right?* when your worldview is challenged. Your sense of self will become less about being correct, and more about being receptive to new information—being open. Kinda cool. But guess what? Our work is not yet done—because it's time to talk about the importance of self-disclosure.

Close Social Bonds Require Mutual Self-Disclosure

As previously noted, validation is only one of the ingredients when it comes to making a close friendship. Genuine friendship takes more than communicating understanding—it involves revealing vulnerability and mutual self-disclosure. After all, for someone to really know who you are, you must be willing to reveal that (warts and all, tee hee). The more people know about you, the more they're likely to trust you. And trust is a cornerstone of any healthy intimate relationship. So, how do you go about doing this? Let's start by thinking about someone you already have a relationship with.

Bring to mind someone you'd like to get to know better or desire a closer relationship with (but not a perfect relationship, tee hee). It can be any relationship. Perhaps you want to feel closer to your partner, or maybe there's an acquaintance at work you'd like to make a friend. Once you have an image of this person in mind, rate the current level of intimacy you have with them—using the very cool RO DBT Intimacy Rating Scale below. Simply read the description under each level and pick the level of intimacy you think best describes your current relationship (as best you can).

RO DBT Intimacy Rating Scale

Levels 1–2	Levels 3–4	Levels 5–6	Levels 7–8	Level 9	Level 10
Talking about everyday, nonemotional events (like the weather); stating opinions about nonemotional topics (like service at a restaurant)	Making nonemotional disclosures about personal goals or values (like politics, parenting, or philosophy), nonpersonal topics (like world peace), or socially acceptable personal preferences (like "I love to go mountain biking")	Revealing private feelings or emotional judgments about personal events (like true feelings about a boss or coworker), or revealing possibly socially unacceptable judgments or preferences (e.g., "I detest disorganized people")	Revealing personal opinions or thoughts about the relationship ("I really like you"), revealing private judgments or feelings about highly emotional personal events (like one's unhappy marriage), engaging in open expression (like tears or uninhibited laughter)	Revealing feelings of affection or desire for more intimacy ("I want to spend more time with you"), sharing stories of shameful or embarrassing experiences that could be damaging if known publicly, being willing to be highly vulnerable (sharing extreme self-doubt or weakness)	Expressing love or intense feelings of caring and desire for a committed, long-term relationship, and being willing to reveal deep-seated vulnerable emotions that one may never have expressed before and to make serious personal sacrifices for the relationship

Next, pick the level of intimacy you'd like to have with this person. Notice that each level of intimacy varies according to the level of vulnerable self-disclosure. So, don't rate what you think it "should" be—simply rate the level of disclosure you currently have or have had, and then rate the level of disclosure you'd *like* to have in the future. BTW, you can use the scale to rate other relationships too—but make sure you rate at least one relationship, because we'll be using your example when we practice skills later in the chapter.

Note: don't assume that higher ratings of intimacy on the scale are better. For example, Nicole would rate her relationship with her mail delivery person at Levels 1–2, despite seeing them every day. That doesn't make the relationship "bad" or a "poor" one; rather, the intimacy level reflects the relationship's particular context, as well as Nicole's desire for intimacy with this person. If Nicole were interested in becoming friends with the mail delivery person, she would need to increase her level of disclosure and see if it was reciprocated. Likewise, you may have a friendship currently at Levels 5–6, but you desire more closeness with that person—meaning you desire a higher level of intimacy with your friend. The point: there's no ideal level of intimacy for all relationships or all people. The higher the level of intimacy, the higher the level of vulnerable self-disclosure and trust needed. That said, learning how to increase our intimacy level with someone is a core part of emotional health, because when we feel socially connected, we naturally feel safe and worry less. And you only need one close social bond to reap the positive benefits of social connectedness. So, how does one get better connected? The skill to use is Flexible Mind ALLOWs (Lynch, 2018b).

Flexible Mind ALLOWs

As you work through each letter in the acronym ALLOWs, use the relationship example you chose above as a template for practicing each skill.

A: Assess your current level of intimacy and the level of intimacy you desire with the other person (using the RO DBT Intimacy Rating Scale), and determine the extent you're committed to improving the relationship. Use the questions below to facilitate your assessment.

- *What do I find rewarding about interacting with this other person? What attracts me to this other person? What do I admire about them? What do I find interesting about them? What do I want from them?*
- *Would an improved relationship help me obtain an important goal or help me live by my values? What has prevented me from trying to improve the relationship in the past? What is preventing me from taking the first step towards a closer relationship? Am I waiting for them to make the first move?*

L: Look for beliefs, assumptions, judgments, and emotions that may be interfering with your willingness to get closer to this person, share feelings, reveal vulnerability, or trust them. Use the questions and skills below to facilitate this.

- *Are you reluctant to attempt to improve the relationship or get closer to them because you feel embarrassed, guilty, or ashamed about a past behavior that may have disappointed them, caused them harm, or damaged their positive regard of or trust in you?* For example, say you did something in the past (that you're not proud of) which you are afraid to admit—and this is somehow preventing you from taking the steps needed for a closer relationship.

  When we've harmed someone we know, especially someone we know closely—that is, betrayed, cheated, lied, stolen, said nasty things about, broke promises, or sabotaged their work—it's common for us to avoid them, especially if we were caught in the act. Less serious acts—like failing to follow through with a prior commitment or obligation, overstepping the nature of the relationship, misspeaking, making a social gaffe, or breaking a social norm or rule of etiquette—can also trigger avoidance. Although avoidance of the other person seems like a good way to prevent feeling painful, self-conscious emotions, it's also a surefire way to undermine the goal of enhancing intimacy. The good news is that there's a way to restore both the relationship and your self-respect—even if you might've caused serious damage. But spoiler alert: it doesn't involve avoidance (aww shucks!). What it does involve is following these steps:

  - **First, practice self-enquiry.** For example, ask yourself, *What is preventing me from making a repair or admitting to my mistake?*
  - **Second, block urges to avoid the other person, or to avoid taking responsibility, by revealing your wrongdoing to them.** Use the outing-oneself principles in chapter 7. Remember, people who openly admit warranted shame or guilt are universally perceived as

prosocial, responsible, and mature, and doing so is an important first step toward regaining trust, repairing a damaged relationship, and enhancing intimacy.

- **Third, actively repair the transgression by apologizing.** Remember to include an appeasement gesture when apologizing for it to be taken seriously: for example, a slight bowing of head, slight shoulder shrug, openhanded gestures, furrowed brow, and slight grimace of pain (see chapter 5 for more on appeasement gestures).

- *To what extent do you find yourself judging, thinking negatively, or resenting this person in a way that interferes with your desires for closeness?*
  - **Remember that old hurts and current mood can color our perceptions.** Our perceptions are, again, biased: we tend to pay attention most to these things that confirm our beliefs, ignoring or dismissing information to the contrary. So, practice looking for benign, alternative, and nonjudgmental explanations for the other person's behavior, rather than assuming the worst. Remind yourself of times you thought negatively about someone and later realized that you'd misjudged them.
  - **Rather than keeping your dislikes, feedback, or desires for change a secret, reveal them to the other person—with humility.** For example, are there specific behaviors or habits they exhibit that you strongly dislike or find uncomfortable? If you haven't ever told them what these are, how can you ever expect them to do anything different? Of course, just because you reveal your dislikes or desires for change doesn't mean that the other person should (or will) change. But, if you never say anything, you can be certain that nothing will ever change. As we'll learn in the next chapter, when you're giving corrective feedback in close relationships, what may matter most is how the feedback's delivered. Use the tips below as a guide, and make sure you also read chapter 9.
    - **Allow yourself time to reflect on what you want to say before you give feedback.** Not every problem needs immediate fixing. Let two to three days pass (if possible) before deciding how you will respond. Take this time to practice self-enquiry and examine how you may have contributed to the problem.
    - **When the feedback you want to give isn't meant to be taken as literal "truth,"** or isn't for a serious problem requiring immediate resolution, use the skills outlined in "The Art of Teasing and Being Teased," in chapter 9, to deliver your feedback with an open mind, a little humor, and a dash of humility.
    - **When the feedback is meant to be taken seriously, or requires immediate attention or resolution,** use chapter 9's "Tips for Talking to Friends About Friendship" to manage the discussion. Allow the other person time to adjust to the new information—especially if this is the first time you've ever discussed something like this with them.

L: Lean in to the relationship by changing your social signaling.

- **When you're unsure about the other person's intentions or feelings, behave "as if" their intentions are good.** Practice giving them the benefit of the doubt. Research shows that if you signal to others that you believe they're trustworthy, they'll strive to meet your expectations. (Wilson & Miller, 2018). For example, use the Big Three + 1 to signal an easy manner; listen with raised eyebrows, eyebrow wags, eye contact, cooperative closed-mouth smiles, affirmative head nods, and open-handed gestures to signal friendly interest; and use appeasement and non-dominance gestures when stating opinions to signal humility and openness (see chapters 4 and 5 for additional ideas). What's cool is that you don't have to fully believe the other person is trustworthy to reap the benefits of prosocial signaling. You only need to change how you behave when you're around them.
- **Use connecting gestures, light touch, and voice-tone to signal affection, caring, and desires for closeness.** *Connecting gestures* involve the use of signals, like smiles and head nods, that don't interrupt the speaker. Statements of affection or sympathy are more powerfully communicated when they're combined with light touch, such as a comforting hand on a shoulder or a light tap on an elbow. You can signal caring and affection by slowing the pace or rate of your speech and slightly lowering the volume of your voice—and, when combined with a warm closed-mouth smile, an eyebrow wag, and affirmative head nodding, this prosocial blend signals noncritical appreciation and warmth. Raising eyebrows when meeting and greeting someone or when saying goodbyes signals affection, and that you're happy to see them or that you had a good time. Chuckle, laugh, or smile when they do, to signal you consider them a friend. Use validation (particularly Level 7, reciprocity) to signal understanding and match their emotional expressivity during interactions—unless they tend to always be serious: meaning, don't match a flat facial expression if your aim is to signal desires for closeness. Go opposite instead via closed-mouthed smiles, eyebrow wags, and head nods.

O: Out yourself by revealing inner feelings.

True friendship begins when we can share not only the positive aspects of our lives but also our secret doubts, fears, and past mistakes. Signaling vulnerability by revealing our feelings to others transmits two powerful messages: 1) that we trust them (because when we don't trust someone, we hide our true intentions and mask our feelings), and 2) that we a share a common bond of human fallibility (i.e., no one is perfect, tee hee).

To create and build genuine close social bonds, use RO DBT Match + 1 skills (Lynch, 2018b).

Stop the Presses! What Are Match + 1 Skills?

Imagine that you're playing tennis. One person serves; the other just holds their racket. Not much of a game, is it? The same can be true for establishing or improving existing relationships. Match + 1 rests on the simple principle that we must reveal personal information to get close to another person! What's cool about Match + 1 is that it can be used when forming a new relationship with someone you just met as much as with existing relationships or friendships (e.g., to enhance intimacy with your partner, or develop a closer relationship with your neighbor). So how do we do it?

1. **Step 1: Immediately after greeting the other person, begin Match + 1 by revealing something personal about yourself (rather than waiting for the other person to begin).** For example, after saying "Hi, how's it going?" reveal something personal about yourself—say, about an activity, experience, memory, or interaction you had recently. It can be about any topic or anything on your mind at that time. It doesn't need to be profound, witty, wise, or scholarly to work its magic. Indeed, Match + 1 interactions are best when not carefully timed, planned, or rehearsed in advance.

   Keep in mind that the level of intimate disclosure should vary depending on the nature of the relationship. For example, with someone you've just met, a comment about the weather might be a good first start. For someone you know a little better, you might say something like, "I went on a really nice bike ride today—but phew, what a workout!" The basic principle is to begin a Match + 1 exchange with disclosures that are *at or slightly above* the current level of intimacy of the relationship. If you're with a very close friend, for instance, you might choose to reveal something personal about yourself they don't already know. For instance: "You won't believe this, but—I had a dream about you last night! We were both some sort of secret agents on a mission that had gone wrong and being chased by laughing clowns. Not sure what the clowns mean. But I do think we'd make a good spy team!" Notice what makes this example personal is the dream—it's a good way of signaling that this person matters to the speaker, and it's also flattering for the recipient. Plus, did you notice the use of "we" statements? That signals togetherness.

   Another way of beginning a Match + 1 exchange with a friend is to start off the conversation by noticing something you admire about them: for instance, "You know, after our conversation yesterday, I wanted to say—one of the things I admire about you is your willingness to hear differing perspectives, like the ones I shared with you yesterday. It makes me feel closer to you." Notice the level of intimacy expressed corresponds to a Level 9 on the Match + 1 intimacy rating scale—suggesting the relationship is already close.

2. **Step 2. Mindfully listen to how the person responds—i.e., notice if they match your level of self-disclosure—or go higher.** Let go of expectations about how they should respond.

3. **Step 3. Assuming you still want to get to know the person better, simply match the level of self-disclosure in their response to you, and go one level higher**—by revealing more personal

details, genuine opinions, and emotions about yourself. For example, say they reveal they also like bike riding. Step it up and say, "I prefer Thetis Lake during the week, as it's less busy on the trails. The arbutus grove is quite spectacular!"

4. **Step 4. Then mindfully listen to how they respond to your more intimate revelation—without expectation of how they "should" respond. And keep on going.** Don't stop providing details about your life just because the other person doesn't immediately respond similarly. Remember that getting to know someone takes time—*and* the more you reveal, the more likely a person will reciprocate! For example, if the person responds with, "I like bike riding, but I'm not into trail riding," you might say "That's cool. I like the Dallas Road loop myself—the ocean views are amazing! In fact, I just love being in nature."

Importantly, Match + 1 means revealing personal information about yourself, not asking personal questions about another person's life. Though asking questions is okay too, as long as it's not the *only* thing you do.

Remember, closeness takes time, so keep practicing!

Now, finally, the W—which stands for WOW! (Just kidding, but it is pretty wow-worthy.)

W: Welcome, and listen to their disclosures with an open mind, evaluating the level of intimacy afterwards.

- **During the interaction, adopt a stance that signals openness and willingness to hear what the other person has to say.** Listen with raised eyebrows and a warm, closed-mouth smile, interspersed with affirmative head nods and occasional eyebrow wags.
- **When silence occurs during the interaction, don't immediately say something; give the other person time to reply.** And if they seem less forthcoming than you, don't stop revealing; match their level of disclosure instead, using the intimacy rating scale.
- **After the interaction, evaluate the level of intimacy that occurred, using the intimacy rating scale.** Nonjudgmentally evaluate the level of intimacy you imagine you achieved, and use the following self-enquiry questions to guide your evaluation.
  - *How much personal information did I reveal?*
  - *To what extent did I use prosocial signaling to communicate affection, interest, or my desire for a closer relationship?*
  - *What level of intimacy, on the rating scale, do I believe best describes the interaction I had with this person?*

- ▸ *Did the person I was interacting with match my level of self-disclosure? What did they specifically do or say that helped me make this determination?*
- ▸ *What skills do I need to practice to go higher on the Intimacy Rating Scale with this person?*

- **If the interaction didn't go as well as you hoped, try again another time.** And keep trying—because it's possible that revealing personal information is difficult for them too. Allow them time to respond. Block Fatalistic Mind thinking, and don't automatically assume that they aren't interested in getting to know you; remember, relationships require time to build.

  However, if the intimacy level appears unchanged after multiple Match + 1 attempts, consider the possibility that the other person has maxed out the level of intimacy they want with you or are able to achieve. Fortunately, this doesn't mean you need to stop seeing them; instead, it means you need to lower your expectations. You might practice matching their level of self-disclosure during interactions. instead of always trying to increase it. Remember, not everyone is going to want to get close to everyone they meet, so don't take it personally! You cannot force someone to become your friend. Instead, keep practicing and keep on disclosing with other people. Your ideal close relationship is out there, waiting for you!

Ok, well done! That takes us through ALLOWs. Let's check in with Tula to see how she's applied this skill.

> *So, the relationship I identified for this chapter is a neighbour in my building. I'd rate our current intimacy as a 3–4, actually—we exchange opinions about building management and what we like to do on our days off. She just seems like someone fun to hang out with. But it's kinda hard to cross the threshold from friendly neighbour to friend. I recently saw her pull a magazine out of her mailbox, so I seized the opportunity to practice Match + 1. The magazine was about midcentury modern art and design, so I said, "Hey—looks like we have similar taste! I just bought a sofa from The Fabulous Find on Second Avenue!" I was aware that I was trying my best to raise my eyebrows and have an open posture. Her response? "That's cool—what color did you find?" At this point, I wasn't sure if she was just being polite—or, giving her the benefit of the doubt, maybe she's also a bit awkward meeting new folks. So, I responded, "Oh you know, the usual neutral—I'm not, like, a bright orange gal." And she laughed! So, I followed up with, "I'm going next Sunday to look at some lamps. Want to come and browse with me?" I couldn't believe it, but she said yes! She even offered to buy us coffee on the way!*

Tula's example includes several skills: prosocial social signaling, outing herself, and giving the other person the benefit of the doubt. An A+ for Match + 1!

Moving Forward

Well, holy cow! Who thought there'd be so much to know about friendships? In this chapter, we've discussed the qualities that make a healthy and genuine relationship, stressed the importance of validation and taught the seven levels you can use, practiced using the Intimacy Rating Scale, and learned how to go about making or improving a close social bond using ALLOWs. Wow!

At the risk of being repetitive: don't forget it's quality, not quantity, that matters most, when it comes to close social bonds.

Phew! Now might be a good time to take a mini-break. Because, in our very next chapter, we'll be exploring how to give feedback to friends—and still keep them as friends. Double wow!

CHAPTER 9

How to Give Feedback (And Not Lose Your Friends)

Now that we've learned how to make friends and keep them, we're ready to give them a hard time (tee hee). Just kidding! But, as we learned in chapter 7, corrective feedback is one of the most effective ways to acquire new knowledge, and it can highlight areas in our life that may need to change. It's also an inevitable part of any close relationship! Of course, receiving feedback isn't always easy, and neither is giving it—especially if the relationship's important. Thus, the primary aim of this chapter will be to address this dilemma by helping you learn how to give feedback effectively to the people you most care about (just as you learned to take feedback last chapter). We'll also explore the vital role that teasing can play in building and sustaining close relationships. Yowsers!

The Art of Teasing and Being Teased

The reason feedback is a gift that's hard to give (as much as receive) is that we innately recognize that it can be experienced as painful, even when carefully worded and delivered with the best intentions. But that doesn't mean we should simply stop giving feedback. Sometimes kindness means telling a good friend a painful truth to help them achieve their valued goals. Plus, *to grow, we must discover what we don't know*—that is, our blindspots, the areas of growth that we literally can't see for ourselves. Only other people—hopefully, our friends—can point those out. (Any blindspot we believe we've discovered on our own probably isn't a true blind spot.)

If corrective feedback is potentially painful, but important for both our own and others' well-being, how do we go about delivering it in a way that actually works? Spoiler alert: it's not simply being frank or forthright with our opinions, observations, feelings, or beliefs without consideration. That's a good way to make enemies, not friends. Rather, what matters most—especially in close relationships, which are the ones we'll focus on in this chapter—is *how* feedback is delivered: whether it's delivered with an open mind, a little humor, and a dash of humility. But how do you go about doing that? Hint, hint: It rhymes with breeze (😊). The answer is—of course—learn how to *tease*! So, would you like to learn how to give feedback or point out flaws in your friends—without being too heavy-handed about it? If so, then let's learn a set of skills that we broadly refer to as The Art of Teasing and Being Teased (and we're not joking…tee hee).

Teasing is an important part of healthy social relationships, and kind-hearted teasing is how tribes, families, and friends give feedback to each other. Indeed, some of the very first laughs infants exhibit are when a safety signal (such as a smiling mother) is combined with a danger signal (such as a game of peek-a-boo). Similarly, friendly teasing involves a combination of danger and safety signals, most often accompanied by displays of mutual laughter and light touching. Friends playfully and affectionately tease each other all the time. Research shows that teasing and joking are how friends point out flaws in each other, informally, without being too aggressive or pointed. It's how we provide light-hearted feedback about minor violations of social norms (like when a friend farts aloud: "Oops—did you just body-burp?"), correct minor mistakes (like untidiness: "Uh oh, look at this—somebody made popcorn but forgot to clean up. I wonder who that could have been?"), or give feedback about violations of social status (like with a friend who's being a little bossy: "Of course, Your Majesty, we'd be delighted to serve you").

Let's take a moment to practice a little self-enquiry around teasing and how it's manifested in your life. If any edges emerge, note them, and save them for later (e.g., for your daily self-enquiry practice).

To what extent do you enjoy being teased and teasing others? Have others in your life suggested that you need to lighten up or that you take life too seriously? What might your answers tell you?

____

____

____

____

How often do people you know tease each other? How playful are you during interactions with others? What might your answer tell you about yourself? About your relationships?

____

____

____

To what extent did your family members enjoy teasing each other when you were young? To what extent are you able to laugh at yourself, in a kind-hearted way. without getting down on yourself? What is it that you might need to learn?

Who do you tease? Who do you avoid teasing? What might this tell you about yourself and your relationships? What is it that you might need to learn?

It's not unusual for OC folks to report that they don't enjoy teasing because they don't always know when they are being teased or how to tease back—which can lead to awkward interactions.

Let's hear from Elijah.

> *My partner is notoriously forgetful and once forgot the coveted birthday cake we were supposed to bring to their sister's birthday party. I was absolutely mortified. But their sister just put her hands on her hips and announced: "Well, that's what happens when you ask an elephant to be in charge of the birthday cake!" and then warmly smiled with a slight shoulder shrug and playfully slapped him on the arm—and then everyone had a good laugh. If it were my family, my sister would have sternly told me to get back in the car and drive the 20 miles home to get it.*

We can see from this example that family modeling can be significant in the messages we receive about teasing. Elijah partnered into a family where teasing was a normal and fun part of family life, but came from a family where teasing was not an option.

Generally, people who are okay with being teased tend to have an easy manner. They don't take themselves or life too seriously and can laugh (with their friends) at their personal foibles, gaffes, and mishaps. This reflects two important features of effective living. First, being able to chuckle at your own foibles is socially bonding. It signals to others that you recognize you don't know everything and that you're able to examine your personal responses to the world—without falling apart. Second, not taking oneself or life too seriously allows problems to become opportunities for growth, rather than catastrophes or crises requiring immediate fixing—which makes life feel like less of burden and a little more fun (tee hee).

Conversely, have you ever noticed how hard it is to playfully tease (or joke) when you're feeling uptight? An uptight state is a threat state, in which our social safety system (VVC) is turned off or dampened (see chapter 3)—making it more difficult for us to flexibly express ourselves in an easy manner (e.g., we can only fake laughter). Thus, for a tease to be experienced as humorous, it's best delivered from a place of social safety—which is why we usually only tease people we feel safe around, people around whom we can relax and be ourselves, rather than self-conscious or on guard. Essentially, we tease people we feel are part of our inner circle. Think about it: when was the last time the pizza delivery person teased you when dropping off your pizza? Of course, it may be that your pizza delivery person *does* tease or joke with you. And—while that can sometimes feel off-putting—it's likely something to celebrate, as a sign they feel close to you, or want to be!

Friendly teasing, among family and friends, is often about eccentric or idiosyncratic social signaling habits and personality quirks—for example, never putting the lid back on the toothpaste, a tendency to snore, trouble reading maps, habitual forgetfulness, always eating dessert first, a tendency to repeat oneself or tell the same stories, and so on. Sometimes teasing can be part of a long-standing insider or family joke, like a fun, ongoing battle over who loads the dishwasher the most efficiently. From the outside, such insider jokes might seem quite contentious—but for those involved, it's part of a ritual or game of sorts (roasting as a sport 😊)!

Research shows that teasing and its accompanying signals of friendly nondominance are universally displayed across cultures (Mizushima & Stapleton, 2006; Keltner et al., 2001). That said, within a single culture there is a wide range of individual differences regarding the types of teasing that are deemed acceptable; the types of occasions deemed suitable for teasing (for instance, at funerals, some families celebrate the life of the deceased by teasing and joking; other families might see such behavior as disrespectful or uncouth); and who's allowed to be teased by whom (in some families or cultures, for instance, a child teasing an adult is considered inappropriate). Teasing is also moderated by individual differences in biotemperament, social status, and personality or coping style.

What a Friendly Tease Looks Like

In RO DBT, a *friendly tease* can be recognized by three core features—it's always provocative, playful, and kind. Although each feature can be and often is expressed independently (e.g., someone can play without being provocative), a friendly tease has all three (yowsers!). Importantly, friendly teasing is not the same as silly social signaling (see chapter 5), nor is it just telling jokes. Although teases, jokes, and silly behavior all use humor to elicit a reaction from the recipient (e.g., laughter, a nod, or at least a little smile), silliness and joking differ from teasing, because they lack corrective feedback. They're meant to be funny, not challenging, and are used to entertain, signal affection, or lighten up a tense social interaction. There's no intended message other than "let's play," "I like you," or "we're in this together." A friendly tease, on the other hand, is intended to provoke change by commenting on something relevant to the recipient, like a personal habit or social gaffe, and uses humor to ensure that the feedback isn't taken too seriously or seen as offensive or aggressive.

Provocative

Most often, a friendly tease begins with an *unexpected provocative comment* that's delivered with an odd, incongruous, or unsympathetic tone of voice (e.g., expressionless, arrogant, or overly sing-song) or an intimidating facial expression (such as a blank stare), gesture (such as finger wagging), or body posture (such as hands on hips). This provocative comment, challenge, or "poke" is then immediately followed by some form of appeasement gesture, nondominance, and cooperative playful signals (e.g., giggling, gaze aversion, postural shrinkage, eyebrow wags, shrugging shoulders, and smiling). In other words, a friendly tease momentarily introduces conflict and social distance but quickly reestablishes social connectedness by signaling nondominant friendliness. The nondominance signals are critical for a tease to be taken lightly, as a friendly poke (Keltner et al., 1997). They're also what make a tease kindhearted and the recipient more receptive to the feedback embedded within the tease.

Playful

Again, playful teasing between people is a statement of intimacy and trust. It occurs only among friends (or potential friends) and always ends with a nondominant or friendly signal, such as a smile, a bow of the head, or an appeasement gesture. Importantly, as you learned in chapter 5, the nondominance gestures signal that you, as the teaser, aren't *insisting* on change, you don't consider your provocation absolute truth, and you see the other person as an equal. In this way, delivering feedback through teasing is a way for you to be a friend to others you feel close to, and to point out the times they might forget to, say, tie their shoes (tee hee).

Importantly, the *exaggerated social signals that accompany the provocative part of a tease* are essential for the tease to be seen as playful or amusing. They signal affection to the recipient—since we don't play with people we dislike, and, when teasing is playful and reciprocal, it's socially bonding. The exaggerated facial expressions, gestures, and voice tones you use when delivering a tease also clarify that the tease is *off-record*—that, again, the feedback isn't meant to be taken as literal "truth," or seen as a serious problem requiring immediate resolution. This explains why teasing rarely occurs during life-threatening, grave, or dangerous events (like major accidents, physical traumas, funerals, or earthquakes). Researchers have identified a wide range of exaggerated signals and *off-record cues* that teasers might use to signal their playful intentions—e.g., unexpected shifts in voice tone, sudden changes in voice volume, unexpected slowing down or speeding up rates of speech, prolonged pauses, winking, dramatic sighs, exaggerated facial expressions and gestures, use of metaphor, and atypical language (e.g., Eisenberg, 1986; Miller, 1986; Keltner et al., 2001). *On-record* feedback, by contrast, is more serious. It's the social signaling style a doctor might use when delivering a diagnosis to a patient or that a lawyer uses when counseling a client about how to behave in court. It explicitly describes the behavior that needs to change, makes direct suggestions, is meant to be taken seriously, and is intended as a statement of fact or an important directive.

Kind

The third feature of a friendly tease is that it's *always kind*. This means that when you're delivering a friendly tease, you not only playfully exaggerate the provocation and signal nondominance but are also *responsive to the reactions* of the recipient. For example, friends know when to stop. They don't continue a tease if it becomes clear their friend isn't enjoying it. Unkind teasing, on the other hand, can be recognized by its lack of responsiveness to feedback. The tease just keeps going, even when the recipient of the tease makes it clear, verbally or nonverbally, that it's gone on too long, they're not enjoying it, they don't find it amusing, and they'd like it to stop. Ultimately, the best teases are fun to give and fun to receive—they generate mutual laughter. So, if you're friend doesn't seem to be having good time, your tease may not have been received as friendly.

If you're wondering what to do when this happens, no worries! We'll cover tips for managing this later in the chapter. In the meantime, let's look at some examples of teases and then put what we've learned into practice.

Think back to Elijah at his partner's family's party. There, the feedback was that you shouldn't trust the person with the poorest memory to be in charge of the birthday cake (with a nice ironic nod to elephants, who are famous for their memory)! The tease was followed by an appeasement gesture: a warm smile with a slight shoulder shrug and light touch. These are *critical* to communicate to the recipient and others, that no harm is intended. Without them, your tease may be experienced as not-so-friendly.

Friendly teasing can also be used to help our friends live according to their valued goals—for example, by highlighting inconsistencies between what a friend says they'll do and what they actually do. Imagine having a friend at your workplace who's talked frequently about the importance of being on time and forthright in her dealings with others. One day, she tells you, somewhat sheepishly, "I had this report for work due that I kept putting off writing. So I told my boss a little lie—I told her I just hadn't gotten the email about it." Can you spot the discrepancy between what she says she'll do and what she actually did? There are two in this scenario: (1) she says she values being on time but procrastinated, and (2) she values honesty but told a lie. Now, can you think of a friendly tease that would point out these discrepancies? Record below what you came up with.

____

____

____

____

____

____

Here are a few examples of what we came up with:

- "Yeah, you're right, being on time is overrated. Maybe your boss will write the report for you now…eh?" *(Enthusiastic grin with a wink-wink and a nudge.)* This tease reminds your friend about their value for being timely and not putting off work—by suggesting they believe the opposite.
- "Someone's getting Employee of the Year!" *(Enthusiastic grin.)* This tease reminds your friend about their value of forthrightness by playfully highlighting her lying as a sneaky way of getting ahead.

Notice that each tease had feedback embedded, that was also accompanied by friendly, playful, or nondominant signals.

Tom reflects: *One of the teases in my family—that's evolved, over time, into an insider family tradition—began years ago. It first appeared during a long-distance drive I had with my daughter, just after finishing my PhD in clinical psychology. During a rest stop, she bought herself a huge chocolate fudge ice cream sundae with all the fixings to eat in the car (yummy). I'd been trying to reduce my sugar intake at that time, so I settled for a bottle of water. And my daughter took advantage of this! It all began innocently enough; as I drove, she quietly sat beside me licking the sprinkles off the top. But very soon, she started making little comments, like "Ohhh, this is so good, Dadddd," "It's soooo delicious."* (In a sing-song voice with a cheesy grin.) *She then said, "Too bad you can't have anyyyy…because I think there's too much here for me."* (Heavy sigh). *And then, while extending a huge spoonful of the ice cream towards me, she said, "Come on, Daddddd… Help me out… Why don't you take a break from your diet… It's sooo good."* (Waving spoon around, cheesy grin.)

Although this sounded very enticing, I remained resolute: "No, no, that's okay, I'm not really hungry." She then replied, "Okay, but you don't know what you're missing…because I think it's the best ice cream, I've ever had… It's sooo veryyyy delicioussss… Let me know if you change your mind!" (Mischievous smile, smacking lips, singsong voice.) *She then slowly continued to eat, punctuated by occasional pauses where she would stop, smile, and gaze up at me, while loudly smacking her lips or moaning in apparent ecstasy. I tried to ignore her and concentrate on my driving. But finally, I couldn't stand it anymore! I turned towards her and said "You know what? I think I could drop my sugar restriction for one day. So, I'll not only take that scoop you just offered, but let's see if we can finish this off together!" She smiled widely and said, "Sure thing!" And then, after cleaning her spoon, she carefully dipped the tip into a tiny bit of whipped cream—about the size of a pinhead—and offered it to me with a cheesy grin, saying, "Here you go!" I was surprised—what happened to that huge scoop she'd offered earlier? But I also recognized that she was playacting—having fun, giving her dad a hard time (tee hee). So, I played along, but with a little feedback attached (tee hee). While the miniscule drop of whipped cream dissolved on my tongue, I said, using a weird, whiny voice tone, "Thanks...a lot!" followed by a cheesy grin. We both laughed uproariously.*

And soon, this little tease became a family insider tease. The "Thanks...a lot!" tease most often occurs in our family when a gesture of support or offer of help isn't big enough to make much of a difference (similar to the benefits gained from a pinhead of whipped cream; tee hee) or when a suggestion (like "Maybe you should work out") is something the recipient already knows about. Although there's always a little feedback embedded, the exaggerated whiny singsong voice tone or monotonic voice and flat face that accompanies the "Thanks...a lot!" always softens the message and signals playful, nonserious intentions. Plus, it's usually followed by mutual laughter (tee hee).

This example demonstrates how important it is to embed silly, exaggerated, and off-record markers into teases for them to be taken lightly, and to maximize humor. (It also reflects the difference between teases and jokes. Tom's daughter's play with the ice cream was a joke, since there was no intended feedback; it was just about playfully surprising her dad.)

So, let's practice the "Thanks...a lot!" tease! (Tee hee.) As before, get your smartphone out and record yourself during your practice (or use a mirror).

1. We'll start our practice by doing what you should *not* do (if you want to tease, that is)! Yowsers! So, first, record yourself saying "Thanks...a lot" as if you really mean it—meaning it's on record, and intended as a genuine expression of appreciation. BTW, this means you won't be exaggerating your social signals (e.g., using a whiny or monotonic voice). Instead your voice tone should be earnest and warm. Record yourself saying "Thanks...a lot" like this several times.

2. Next, say "Thanks...a lot"—but now as a friendly tease. Meaning, in a way that signals you don't really mean it (i.e., you don't really have much appreciation)—and instead are giving your friend a little friendly feedback (tee hee). Record yourself multiple times—using different voice tones or pacing. For example, try saying "Thanks...a lot!" using a whiny, weird singsong voice. Try it out using a slow, monotonic tone of voice. Have fun experimenting.

3. When you're done, watch the recording of yourself and evaluate what it feels like to be on the receiving end. Notice the social signaling differences between the first practice, where you said "Thanks...a lot" using a genuine voice tone, and the second practice, where you purposefully

exaggerated how you said it to ensure it would be received as non-serious feedback. Notice that the first practice is on-record communication, because the voice tone that you (hopefully) used made the statement feel like genuine appreciation. The second practice, conversely, featured exaggerated, off-record markers to signal that the "Thanks...a lot" was not meant to be taken literally—and instead a friendly tease.

4. Wow! For added fun, show your recordings to a friend. Ask them which expression feels more genuine (hopefully the first practice), and which more like a tease (the second practice).

5. Finally, start looking for opportunities in the real world to practice the "Thanks...a lot"—say, when you want to tease someone about an offer of help that doesn't really help. And don't forget to add non-dominant friendly gestures and expressions (like smiling or eyebrow wags) after each tease (tee hee). Record your observations below, or in your self-enquiry journal. *What happens when you use this tease? How does it change the interaction at hand? How does it affect your ability to be or feel closer to others?*

____

____

____

____

____

How Is Your Tease Being Received?

A friendly tease is both provocative and affectionate. It combines a danger signal (e.g., an unexpected challenge) with a safety signal (e.g., a smiling friend). But finding the right balance can be tricky. When a tease is too provocative, it's less likely your friendly intentions will be received. Yet, being *too* affectionate loses the fun. Teasing is fun because it's a *little* scary (notice the emphasis on little). And we like feeling a little scared sometimes—otherwise, why would horror films be so popular? The good news is that even if you don't like horror films, there are several nonverbal and verbal indicators that suggest your tease is being received as intended (as a friendly poke). These include mutual, shared laughter or giggling, chuckling, maintaining eye contact, or teasing back. On the other hand, if the other person frowns, looks away, has a flat face, becomes serious, talks less, or justifies or defends their actions, these suggest that the tease isn't being received well—and stopping becomes important.

So, when gauging whether your tease is being received as friendly, it's all about how the other person responds. For example, examine the extent they appear to genuinely enjoy your tease or respond playfully in return, say by joking or teasing back. The questions below can be used as additional guides. The more "yes" responses, the more likely your tease was received as friendly.

Does the other person…

- ☐ *maintain eye contact?*
- ☐ *laugh, smile, or chuckle when you do (even if just a tiny little bit)?*
- ☐ *use full sentences when responding, not one-word answers?*
- ☐ *continue conversing with an easy manner after the tease?*
- ☐ *tease you back?*

When Teasing is Not Nice

Unfortunately, humans aren't always nice, and teases aren't always kind. We can be ruthlessly callous and deceptive to those we dislike, or to rival members of another tribe. And teases, even as "friendly" pieces of feedback, can be conflated or commingled with sarcasm, niggling, and bullying. The paradox is that teasing is both a crucial part of healthy relationships, and it can also serve as a malicious weapon. This may make you a little leery of using it altogether! The solution to this dilemma is to recognize that not all teases are the same—just as not all smiles are the same, nor do all smiles reflect friendly intentions.

Imagine a continuum:

Friendly Teasing	Unkind Teasing and Niggling	Bullying
Provocative, playful, kind	Provocative, apparently playful, unkind	Highly provocative, not playful, unkind

On the extreme *unfriendly* side of feedback is bullying—the opposite of friendly teasing, which is always playful and never delivered with an intention to cause harm. Bullying can involve a wide range of behaviors, from aggressive taunting to spreading rumors, directly criticizing, excluding, making fun of someone in an intimidating fashion, physically attacking someone, name calling, or taking valued objects. Interestingly, bullying is never playful (see Keltner et al., 2001). Even when it's done in a teasing manner, using off-record markers like an exaggerated, mocking voice tone, the bully's usually the only one laughing. This creates a power dynamic in which the bully feels 'better than' or superior to the person being bullied. (As for bullying that doesn't also involve off-record markers, that's better considered a direct act of hostility, not teasing.) Thus, bullying can be characterized as highly provocative, not playful, and unkind. Interestingly, its extremely provocative nature can make it easier to identify, even when delivered off record and indirectly expressed—the unfriendly intentions are typically clear.

In the middle part of the continuum is what we refer to, in RO DBT, as unkind teasing, or *niggling*. Niggling is a way of getting back at someone, punishing someone, or undermining the efforts of a rival without ever having to admit or take responsibility for one's nefarious intentions: "Who, me? No, I'm not trying to give you a hard time. Can't you take a joke?" It is the essence of dirty fighting and a source of secret pleasure (akin to *schadenfreude*, the phenomenon of experiencing pleasure when a rival is in pain or suffers a loss). And it's scary, because it is usually disguised as a friendly tease. Though it's never friendly, it pretends to be—for example, "Don't worry—I like you. The reason I never laugh at your jokes is simply because I don't find them funny." The secret is plausible deniability. Niggling uses off-record communication and indirect signals—which are precisely the things that make friendly teasing friendly, by suggesting that a tease shouldn't be taken literally, and that its feedback is benevolent in intent even as it humorously provokes—to confuse, punish, or cause harm instead. Thus, niggling and unkind teasing are powerful because they function to secretly control others or put them down, and yet the indirect way they are expressed makes it plausible for the sender to deny doing so: "I really don't know what you're getting all upset about. I was just playing with you." In fact, the more upset the recipient of a niggle becomes, the more powerful the unkind teaser is likely to feel.

Interestingly, we usually keep our acts of unkind teasing to ourselves, as secret—meaning we don't reveal them to others or admit malicious aims. The exception to this is when we form harsh gossip groups, whereby "badmouthing" and "making fun" of people we dislike evolves into a cruel sport. The reason we hide our acts of unkind teasing from others (and often ourselves) is because, inwardly, we recognize it's an indirect way of communicating disapproval or dislike and that its sneaky nature is a form of deception—designed to wound or cause harm, rather than join with or truly help the other person. We also recognize that it goes against our valued goals (e.g., fairness, honesty, or direct communication), and that we wouldn't like to be treated by others in a similar sneaky fashion.

The good news is that friendly teasing isn't niggling, so you can relax (phew!). But don't relax too much—because it's now time for a little self-reflection. Use the questions below to determine the extent you may engage in unfriendly teasing. If you discover any "edges" about a particular question, practice self-enquiry (e.g., in five-minute practices, across three to four days), using your self-enquiry journal.

Do I possess a cutting sense of humor? Am I an expert at the humorous put-down? What might this say about how I see other people or my social interactions? Is there something here to learn?

____

____

____

____

Do I ever secretly pride myself on being able to make clever or barbed comments disguised as innocent jests? What prevents me from being more direct?

____

____

____

Do I like it when other people niggle me? What might this tell me about my values?

____

____

____

____

____

Have I ever purposefully used humor or teasing to block another person from achieving their goals, make their life difficult, teach them a lesson, or punish them? What might this tell me about how I manage competition or conflict? Is there something here to learn?

____

____

____

____

____

To what extent do I enjoy using a tease or joke to make another person squirm or get upset?

____

____

____

To what extent do I engage in harsh gossip, badmouthing, or making fun of other people? Am I proud of my behavior when I do this? Would I teach a child to behave similarly? What might this tell me about my values? Is there something here to learn?

____

____

____

____

____

Distinguishing Between the Nice and the Not-So-Nice

How do you tell the difference between a friendly poke and a not-so-friendly-poke? First, you can never know for certain what another person's intentions are unless they openly reveal them to you—assuming otherwise would be arrogant (and anti–RO DBT). But since it's our job to answer questions (tee hee), we thought we'd give it our best shot. Our first thought is that intention matters. (Oops, did we just contradict ourselves?) What we *intended* to say (tee hee) was that acts intended to aggravate or irritate are never friendly teases. Thus, one difference between a friendly tease and an unkind tease is the extent to which the sender is using the tease to attain an aim, win, control, dominate, or punish the person they're teasing, as opposed to playfully suggesting, advising, or helping them achieve their goals or live by their values. And unfortunately, this just leads us back to our original point—"you can never know another person's intentions unless they tell you," blah, blah, blah. So, perhaps we'd be better served if we looked at behavioral indicators—things you can actually see. For example, most folks would agree that teasing someone about a feature or trait they possess that they're unable to change isn't particularly nice (e.g., "Ha ha...you've got freckles!"). The recipient can't actually *do* anything about the feedback.

Fortunately, there are several additional behavioral markers available to identify whether a tease is a friendly or a not-so-friendly poke. These behavioral markers can be distilled into one basic principle: *It all depends on how the tease was delivered*. For example, a tease can suddenly feel more like a putdown when a smile or other appeasement signals arrive too late. The questions below summarize these markers; you can use them to guide your assessment of any teases you receive. (For a handout version, visit http://www.newharbinger.com/50782.)

- *To what extent did the sender signal friendliness, deference, receptivity, and sincerity, after the tease, via nods, smiles, open and sincere social signals?*
- *Did the sender apologize or attempt to repair, appease, or signal nondominance when the recipient failed to find their tease amusing (e.g., didn't laugh or chuckle)?*
- *Did the sender prolong the tease regardless of how the recipient responded?*
- *Did the sender stop the tease when asked to do so?*

Of course, in addition to the indicators above, when you're unsure of a teaser's intentions, you can also ask them directly, "Are you teasing?" and evaluate how they respond. Note asking directly works best when your relationship with the other person has generally been friendly or close in the past. Use the questions below to evaluate how they respond to your query.

- *Was the sender willing to "own the tease" when asked directly about it?*
- *Was the sender forthcoming about their intentions (e.g., that they meant the tease to be taken lightly)?*

And if after trying out all the above you remain unsure, there's still a basic rule for how to respond. (BTW, we know we're not supposed to be giving out rules to people who are rule-governed and OC—so, don't tell anyone, tee hee.) *In general, if the sender is a friend, practice giving them the benefit of the doubt by assuming the tease was intended to be friendly.* This may feel like a self-sacrifice at times, because it often requires letting go of strong convictions or beliefs about what's happening. It can help to remind yourself that being a good friend sometimes means making sacrifices, for the benefit of the relationship, without always expecting something in return. Of course, if you find you often need to give a certain friend the benefit of the doubt about friendly intentions, it may be time to evaluate the relationship more broadly. And fortunately for us, that is our next topic.

Close friends are relaxed when together. They feel safe because each trusts the other to be non-exploitative. Thus, friendly teases between them, though always provocative, are also always playful and kind. So, when it comes to evaluating the nature of your relationship to determine the likelihood teases from a particular person are friendly or not so friendly—it helps to reflect on the extent you feel safe around the other person. Use the questions in the box below (adapted from Lynch, 2018b) to facilitate this. (You can also find a handout version at http://www.newharbinger.com/50782.)

Box 9.1. Tips for Knowing If You're in a Toxic Relationship

If there are more NO responses than YES responses to the following questions, then it's possible the relationship is damaged or unfriendly.

1. Do I consider them a friend?
2. Have I enjoyed playfully teasing or joking with them in the past?
3. In general, when I laugh, do they laugh with me?
4. Do I trust them to tell me what they really think?
5. In their presence, do I generally feel safe?
6. Do I have evidence or experience suggesting that they have my best interests at heart?
7. Do they allow me time to express my feelings or ideas?
8. Are they open to me giving them critical feedback or differing opinions?

If the relationship's not particularly important to you—or you believe it's highly toxic—you may need to consider ending it. If the toxicity involves a long-term relationship, seek independent counsel (for example, a marriage counselor). However, if the relationship is one you value or wish to improve, then: *If possible, talk to the person about your feelings*. But before you do, allow yourself the grace of time to reflect. Not every problem needs immediate fixing; and interpersonal conversations should be conducted thoughtfully. Let two to three days pass before deciding how you'll proceed. Take this time to practice self-enquiry, here or in your journal, and examine how you may have contributed to the problem.

____

____

____

____

____

____

____

For the meeting itself:

1. Choose a place and time for the discussion that's private and likely to maximize feelings of relaxation and safety for the both of you. For instance, invite the other person out to lunch at a favorite restaurant, or take a walk together on a beach.

2. Begin the discussion by providing a brief description of the underlying circumstances motivating your request for the discussion—without defending, justifying, or rationalizing your point of view. For example, "As you know, I've been working on being more open to critical feedback, but also on being more open to revealing my feelings to people I care about. And since I really value our friendship, rather than pretend everything is okay, as I might normally do, I wanted to let you know that I have been feeling a little confused about our relationship ever since the other day when you teased me about [describe the teasing event]. So, I was wanting to talk with you about your experience of what happened that day—and hopefully repair any damage that may have occurred in our relationship. Is that okay with you?" *(Shoulder shrug, closed-mouth cooperative smile.)*

3. During the interaction, don't forget to use your body to signal openness and activate social safety. For example, while listening to feedback, use an eyebrow wag; if sitting, lean back in your chair; slow the pace of the conversation by taking a deep breath; allow time for the other person to respond to questions or complete observations before you speak; use openhanded gestures; signal nondominance by shrugging shoulders when uncertain; and maintain a musical tone of voice.

4. If you feel misunderstood or challenged during the interaction, don't react right away. Instead, silently ask yourself, *Is there something here for me to learn?* As we've been learning, asking this question, rather than automatically assuming your position is correct or that you are being attacked, facilitates receptive listening and loosens the grip of rigid, closed-minded thinking, even in the heat of the moment. It's the cure for defensiveness that can lead to new learning or a change in perspective. (But don't forget: This doesn't mean that you must mindlessly agree or automatically abandon your point of view. It simply means allowing yourself the grace of listening to another).

5. Lastly, give the other person time to adjust to the new information—especially if this is the first time you have ever discussed something like this with them. And don't assume that minimal self-disclosure on their part during the discussion means that they don't desire a closer relationship. They may struggle with vulnerable self-disclosure too!

Some additional tips for talking with friends follow.

Box 9.2. Tips for Talking with Friends

- Openly and directly reveal how you feel, without assuming your emotions represent truth or facts. This will make it more likely that your friend will respond nondefensively.
- Use qualifiers when speaking to signal open-mindedness and humility. For example, "From what I can tell..."; "Is it possible that...?"' "I'm aware of imagining that you..."' "I'm not sure if I'm correct, but it seems to me that you..."
- Use I-statements when revealing inner experience, to signal that you're taking responsibility for your emotions, thoughts, and beliefs, not blaming your friend. For instance, "I feel annoyed when you..." rather than "You make me annoyed when you..."
- Admit to your friend how your actions may have damaged the relationship, and apologize, if an apology is warranted. Taking responsibility for our actions that may have caused suffering (even if unintended) signals openness, nonarrogance, and desire for an improved relationship.
- Don't assume you know your friend's inner thoughts, emotions, or motivations with certainty.
- Let go of expectations that your friend behave as you believe they should. Practice listening to what your friend needs or wants instead.

How to Respond to a Tease

Take a moment to reflect: *How do you typically respond to a tease?* Research suggests that there are three ways most people respond: (1) ignore it, (2) confront it directly, or (3) laugh it off. But which way is best? (Drum roll, please…) The most effective response to a tease—friendly or not—is to *laugh it off*. Generally, laughing it off saves face for both sender and recipient, making conflict less likely. Laughing at a tease (or at least chuckling) signals that you're not getting uptight about being teased, creating a win-win situation for everyone involved. Ultimately, laughing at a tease—even when you can't quite see the humor in it or what the feedback was, and regardless of the sender's intentions—is an act of kindness. By behaving "as if" their intentions are friendly, you give the sender the benefit of the doubt, and imply that you consider the teaser a friend—or at least, not a threat.

Interestingly, research suggests that laughing at a tease increases likeability and positive feelings between the sender and the recipient—even when the tease was meant to be *un*friendly. It's almost like magic. Plus, in cases when a tease is definitely intended as unkind, laughter signals that you're not taking the niggling or bullying seriously, or giving it merit—meaning, you're not threatened by the teaser. It makes it harder for the teaser to take pleasure from your pain—since you don't seem to be getting all worked up about it. It also has the added benefit of decreasing the likelihood of future unfriendly teasing by the teaser (Scambler et al., 1998; Georgesen et al., 1999; Bias et al 2005), by taking away the "fun" of your hurt reaction, which might reinforce the unkind teasing. And of course, when a tease was intended as friendly, laughter reinforces the relationship and signals your openness to feedback, with an easy manner. So, go on, laugh about a tease, whenever you can—because the most likely outcome will be more laid-back interactions and more fun with friendly teasers. Cool! (Of course, for unfriendly teasers, this means less fun. Sorry. ☹)

What if laughing doesn't seem to stop unfriendly teasing? Then, we can move to option two, behaving "as if" you don't notice the tease—by *ignoring it.* Intentional ignoring is an indirect social signal—meaning, it intends to influence, but without making it obvious (or having to admit to it). Despite this, ignoring is often an act of kindness, because it avoids direct confrontation and escalating a potential conflict. Its indirect nature saves face, for both the recipient of the tease and the unfriendly sender. (Of course, ignoring can also be used unkindly—for instance, when it involves long periods of purposefully not looking or talking to someone; a.k.a., the silent treatment). Helpful ignoring can manifest in many ways: for example, changing the topic, pretending you didn't hear the tease, carrying on with the conversation "as if" the tease had never occurred, engaging a nearby person in conversation, picking up a book and reading, excusing oneself to go to the bathroom, acting distracted, checking on a text message, or quietly exiting the interaction. Perhaps unsurprisingly, ignoring a tease works best when you don't know the teaser very well or are unlikely to interact with them in the future.

Lastly, if laughing or ignoring don't work with unfriendly teasing, you should consider *confronting directly*. This often translates into directly communicating to the teaser that you're experiencing their teasing as unkind and it's negatively impacting the relationship. Often, this can work—especially in adult relationships. In some cases, having an independent, objective observer present with you can help. Finally, if you're dealing with a malevolent teaser—someone who purposefully desires to cause you distress—the healthiest response may be to abandon the relationship entirely, while continuing to laugh off any additional unfriendly teases that occur in the meantime, acting as if you aren't bothered or that you don't take them seriously (which can be protective). It can also be useful, considering the unique challenges arising from these types of relationship ruptures, to discuss your problems with an unkind or malevolent teaser with an independent observer, like a therapist.

Pulling it All Together

So, what have we learned about feedback and teasing? One: to deliver a good tease, you need to know what you want to give feedback about. Of course, that can be hard to do beforehand—most social situations are fluid, and the behavior we and others display is often unpredictable. (But not always—the "Thanks…a lot!" tease you practiced is the kind you can plan for and repeat!) Ultimately, what you need to be alert for, in your friends—in order to tease—is: something you wish they might change, but don't *insist* that they change or believe to be a serious problem. (If there's a serious problem you want to give feedback about, use the on-record tips in box 9.2 above.) Generally, there are three broad categories of behavior that we tease our friends about:

1. Things they do that mildly annoy us
2. Things they do that make us embarrassed *for them*
3. Discrepancies between what they say they will do (or value) and what they actually do

Let's take a closer look at each category.

Category-one teases are about the things a friend does, repeatedly and often unknowingly—their habits or traits—that you personally find mildly annoying, perplexing, or odd, and wish they would change or do differently. They're not serious problems or issues requiring immediate attention; nor would they necessarily be seen as annoying or problematic by all people. The behaviors that work best for teasing in this category are things you might've already asked your friend to consider changing or become more aware of—yet despite your friendly feedback, they continue to appear at least occasionally, perhaps without your friend being aware of it. Examples include

- forgetting to put the toothpaste cap back on,
- regularly repeating themselves or telling the same story,
- forgetting to turn off lights,
- working when on vacation,
- leaving their clothes on the floor,
- insisting there's only one way to pack the dishwasher, and so on.

Take a moment to think about category-one behaviors you've observed in your friends that you might like to target for feedback.

___

___

___

Because not everyone will find such behaviors annoying or problematic, they represent personal desires on your part for how you would like the world to be and your friend to behave. Thus, the things you personally desire to change in your friends may also represent areas for *your* personal growth—i.e., *your* edge, and opportunities for self-enquiry. That said, if your friend complies with suggested changes, it can benefit both them and you. Remembering to put the toothpaste cap back on, for instance, because it matters more to the teaser than to the target can be a nice way of saying "I love you."

Tom reflects: *My wife Erica will invariably tease me whenever I start talking about quantum mechanics or quantum physics —usually by beginning to yawn, then appearing to fall asleep, followed by loud snoring, which increases in volume if I don't seem to get the message. As soon as I change the topic, she miraculously "wakes up" with a big cheesy grin—often saying something like; "Sorry, were you saying something?" Her feedback to me, as you've probably guessed, is that she finds quantum mechanics (or QM, as she likes to call it) boring. It's funny because it's opposite to how she responds to other scientific topics (she is a bit of a science geek)—but also because somehow, I never seem to get the message; I still repeatedly and excitedly bring up QM whenever I feel the urge. Does this mean that I haven't heard her feedback? No, because it has changed my behavior. I no longer try to engage her in serious or long conversations about QM, which is respectful of her genuine wishes. But sometimes I pretend I might—just for the fun of it (tee hee).*

Category-two teases are about the things your friend might do in public that you feel embarrassed about *for them*—not for yourself. These teases, when delivered with humor and kindness, are protective; they're designed to alert a friend about a minor gaffe or error they've inadvertently made, without making a big deal out of it. They target your friend's blindspots—like unwitting or unconscious displays that potentially could have embarrassing consequences for them (like going to a party with their pants zipper down), inadvertently offending someone (for instance, by assuming everyone they meet speaks English), unintentionally interfering with the goals of others (say, by talking too loudly in a restaurant), or being misunderstood by people who don't know them (e.g., a tendency to frown when listening, which may be misinterpreted as dislike rather than interest). Other examples of behaviors that lend themselves to category-two teases include habitually showing up late for meetings, checking messages or texting during conversations.

When and where you deliver a category-two tease (e.g., in public or in private) can affect whether it's received as intended; the nature of the relationship (e.g., the level of intimacy, the extent teasing is already part of it) is also a factor. What makes a category-two tease an act of kindness is that compliance with suggested changes benefits your friend (e.g., pants zipper now secure, tee hee). Conversely, in category-one teases, compliance benefits the teaser and the relationship.

Tom reflects: *A helpful type of category-two tease for me, usually delivered by my wife Erica, is designed to help me recognize times when I'm being a little long-winded. Most often it stems from excitement about a discussion or when I feel confident and knowledgeable about a particular topic. I sometimes joke that the problem is an occupational hazard of being a professor, but I also recognize it can be off-putting to other people, depending on the situation. And it's exacerbated by the fact that, when I'm being long-winded, I'm often not aware of it. So, sometimes I need a little help from my friends—especially in the heat of the moment. Once, when I was teaching an RO DBT course, I recall* *being asked a question that could've been answered simply—but instead I launched into a long, convoluted theoretical response that increasingly seemed unlikely to ever answer the question. As I continued pontificating, I gradually began to notice that Erica, who was my coteacher, was busily waving her arms about—presumably to get my attention. Stopping my discourse mid-sentence, I turned to her and said, "Yes? Do you have a comment?" Erica stood up, and with a smile, eyebrow wag, and a slight shoulder shrug—said, "Yes, I do. But actually it's more of a question. Would you mind terribly if I tried to answer this particular question for you?"* (Mischievous smile.) *And since teaching RO DBT means practicing RO, I said with a smile, "Sure, go for it." Erica then turned to the questioner and asked them to repeat their question. After confirming she had it right, she smiled and turned to the room "So, is everyone ready for my response? Because I think it's going to be big." Then she turned towards me, with a big, cheeky grin. "OK, drum roll, please! Because the answer to your question is"—a dramatic pause—"No." And then she promptly sat down, with laughter rolling all around (including from me, tee hee). Her answer was not only correct, but the striking difference between it and mine, and her theatrical and playful manner, made it clear to all that she was also giving me some friendly, off-record advice in the form of a tease. It was a category-two tease because it blocked me from being too verbose while playfully demonstrating a pithy alternative. Plus, a lot of fun too! (BTW, did you notice how pithy that last sentence was? Tee hee!)*

Category-three teases are about discrepancies between what a friend says they'll do (or value) and what they actually do. Like category-two teases, they're done with the intention of helping your friend—in this case, to live more fully according to their valued goals and expressed wishes. Thus, any changes that these teases provoke will be for your friend's benefit, not yours per se—and that's kinda cool.

Examples of valued goals and behaviors that lend themselves to category-three teases include:

- a friend who values honesty repeatedly cheating when playing cards
- a friend who values kindness laughing at the misfortune of others
- a friend who values contributing to their community neglecting their duty
- a friend who values treating others as equals behaving as if they're superior
- a friend who likes to see themselves as always polite and considerate habitually succumbing to road rage
- a friend who values planning ahead abandoning their plans at the first sign of trouble

Now, imagine you had a friend who values sharing, but tends to grab the communal box of doughnuts and gobble up their favorites before anyone else has a chance. A category-three tease for such a friend might look something like this: You loudly clear your throat to get their attention: "Hrrmph, hrrmph!" And then, looking directly at them, you say, "Please ignore my drooling—my doctor says it's just a symptom of an acute case of sugar deprivation." *(Cheesy smile.)* Imagine giving the same feedback (i.e., "Please share") directly and on-record—it could easily be seen as more serious than intended. The off-record nature of a friendly tease gets the point across without it feeling like a formal warning.

Phew! And yippee! The *pulling it all together skill* we'll learn next, to help you learn how to use these teases in day-to-day life, uses an acronym known as Flexible Mind BANTERS. Let's get going!

Flexible Mind BANTERS

B: Briefly identify the feedBack you want to give the recipient of the tease.

The **B** in the acronym BANTERS refers to the **B** in **feedBack**. Without feedback, a tease is just being playful or joking around. Of course, just joking around also has its place! But to deliver a good tease, specifically, *you need to know what you want to give feedback about*. In other words, what you need to look for in your friends—in order to tease—is something you wish they might change but that you don't believe *must* change or consider a serious problem. And—don't overthink it! Remember, teasing is a way to help give feedback without getting all serious and heavy about it. Thinking too much about a tease can make teases come off stilted and stiff. So, how do you *not think too much* about a tease? It's a bit like trying not to think of a yellow alligator—the harder you try not to think about them, the more alligators you see. (Yikes!) Ultimately, our best advice here is: practice makes perfect. (But wait, we forgot—as OC folks, we're *not* supposed to be trying to make things perfect. If you're OC, you are already too good at this!) (Still—practice anyway, tee hee.)

You can also use our super-practical tip for creating spontaneous, non-stilted teases: do the exact opposite of what you'd do if you were to give the feedback directly, seriously, and on-record. For example, if the on-record, serious feedback is, "I really don't appreciate your offer because it hasn't done me any good," said in a serious voice-tone, the exact opposite of this could be our previously practiced tease "Thanks…a lot!" (delivered with a cheesy grin). Or if your serious, on-record feedback to a friend who's talking too loudly in a restaurant would be to nudge them and whisper, in a serious tone of voice, "Keep your voice down—you're disturbing the other diners," the exact opposite would be cupping your hand around your ear and faux-exclaiming, "What? I can't hear you. Could you speak a little louder, please?" followed by an "Oops!" or a cheesy grin. But don't take our word for it; try it out yourself. You may be in for a pleasant surprise (tee hee)!

In this exercise, we'll practice turning feedback into teases (hopefully, without thinking too much). To begin, think of a friend—someone you feel safe around—whom you'd like to practice teasing or get better at teasing. (BTW, since we'll be thinking of teases in all three categories, you might think of more than one friend.)

Category-one teases. Below, write something your friend repeatedly and often unknowingly does (habits or traits) that you find mildly annoying, perplexing, or odd and wish they'd change or do differently.

____

____

____

____

And then, see if you can come up with a way to playfully tease them about it. If you get stuck, write out how you'd give your friend the feedback on-record, including the words and expressions you'd use to communicate that your feedback was meant to be taken seriously. And then, write out its exact opposite to arrive at your tease. Don't forget to describe the nonverbal social signals (voice tone, gestures, facial expressions) that need to accompany the words for your tease to be taken as off-record and friendly. And don't lose the tease you come up with; we'll be using it again later in this exercise.

____

____

____

____

Next, using the same friend (or a different one), *let's practice coming up with a category-two tease.* Below, write the things your friend does in public that you feel embarrassed about *for them*—not for yourself. These behaviors should reflect your friend's blindspots—social mishaps, mistakes in etiquette, etc.—not serious problems.

____

____

____

____

And then, see if you can come up with a way to playfully tease them. If you're struggling to think of one, use our super-practical teasing tip to help loosen things up. Then, hold on to this category-two tease, because we'll be using it again later in BANTERS.

____

____

____

____

Now, using the same friend (or a different one), *let's practice coming up with a category-three tease*. Below, write about things your friend does that don't quite align with what they say they'll do or say they value—but isn't a serious problem that requires immediate fixing.

____

____

____

____

And like before, see if you can come up with a way to playfully tease them about this (using the super-practical teasing tip as you might need to). Hold on to this category-three tease, because we'll be using it again later.

____

____

____

____

A: Activate your social safety system.

The **A** in the acronym BANTERS refers to the **A** in **Activate**—and specifically, your social safety system. It's almost impossible to tease if you're uptight and in your threat system! When in threat, our facial muscles tighten up, our body movements are more constricted, and it's hard to be playful—so our teases can sting the other person or come off a little too harsh or unfriendly.

To activate social safety, you can use the Big Three + 1, closed-mouth cooperative smile, eyebrow wags, and other signals we discussed in chapter 5. That said—*hopefully, most of the time, you can just forget about this step anyway* (tee hee). Why? Because teasing usually occurs among friends—and friends are the people we feel safe around. Thus, there's a good chance you won't need to worry about activating your social safety system before delivering your friendly poke—because hopefully, you'll already be there. If you find you *are* feeling uptight, even around your friend, it's probably wise not to tease anyway, but instead to speak directly and on-record with your friend about what is troubling you, using box 9.2, "Tips for Talking with Friends," as your guide. But don't hold this as a rigid rule, either. We all get uptight around our friends sometimes—and often, what's stressing us out has nothing to do with our friendship; instead, it's to do with *us*: say, work stress, illness, hungriness, recent loss, or any number of other factors. And of course, most OC folks are biotemperamentally predisposed to be comparatively uptight around most people most of the time, whether friend or foe.

Ultimately, when your uptight feelings around a friend seem to stem more from you (e.g., due to biotemperamental predispositions) or from outside stressors specific to you, rather than from a problem in the relationship, you can use the **A** skill in BANTERS to loosen things up a bit first before you tease, deploying social signals that put you and your friend both in a state of safety. *And then you can go in for the kill.* Oops! We meant to say: *and then you're more likely to experience the mutual thrill of a well-delivered tease!* (Tee hee.)

N: Non-verbal playful signals need to stand-out!

The **N**, in BANTERS, refers to the **N** in **Non-verbal.** In many ways, this is the most important step in BANTERS, if you want to ensure that your tease is received as friendly.

What makes playful teasing fun and exciting is how often it boldly violates societal norms or personal expectations. But because teases are intentionally provocative and challenging, it's imperative for playful social signals—voice-tone, gestures, and facial expressions—to stand out. And they need to be both obvious (exaggerated) and unexpected (atypical) to be received as friendly, playful, and off-record. Examples of exaggerated non-verbal provocations include excessive finger wagging, theatrical displays of hands on hips, elongated pronunciations, dramatic gestures and facial expressions, and wide variations in vocal pitch.

Keep in mind "exaggerated" doesn't always mean "big"—as in wildly expressive, expansive, or loud—because what also makes a playful tease stand out, and be recognizable as off-record, is the fact that it's *unexpected or atypical behavior,* either *for the situation* (the social context) or *for the person displaying them* (the teaser). For example, you can't exaggerate a flat face and make it more expressive, since it's nonexpressive by definition. But you can still use it as part of a tease by making its appearance a surprise or unexpected. Say you wanted to tease a friend who tends to repeat not-so-funny old jokes; the next time you hear one of those jokes, you might morph your initial display of polite laughter into a flat-faced stare. Or, with a friend who offers you a food they know you dislike, you might say, with a flat face and monotonic voice, "Oh, that sounds just wonderful." It's the *change* in voice tone, and the *discrepancy* between what's said and how it's said, that makes this tease provocative and funny, and conveys that you're not too thrilled about tasting a disliked food. Note both examples use low-intensity signals to make playful intentions clear. And of course, what's crucial to both these teases being received as friendly is that they be followed by a giggle, smile, or some other form of nondominance signal.

As a general rule (BTW, we know, we're not supposed to endorse rule-governed behavior in this book—so, don't tell anyone, tee hee), *the less you know someone, the more exaggerated your playful social signals should be.* These signals must be seen to make friendly intentions known. And when someone doesn't know you well, the best way to ensure this is to make the signals conspicuous and hard to miss.

T: Practice teasing and then Tease some more!!!

The **T** in the acronym BANTERS refers to the **T** in **Tease** (of course). At this point, you have no excuse but to go out and start teasing your friends, family, and other people you care about or feel affection for (tee hee). For example, if your mom always puts her hair in a bun when she gets overly serious about something, you might put your hands on your cheeks, when you see her, and—looking around, using a sing-song voice—say, "Uh oh, we better alert the family—no more or smiling or laughing allowed. Mom's hair bun is back!" Or, rather than directly expressing your irritation at a sibling's repeated call for more ice for their drink, tease them by bowing and adopting a posh British accent while saying, "Of course, Your Majesty, I exist only to serve you!" With practice, you can become a master in the art of teasing and being teased. (But don't try *too* hard—because if you're OC, you do enough of that already, tee hee.)

A few reminders:

- Keep your teases short (as in, seconds). Prolonging a tease can start to feel like taunting or a putdown—especially if the target has signaled that they're not finding it funny. The guideline to keep in mind: when your friend doesn't find it funny, your tease has likely gone too far. So, stop teasing and use the skills in the letters E and R of BANTERS (below) to make your friendly intentions clear.
- Teasing also works best in person and face-to-face. An anonymous tease can easily be misinterpreted as harsh, unfriendly, or trolling. In-person interactions make it easier for the recipient to

recognize the non-serious nature of the feedback, since your exaggerated and playfully unexpected social signals can be clearly seen. Teasing in-person also allows you the opportunity *to observe how the recipient responds* and adjust accordingly, to ensure your friendly intentions are received. Granted, teasing can be done over text or email—but it's much more difficult. Signals need to be exaggerated even more to make sure the other person recognizes the tease's non-serious nature (which is probably why emojis were invented, tee hee 😊).

E: Express nondominance immediately after your tease to signal friendly intentions.

The **E** in BANTERS refers to the **E** in **Express**. Again, immediately following your challenge or "poke"—the provocative part of a tease—express nondominance, using signals of nondominance, appeasement, and cooperative play to communicate affection and re-establish social connection. As we've learned, it's important to exaggerate the *provocative* side of a tease; but it's equally important to exaggerate (and make obvious) the *friendly* side of a tease, to ensure that a tease is not taken as harsh judgment or "truth." Nondominance and appeasement signals are critical for a tease to be taken lightly (Keltner, Young & Buswell, 1997). And one of the most powerful means of doing this is the "Oh, My Gosh!" silly social signal we learned in Chapter 5. Others include giggling, smiling, eyebrow wags, shrugging shoulders, a light touch or hug, or slight gaze aversion to break direct eye contact (which can come across as aggressive). The idea is to be playfully provocative with your friend, not to stick it to them (tee hee).

R: Be Responsive to the reactions of the target of your tease and repair, if necessary.

The **R** in BANTERS refers to the **R** in **Responsive**. During your tease, notice how the target reacts to it and respond accordingly. Does your friend appear to genuinely enjoy your tease—to find it amusing, or laugh with you? Do they respond playfully in return? The best teases are fun to give and to receive; they generate mutual laughter. Again, there are several nonverbal and verbal indicators that suggest your tease is being received as intended. These include shared laughter or giggling, chuckling, maintaining eye contact, or teasing back. When all seems to be going well, there's no need to do anything more than enjoy the moment.

But sometimes, teases fall flat, and not every tease you deliver will be received as intended. Thus, you also need to be *responsive* to the reactions of the person on the receiving end of your tease. Be alert for clues that the tease isn't being received well—like the other person frowning or looking away, having a flat face, becoming serious, talking less, or justifying or defending their actions. Then, change how you respond, with the aim of reestablishing social connectedness.

Sometimes teases fall flat because they're expressed too weakly; other times, they fall flat because they're expressed too strongly. Regardless of what happened, or why, whenever you sense that your tease is not being received as intended, drop it and attend to the relationship.

When a tease falls flat, acknowledge that things didn't go as planned. Reassure your friend that you didn't intend the tease to be taken seriously, and acknowledge your own potential for fallibility—that your tease was not "truth" or a "statement of fact." Openly admit to a poor delivery of humorous intentions—without getting down on yourself, or overapologizing. For example, you might say, "Oops, I don't think that came out the way I intended," or "Oops—well, that was a bit over the top?" or "Oops—that was meant as a tease, but I think I need a little practice." Complement such statements with nonverbal signals like the "Oops!" or the cheesy appeasement grin from chapter 5. These particular signals take the heat off the recipient of the tease by keeping things light-hearted and playful—again, allowing you to say "I'm sorry" without getting too serious about it.

Let's take an opportunity to practice responding this way. As before, get your smartphone out and record yourself during your practice, or use a mirror. Record yourself saying "Oops," with raised eyebrows, a slight shoulder shrug, and a cheesy grin, as you try each phrase: "Oops, I don't think that came out the way I intended," "Oops—well, that was a bit over the top?" and "Oops—that was meant as a tease, but I think I need a little practice." Consult illustration 5.4, from chapter 5, if you need to. Repeat until it starts to feel natural.

When you're done, watch the recording of yourself. What does it feel like to be on the receiving end of your social signal? Were there any gestures or expressions you found difficult or awkward to display? (These are the ones you need to practice most.) Finally, show your recordings to a friend. Ask them which expression feels more friendly or which they'd prefer to spend more time with. Then, start looking for opportunities in the real world to try out what you have learned. Record what you observe below or in your self-enquiry journal.

____

____

____

____

____

Note there may be times when a lighted-hearted approach fails, and your friend still appears upset, despite your use of a lighthearted acknowledgment like the "Oops." If this happens, openly reveal your intentions—for example, to be provocative and funny, *not* to criticize, make them squirm, or give them a hard time. Apologize more formally—for example: "I'm aware of imagining that my tease didn't go over very well—and I just want to let you know that I'm not trying to give you a hard time. So, I'm genuinely sorry you experienced it as hurtful." Combine nondominance and appeasement signals with cooperative-friendly signals to signal sincerity—e.g., a warm smile, eyebrow wags, eye contact, slowed pace of speech, and a soft tone of voice. Plus, use box 9.2, "Tips for Talking with Friends," to guide your discussion.

Let's practice this! As before, get your smartphone out and record your practice, or use a mirror. First, let's demonstrate *what you shouldn't do*—that is, make an apology without an appeasement gesture. With shoulders back, chin up, and a commanding voice, record yourself saying, "I'm aware of imagining that my tease didn't go over very well—and I just want to let you know that I'm not trying to give you a hard time. So, I'm genuinely sorry you experienced it as hurtful." Then, record your observations (e.g., thoughts, emotions, sensations).

____

____

____

____

____

Next, let's practice *what you should do*—using appeasement gestures and concerned expressions when making an apology. Record yourself saying the same words—"I'm aware of imagining that my tease didn't go over very well—and I just want to let you know that I'm not trying to give you a hard time. So, I'm genuinely sorry you experienced it as hurtful"—but now with a slight bowing of head, slight shoulder shrug, openhanded gestures, furrowed brow, and slight grimace of pain. Repeat and record yourself multiple times—until it feels natural. Notice which gestures you find most difficult or awkward to display; these are the ones you'll especially want to practice. If it helps, make some notes about the experience below.

____

____

____

____

____

Lastly, go back and watch all the recordings you made during this exercise. Can you notice a difference between apologies made with appeasement gestures and expressions of concern versus those without such gestures? Which feels most sincere? Show your recordings to a friend. Ask them which expression feels more friendly or which they'd prefer to spend more time with. Start looking for opportunities to practice in the real world. Notice how their use impacts your relationships. Record observations below or in your self-enquiry journal.

____

____

____

____

____

Putting It Into Practice (At Last!)

Now, let's really 'pull it all together' by practicing all that you've learned—now in the real world! (Yippy!) Reflect back on the three teases you came up with earlier for your friends (under the **B** skill for **feedBack** in BANTERS). Your mission, should you choose to accept it (and we hope you will), is to practice delivering the teases you came up with for your friends, using the BANTERS skills as your guide. BTW, if you want to change your tease, now that you've learned more about them, that's okay. Also remember that your teases shouldn't be about serious problems or things that require immediate fixing. Don't forget to exaggerate nonverbal behaviors when delivering your tease, and be responsive to your friend's reaction to your tease. Notice the impact your tease has on your relationship, and feel free to talk explicitly with your friend about what happened afterwards. And, regardless of the outcome, keep practicing! Also, keep in mind that though there's a lot to remember, if you forget a skill or a tease falls flat, you can stay chill—because you'll be teasing the people you feel most safe around (i.e., your friends, tee hee). So, have fun! And, after each practice, record your observations for each category below.

Category-one tease (teasing your friend about things you find mildly annoying, perplexing, or odd):

____

____

____

____

Category-two tease (teasing your friend about the things they do in public that you feel embarrassed about *for them*—not for yourself):

____

____

____

____

Category-three tease (teasing your friend about things they do that don't align with what they say they'll do or say they value—and what they actually do):

____

____

____

____

S: After your tease reflect on how it went and practice Self-enquiry as needed.

The S in BANTERS refers to the S in **Self-enquiry**. After the tease, reflect on how you think your tease went. Begin your assessment by asking: *How did the person I teased respond to my tease?* If you thought the tease went well, what behavioral indicators supported your conclusion—shared laughter or giggling, chuckling, maintaining eye contact, or teasing back? (See also "How Is Your Tease Being Received?" earlier in this chapter.) If you believe that it didn't go well or that your tease fell flat, what behavioral indicators supported your conclusions? Did the recipient frown or look away? Did their face become flat? Did they talk less, or began to justify or defend themselves? And then, what did you do—did you drop your tease and attend to the relationship, by signaling that you didn't intend the tease to be taken seriously, or openly admitting to a poor delivery of humorous intentions (without getting down on yourself or overapologizing)? Did you apologize more formally, if that was needed? Finally, to what extent did you find yourself ruminating or worrying afterwards, either about the delivery of your tease or how your friend responded? Record your reflections in the spaces provided below or in your self-enquiry journal.

____

____

____

____

____

Look too for any "edges" that emerge. Rumination, for instance, may indicate an area in your life that needs to change or a place for new growth. Remember to keep your self-enquiry practices short, less than five minutes, and record whatever emerges from your practice in your self-enquiry journal. You can also use the questions below to help locate your edge or deepen your practice. And don't forget: *the best self-enquiry question is often the one we dislike the most* (tee hee).

- *What did I find most enjoyable or easy to do when teasing my friend? What was most difficult? To what extent did perfectionism play a part in how I evaluated my tease or my friend's response to my tease? What might my answers tell me about myself, my friendship, or how I see the world?*
- *To what extent was I able to exaggerate my playful social signals to ensure they were obvious or unexpected? Did I engage in an appeasement gesture? Is there something here to learn?*
- *To what extent was I hoping my tease would make my friend squirm or feel uncomfortable? If any of those actually happened, did I find it amusing or feel pleasure? What might this tell me about how I see my friend or our relationship? Is there something to learn?*
- *What did I hope my tease would accomplish? If my friend were to change their behavior as a result of my tease, who would benefit from the change? Myself? My friend? The relationship? Is there something here to learn?*
- *To what extent was my tease motivated by secret desires to punish or teach my friend a lesson? What might this tell me about how I see my friend or our relationship?*
- *To what extent did my teasing feel like a competition? Do I believe it's important to be better at teasing than my friend? What might my answers tell me about myself? About my relationship with my friend?*
- *Did my friend give me any feedback about my tease? How open was I to hearing it?*

- *To what extent did I use the skills from this lesson—before, during, and after my tease? What might my response tell me about how I learn or my willingness to learn?*
- *To what extent have I resisted this exercise? How open have I been to examining my personal responses, beliefs, and emotions during this practice of self-enquiry? What might my response tell me about myself or my willingness to learn?*

Elijah

Let's see Flexible Mind BANTERS in action with an example. One of Elijah's valued goals is to get closer to his nephew, Jamille; he also values a clean house. The problem for Elijah is that his nephew loves to cook when he visits, but he often leaves a mess. How can Elijah give his nephew feedback without being seen as the critical uncle? By using BANTERS, of course! Let's see how it went.

B: Briefly identify the feedBack you want to give the recipient of the tease.

I want him to know that while I love him cooking and baking at our house, he never cleans up his mess! And I'd like him to—it's helpful to me, both practically and in terms of my household harmony.

A: Activate your social safety system.

When I walk in the kitchen and see all those dishes, I immediately get tense and defensive. So, today, I remembered to raise my eyebrows, take a deep breath, and put on my closed-mouth cooperative smile.

N: Nonverbal playful signals need to stand out!

As Jamille noticed me, I put my hands on my head, opened my eyes really wide, and dropped my mouth open, like I was in complete shock! And then I slowly started to say, "Oh my gosh, Jamille—"

T: Practice teasing and then Tease some more!

"*—Call the police department! Someone's broken in and dirtied all the dishes!*"

E: Express appeasement and nondominance immediately after your tease to signal friendly intentions.

"*I then turned to him and flashed a cheesy appeasement grin, made a tee-hee chuckle, and shrugged my shoulders.*"

R: Be Responsive to the reactions of the person on the receiving end of your tease and Repair, if necessary.

I was alert to his response to my tease. Jamille laughed and joined in, saying "No! We better call the FBI because this looks very, very serious! Don't touch any of the evidence!" Him joining in meant two things to me—he'd heard my feedback, and he knew I wasn't being overly critical. The end result was that we did the dishes together—he washed, I dried.

S: After your tease, reflect on how it went, and practice Self-enquiry as needed.

I was somewhat surprised that I didn't feel a lot of "energy" or stress when I teased my nephew. If I were to do self-enquiry it might be around my initial nervousness about teasing, something like: where did I ever get the idea that teasing could never be helpful? What's cool is that my feedback seemed to have been heard, because he joined in the cleanup without being prompted. Today, "calling the FBI" after one of his cooking excursions is a family joke—because he no longer needs to be reminded to clean up after himself (at least not very often, tee hee).

Of course, when you're first learning how to tease, sometimes things fall flat on their face. Let's look at another example, this time from Tula. Tula has been trying to get back in the dating scene, but she often feels awkward interacting with others. Teasing would be a useful skill for her to learn, since it's adjacent to flirting. So, let's return to her example from chapter 4, where the person she was dating cancelled plans to go away for the weekend. As you recall, Tula actually broke things off despite really being smitten with this person. Let's take a look at how she could've done things differently!

B: Briefly identify the feedBack you want to give the recipient of the tease.

I want them to know that this weekend was really important to me, and being cancelled on makes me feel less valuable.

A: Activate your social safety system.

I was super angry, and I could feel my teeth start to clench. But I remembered to raise my eyebrows, take a deep breath, and put on my closed-mouth cooperative smile, as this would make my voice tone more musical and less defensive.

N: Nonverbal playful signals need to stand out!

When they said sorry for the last-minute cancel, I gave a heavy sigh…

T: Practice teasing and then Tease some more!

Well, I didn't realize that your family was royalty!

E: Express appeasement and nondominance immediately after your tease to signal friendly intentions.

I then smiled.

R: Be Responsive to the reactions of the person on the receiving end of your tease and Repair, if necessary.

"I asked myself: how did my tease land? He wasn't smiling with me—he just looked at me with a confused expression. Instead, he seemed to get defensive about his decision to cancel our trip. He started to explain why it was important to be there for his family. It seemed that he wasn't taking my tease as I'd intended, which meant I should make a repair. So I decided to out myself, saying "Evan, I think I just did an oops. I was trying to tease you about your change of plans—but I think I may have made a mountain out of a molehill instead. I wasn't trying to give you a hard time. I just wanted you to know that I'll miss our time together." He smiled when I said this and seemed to relax. We then started to talk about his family's unexpected visit, and how it might be an opportunity for me to meet them in person and spend time with him too. And BTW, it's become a running joke for us—because he now teases me about my teasing!

S: After your tease, reflect on how it went, and practice Self-enquiry as needed.

When I reflected back on what happened, my first observation was about the tension I felt in my body before I delivered the tease. Had I been able to really activate my social safety system? Maybe my tone of voice had been a bit sharp, or there was bodily tension that communicated something other than I'd intended. I also wondered whether my initial sigh was exaggerated enough to read as playful. Could it have been mistaken to mean serious exasperation on my part? What is it that I might need to learn? Ultimately, I found this old story emerging: "It doesn't really matter, because people only care about themselves." It's a story that tends to regulate me because it justifies my anger, resentment, and despair. I then asked: what am I so angry about? And—if it truly "doesn't really matter," then why am I getting all worked up about this? Is it possible that I'm afraid that if he spends time with his family, I'll become less important in his life? That seemed to generate more energy for me, but I also felt an urge to quickly find an answer—an urge I know to be wary of. And so, I decided to stop my practice and save the question for my self-enquiry practice tomorrow.

Moving Forward

Okay, that's all the preaching and teaching we have about teasing, which was hopefully pleasing (tee hee)! We encourage you to practice, practice, and practice friendly teasing whenever you get a chance (even if you're already great teaser). And don't keep it a secret. Tell your friends that you're learning how to tease, and ask them to join in by teasing you back. What's cool about teasing is that it's not only socially bonding, but a great way to communicate and receive feedback without getting all serious about it! And what's double cool: a good tease is always kind.

Concluding Remarks

A major premise of this book is that maladaptive perfectionism isn't *bad*—it's more about having too much of a good thing. Namely, self-control—a personality trait that's partly biologically based. If you struggle with perfectionism, your self-control is out of control. You can't stop trying to control things—including your perfectionistic tendencies. Yikes! And therein lies the paradox: you can't use your superior capacities for self-control to control your perfectionism. If you try, you only put another thing on your "to-do list" (sigh). And if you try even harder, you end up feeling more exhausted. Thus, maladaptive perfectionism is both a *blessing and a curse*. Perfectionism means that things get done, trains run on time, Olympic medals are won, grammatical errors are uncovered (*but don't tell our editors*), deadlines are met, and expectations are exceeded. Indeed, superior capacities to inhibit impulses, plan ahead, and delay gratification make perfectionistic overcontrolled individuals the doers, savers, planners, and fixers of the world! But when "being good" starts to mean being good *all the time*, it becomes a trap. Being perfect all the time is an impossible task.

The principles and skills covered in this book are derived from a transdiagnostic, evidence-based treatment for disorders of overcontrol known as radically open dialectical behavior therapy or RO DBT (Lynch, 2018a, 2018b). We've covered a lot of ground. Here is a summary of some of the core precepts we've been exploring.

- Our species' survival depended on our being able to form long-lasting social bonds, share valuable resources with unrelated others, and work together in tribes or groups. Thus, we're tribal by nature, and when we feel part of a tribe, we naturally feel safe and worry less.

- Our brains respond "as if" we were still living in primordial times. We're evolutionarily hardwired to be hypersensitive to signs of disapproval—as in, are we "in" or "out" of the tribe?

- Rather than focusing on what's "wrong" with hyper-detail-focused perfectionists, RO DBT begins by observing what's healthy about all of us and uses this to guide treatment interventions. Psychological health or well-being, in RO DBT, reflects three core, transacting features:

  a. *Receptivity and openness* to new experience and disconfirming feedback in order to learn

  b. *Flexible control*, in order to adapt to changing environmental conditions

   c. *Intimacy and connectedness* with at least one other person, since individual and species success depends on our capacities to form long-lasting bonds with unrelated others and work together in groups or tribes

- RO DBT posits that maladaptive perfectionism is fundamentally a problem of excessive self-control, and that the emotional costs of maladaptive perfectionism and overcontrol are primarily social in nature.
- Maladaptive overcontrol is a personality style characterized by decreased openness, excessive emotional inhibition, hyperperfectionism, social isolation, and aloof or distant relationships.
- Perfectionistic overcontrolled coping is thought to result from transactions between our innate biological predispositions (nature) and our family, cultural, and environmental experiences (nurture), like family and cultural expectations that prioritize performance, high achievement, and not making mistakes.
- RO DBT contends that biotemperament may be the driving force behind maladaptive overcontrol. Biotemperament is powerful because it can influence a person's perception and overt behavior at the sensory-receptor or preconscious level of responding, as well as the central cognitive or more conscious level of responding. Put another way, you can't talk yourself out of a biotemperamental predisposition; it's genetically based. There are four dimensions of biotemperament relevant for OC: high threat sensitivity, low reward sensitivity, high inhibitory control, and high detail-focused processing of stimuli.
- RO DBT proposes a novel neuroregulatory model centered around five broad classes of stimuli, or cues: *safety, novelty, threat, reward and overwhelming.* Each is linked to a distinct neural substrate and corresponding autonomic nervous system responses, which impact how a person social signals. RO DBT also teaches skills to activate or deactivate these differing neural substrates—in particular the ventral vagal complex (VVC), a neural substrate associated with social safety and desires for affiliation.
- When we feel safe, we naturally feel relaxed and socially engaged, our social safety system (VVC) is on, our heart and breathing rates slow, we can effortlessly make eye contact, our laughter and smiles are genuine, we're able to listen to others better, and we're likely to want to reach out and touch someone.
- RO DBT is the first treatment in the world to prioritize social signaling as a primary mechanism of change, based on robust research that shows that the ways a person socially signals strongly impacts their relationships. A social signal is any behavior—regardless of its form, its intent, or the performer's awareness—that's carried out in the presence of another person. RO DBT teaches nonverbal social signaling strategies to enhance social connectedness, including gestures,

postures, voice tones, and facial expressions that universally signal openness, nondominance and friendly intentions, across cultures.

- Open expression of emotion increases trust and social connectedness. When a sender openly and candidly reveals intentions and expresses emotions, recipients are more likely to perceive the sender as trustworthy, genuine, and authentic. Consequently, they're more likely to socially welcome, help, or play with them—which positively impacts the emotional well-being of the sender by increasing feelings of safety and security. Social signals are powerful because they can trigger similar neural substrates and emotions in the recipient as those being activated in the sender, via a process called micromimicry.
- There's no "right" or optimal way to socially signal. Each of us has our own unique style of expression. What's important is that our social signaling style help us live according to our valued goals and effectively communicate our intentions and inner experiences to other people—especially those we desire to be close with.
- RO DBT also differs from most other approaches via its emphasis on openness and self-enquiry mindfulness practices. Radical openness is more than awareness—it's actively seeking the things one wants to avoid or may find uncomfortable in order to learn.
- Before you start giving others feedback, it helps to know how to take feedback from others yourself. Being open to feedback enhances new learning. And it's freeing, because we no longer need to defend our point of view as the only correct one possible.
- If you desire long-term, close social bonds, you must be able to signal that you care about someone other than yourself. Validation is a core means of achieving this—it involves understanding another person *and* communicating this understanding back to them. However, genuine friendship involves going still further to reveal vulnerability and engage in mutual self-disclosure. People cannot know who you are unless you reveal who you are.
- When it comes to *giving* corrective feedback in close relationships, what may matter most is *how* it's delivered. Corrective feedback that's delivered with an open mind, a little humor, and a dash of humility works best. Friendly teasing is a core way to do this. It's how friends informally point out flaws in each other, without being too heavy-handed about it.
- Lastly, to end this summary on a high note (tee hee): don't forget that in RO DBT, silliness is no laughing matter. We take silliness very seriously, because perfectionistic, overcontrolled folks tend to take life too seriously. The good news is that even cranky adults can learn to enjoy being silly. It's all about giving yourself permission, throwing yourself into the deep end, and then practicing, again and again and again. Plus, you only need be silly for a second or two for it to create

beneficial social bonding effects. And of course, being silly doesn't mean being silly all the time—that would be silly (tee hee).

The Path of We (Not Me)

In many ways, the central message of this entire book comes back to the core RO DBT assumption that individual well-being is inseparable from the feelings and responses of the larger group or community. We all desire to be loved, admired, and appreciated for our unique contributions to the world. Yet our personal success, sense of self, and emotional well-being is *highly dependent on feedback and support* from our fellow tribal members. Looking in the mirror and telling ourselves that we're lovable, competent, or good doesn't really get the job done. We depend on our fellow tribal members to verify our worthiness—which explains why we care so much about the opinions of others.

The problem for perfectionistic OC people is *not* that they don't care about other people (or their opinions). It's that they care *too much* about personal success. Despite this, they usually have a high sense of moral obligation to do "the right thing" even when it's very difficult or unpleasant, and they frequently endorse values like restraint, temperance, fairness, politeness, self-sacrifice, accuracy, integrity, service, honesty, accountability, and discipline. What's interesting about all these values and traits is that they all depend upon a social context for meaning. That is, they're virtuous not just because they're difficult to live by, but also because they function to contribute to the well-being of one's tribe or community. They allow one to place the needs of others over the needs of the individual.

What's missing, for someone who considers winning and being the best to be what matters most, is the recognition of a basic truth about our species—that our individual success and survival is highly dependent on others. We are better together, as members of a tribe or community, and learning how to form a close social bond with another person is a core developmental task. It's only when we're able to acknowledge our innate dependence on the goodwill of others for our personal success, and the importance of contributing to our tribe for our species success, that the powerful grip of maladaptive overcontrol and perfectionism can begin to loosen.

Fortunately, by working through the skills and activities in this book, you've begun to walk that path. Recall the definition of radically open living you learned in chapter 5: learning how to flexibly adapt your behavior to everchanging circumstances in order to achieve goals or live according to your values, *in a manner that accounts for the needs of others*. That last part's the most important. When we're able to recognize that how we behave around others impacts their well-being, it's no longer just about us, our needs, and our perfectionism. We're on the path of *we*, not *me*, and we can build lives worth sharing.

Building a Life Worth Sharing

Again, a "life worth sharing" is one lived in a manner that goes against older, "selfish" tendencies to individual survival and advantage—a manner that instead contributes to another's well-being, without always expecting something in return. It recognizes too that we can't achieve heightened self-awareness in isolation—we need other people (hopefully, our friends) to point out our blindspots. Plus, a life worth sharing values open dialogue as a core means for personal growth. It's courageous because it actively seeks to find fault in itself and question its motives, and does so without falling apart. It can laugh at its own foibles, too, and share the laugh with others.

Ultimately, each of us must decide for ourselves what a life worth sharing means for us and how it might manifest in our lives. For example, it might mean improving a long-term relationship, or it might mean establishing your first genuine friendship, or it might mean contributing to the welfare of someone you barely know. The choice is yours—but whatever you do, make sure it includes someone other than yourself (tee hee).

Essentially, from an RO DBT perspective, when it comes right down to it, we're all the same, no matter our individual or cultural differences. We're better together. And each one of us inwardly knows this, regardless of how much we may have been hurt or may have attempted to persuade ourselves otherwise. This is why we all fear social exclusion, care so much about what others think of us, are upset when others disapprove of our behaviour, love to gossip, and feel self-righteous about punishing those who have harmed or deceived other tribal members for personal gain. We all desire to be loved and respected; we all want to be treated fairly, believe in equity, and desire to be perceived by others as impartial. Yet our capacity for love is a predisposition, not a given. It can grow or wither depending on how we choose to live our lives. We hope your choice will be the "path of we" (not "me," tee hee. BTW, our editors found this rhyme extremely lame—oh well!).

Final Thoughts

Radical openness is the core philosophical principle and core skill in RO DBT. It's posited to impact not only how we see the world, by making us more receptive to critical feedback, but also how others see us: people like open-minded people! Thus, it's considered both a state of mind and a powerful social signal, influencing both our personal perception and also how others see us.

Yet, practicing radical openness isn't necessarily easy. It requires purposeful self-enquiry, and a willingness to be "wrong" with an intention to change when change is needed. It challenges our perceptions of reality, based on the idea that *we don't see things as they are—we see things as we are.* It can be painful, because it often requires sacrificing firmly held convictions or self-concepts. It means we can no longer automatically assume that our perspective is always correct, or automatically dismiss further self-examination by telling ourselves that we already know the answer, or feel self-righteous about discounting feedback we don't like (bummer). It also means taking responsibility for our choices and responses to the world. We can no longer simply blame others, fall apart, expect the world to change, or get down on ourselves upon discovering a painful truth. (Yowsers!)

Thus, radical openness is also *training ourselves to face ourselves*. It's the primary source of self-integrity, and a core means for us to live by our values. For one, radical openness helps us loosen rigid thinking by celebrating diversity. It recognizes that there are numerous ways of solving problems or perceiving the world, and rarely is there only one correct way. Radical openness also enhances new learning. Being open to critical feedback allows you, as a practitioner of radical openness, to benefit from the collective wisdom of the tribe without needing to learn everything the hard way, via trial-and-error or direct experience. Plus, when you start asking *What do I need to learn?* instead of *How can I prove I'm right?* every time your worldview is challenged, your sense of self becomes less about being correct and more about being receptive to new information. This openness inevitably generalizes to your relationships, as people innately recognize the value it brings. For example, we tend to trust open-minded people because they are more likely to reveal than hide their feelings or intentions during conflict. We desire to affiliate with open-minded people because they don't take themselves or life too seriously—making them fun to be around. We feel safe around them because we recognize that they're more likely to give others the benefit of the doubt during interactions, and they don't automatically assume their way is the only way or right way. Essentially, openness is tribal glue and a powerful social safety signal. It helps you place the needs of others on an equal footing to your own, and is thus the cure for arrogance, selfishness, lack of empathy, and isolation. It also resolves the paradox of perfectionism, and allows you to build that life worth sharing!

Yet practicing radical openness requires, well, practice. It's experiential, not something that you can grasp solely intellectually. It also evolves over time, as a function of your continued practice. So, as we come to the end of our work together—which has hopefully been helpful *and* fun!—we thought we might end with a little self-enquiry practice (yippee!).

Perhaps the best question to start with is: *To what extent did I find the skills in this book helpful?* If they made a difference in your life, then perhaps the next best question would be: *How might I ensure that my practice of radical openness skills grows and is sustained?*

____

____

____

____

____

____

From there, rather than tell you what to do (tee hee), we hope you'll continue exploring for yourself what radically open living and a life worth sharing mean for you. And, regardless of what you decide, you can relax—because the decision to practice or not to practice RO skills is entirely up to you. It'd be arrogant for us to suggest anything otherwise (tee hee)!

For more information about RO DBT, visit http://www.radicallyopen.net.

References

Aloi, M., Rania, M., Caroleo, M., Bruni, A., Palmieri, A., Cauteruccio, M. A., De Fazio, P., & Segura-García, C. (2015). Decision making, central coherence and set-shifting: A comparison between binge eating disorder, anorexia nervosa and healthy controls. *BMC Psychiatry, 15*(1), 6. https://doi.org/10.1186/s12888-015-0395-z

Ambady, N., & Rosenthal, R. (1992). Thin slices of expressive behavior as predictors of interpersonal consequences: A meta-analysis. *Psychological Bulletin, 111*(2), 256–274. https://doi.org/10.1037/0033-2909.111.2.256

Berntson, G. G., Cacioppo, J. T., & Quigley, K. S. (1991). Autonomic determinism: The modes of autonomic control, the doctrine of autonomic space, and the laws of autonomic constraint. *Psychological Review,* 98(4), 459–487. https://doi.org/10.1037/0033-295x.98.4.459

Boone, R. T., & Buck, R. (2003). Emotional expressivity and trustworthiness: The role of nonverbal behavior in the evolution of cooperation. *Journal of Nonverbal Behavior, 27*(3), 163–182. https://doi.org/10.1023/a:1025341931128

Bracha, H. S. (2004). Freeze, flight, fight, fright, faint: Adaptationist perspectives on the acute stress response spectrum. *CNS Spectrums,* 9(9), 679–685. https://doi.org/10.1017/s1092852900001954

Brand, N., Schneider, N., & Arntz, P. (1995). Information processing efficiency and noise: Interactions with personal rigidity. *Personality and Individual Differences, 18*(5), 571–579. https://doi.org/10.1016/0191-8869(94)00203-5

Breen, W. E., Kashdan, T. B., Lenser, M. L., & Fincham, F. D. (2010). Gratitude and forgiveness: Convergence and divergence on self-report and informant ratings. *Personality and Individual Differences,* 49(8), 932–937. https://doi.org/10.1016/j.paid.2010.07.033

Brown, W. M., & Moore, C. (2002). Smile asymmetries and reputation as reliable indicators of likelihood to cooperate: An evolutionary analysis. In S. P. Shohov (Ed.), *Advances in psychology research* (Vol. 11., pp. 19–36). Nova Science Publishers.

Brown, S. L., Nesse, R. M., Vinokur, A. D., & Smith, D. M. (2003). Providing social support may be more beneficial than receiving it. *Psychological Science, 14*(4), 320–327. https://doi.org/10.1111/1467-9280.14461

Butler, E. A., Egloff, B., Wilhelm, F. H., Smith, N. C., Erickson, E. A., & Gross, J. J. (2003). The social consequences of expressive suppression. *Emotion, 3*(1), 48–67. https://doi.org/10.1037/1528-3542.3.1.48

Cannizzaro, M., Harel, B., Reilly, N., Chappell, P., & Snyder, P. J. (2004). Voice acoustical measurement of the severity of major depression. *Brain and Cognition, 56*(1), 30–35. https://doi.org/10.1016/j.bandc.2004.05.003

Clark, L. A., & Watson, D. (1991). Tripartite model of anxiety and depression: Psychometric evidence and taxonomic implications. *Journal of Abnormal Psychology, 100*(3), 316–336. https://doi.org/10.1037//0021-843x.100.3.316

Codd, R. T., III, & Craighead, L. W. (2019). New thinking about old ideas: Introduction to the special issue on radically open dialectical behavior therapy. *The Behavior Therapist, 41*(3), 109–114.

Couper-Kuhlen, E. (1996). The prosody of repetition: On quoting and mimicry. In E. Couper-Kuhlen & M. Selting (Eds.), *Prosody in conversation: Interactional studies* (pp. 366–405). Cambridge University Press. https://doi.org/10.1017/cbo9780511597862.011

Couper-Kuhlen, E. (2012). Exploring affiliation in the reception of conversational complaint stories. In A. Perakyla & M.-L. Sorjonen (Eds.), *Emotion in interaction* (pp. 113–144). Oxford University Press. https://doi.org/10.1093/acprof:oso/9780199730735.003.0006

Couper-Kuhlen, E. (2012). Some truths and untruths about final intonation in conversational questions. In J. P. de Ruiter (Ed.), *Questions: Formal, functional, and interactional perspectives* (pp. 123–145). Cambridge University Press. https://doi.org/10.1017/cbo9781139045414.009

Craddock, A. E., Church, W., & Sands, A. (2009). Family of origin characteristics as predictors of perfectionism. *Australian Journal of Psychology, 61*(3), 136–144. https://doi.org/10.1080/00049530802239326

Depue, R. A., & Morrone-Strupinsky, J. V. (2005). A neurobehavioral model of affiliative bonding: Implications for conceptualizing a human trait of affiliation. *Behavioral and Brain Sciences, 28*(3). https://doi.org/10.1017/s0140525x05000063

DeScioli, P., & Kurzban, R. (2009). Mysteries of morality. *Cognition, 112*(2), 281–299. https://doi.org/10.1016/j.cognition.2009.05.008

Durbin, C. E., Klein, D. N., Hayden, E. P., Buckley, M. E., & Moerk, K. C. (2005). Temperamental emotionality in preschoolers and parental mood disorders. *Journal of Abnormal Psychology, 114*(1), 28–37. https://doi.org/10.1037/0021-843x.114.1.28

Eisenberg, N., & Shell, R. (1986). Prosocial moral judgment and behavior in children. *Personality and Social Psychology Bulletin, 12*(4), 426–433. https://doi.org/10.1177/0146167286124005

Eisenberger, N. I., & Lieberman, M. D. (2004). Why rejection hurts: A common neural alarm system for physical and social pain. *Trends in Cognitive Sciences, 8*(7), 294–300. https://doi.org/10.1016/j.tics.2004.05.010

English, T., & John, O. P. (2013). Understanding the social effects of emotion regulation: The mediating role of authenticity for individual differences in suppression. *Emotion, 13*(2), 314–329. https://doi.org/10.1037/a0029847

Feinberg, M., Willer, R., & Keltner, D. (2011). Flustered and faithful: Embarrassment as a signal of prosociality. *Journal of Personality and Social Psychology, 102*(1), 81–97. https://doi.org/10.1037/a0025403

Ferguson, T. J., Brugman, D., White, J., & Eyre, H. L. (2007). Shame and guilt as morally warranted experiences. In J. L. Tracy, R. W. Robins, & J. P. Tangney (Eds.), *The self-conscious emotions: Theory and research* (pp. 330–348). The Guilford Press.

Flett, G. L., & Hewitt, P. L. (2006). Positive versus negative perfectionism in psychopathology: A comment on Slade and Owens's dual process model. *Behavioral Modification, 30*(4), 472–495. https://doi.org/10.1177/0145445506288026

Flett, G. L., Hewitt, P. L., Blankstein, K. R., & Gray, L. (1998). Psychological distress and the frequency of perfectionistic thinking. *Journal of Personality and Social Psychology, 75*(5), 1363–1381. https://doi.org/10.1037/0022-3514.75.5.1363

Fox, E., Lester, V., Russo, R., Bowles, R. J., Pichler, A., & Dutton, K. (2000). Facial Expressions of Emotion: Are Angry Faces Detected More Efficiently? *Cognition and Emotion, 14*(1), 61–92. https://doi.org/10.1080/026999300378996

Frost, R. O., Marten, P., Lahart, C., & Rosenblate, R. (1990). The dimensions of perfectionism. *Cognitive Therapy and Research, 14*(5), 449–468. https://doi.org/10.1007/bf01172967

Fruzzetti, A., & Worrall, J. (2010). Accurate expression and validation: A transactional model for understanding individual and relationship distress. In K. T. Sullivan & J. Davila (Eds.), *Support processes in intimate relationships* (pp. 121–150). Oxford University Press.

Gailliot, M. T., Baumeister, R. F., Dewall, C. N., Maner, J. K., Plant, E. A., Tice, D. M., Brewer, L. E., & Schmeichel, B. J. (2007). Self-control relies on glucose as a limited energy source: Willpower is more than a metaphor. *Journal of Personality and Social Psychology, 92*(2), 325–336. https://doi.org/10.1037/0022-3514.92.2.325

Georgesen, J. C., Harris, M. J., Milich, R., & Young, J. (1999). "Just teasing...": Personality effects on perceptions and life narratives of childhood teasing. *Personality and Social Psychology Bulletin, 25*(10), 1254–1267. https://doi.org/10.1177/0146167299258007

Gladstone, G. L., Parker, G. B., & Malhi, G. S. (2006). Do bullied children become anxious and depressed adults? *Journal of Nervous & Mental Disease, 194*(3), 201–208. https://doi.org/10.1097/01.nmd.0000202491.99719.c3

Graham, A. R., Sherry, S. B., Stewart, S. H., Sherry, D. L., McGrath, D. S., Fossum, K. M., & Allen, S. L. (2010). The existential model of perfectionism and depressive symptoms: A short-term, four-wave longitudinal study. *Journal of Counseling Psychology, 57*(4), 423–438. https://doi.org/10.1037/a0020667

Grammer, K., Schiefenhövel, W., Schleidt, M., Lorenz, B., & Eibl-Eibesfeldt, I. (1988). Patterns on the face: The eyebrow flash in crosscultural comparison. *Ethology, 77*(4), 279–299. https://doi.org/10.1111/j.1439-0310.1988.tb00211.x

Greville-Harris, M., Hempel, R., Karl, A., Dieppe, P., & Lynch, T. (2016). The power of invalidating communication: Receiving invalidating feedback predicts threat-related emotional, physiological, and social responses. *Journal of Social and Clinical Psychology, 35*(6), 471–493. https://doi.org/10.1521/jscp.2016.35.6.471

Gross, J. J. (2002). Emotion regulation: Affective, cognitive, and social consequences. *Psychophysiology, 39*(3), 281–291. https://doi.org/10.1017/s0048577201393198

Halmesvaara, O., Harjunen, V. J., Aulbach, M. B., & Ravaja, N. (2020). How bodily expressions of emotion after norm violation influence perceivers' moral judgments and prevent social exclusion: A socio-functional approach to nonverbal shame display. *PLOS ONE, 15*(4), e0232298. https://doi.org/10.1371/journal.pone.0232298

Happé, F., & Frith, U. (2006). The weak coherence account: Detail-focused cognitive style in autism spectrum disorders. *Journal of Autism and Developmental Disorders, 36*(1), 5–25. https://doi.org/10.1007/s10803-005-0039-0

Hatoum, A. H., & Burton, A. L. (2024). Applications and efficacy of radically open dialectical behavior therapy (RO DBT): A systematic review of the literature. *Journal of Clinical Psychology, 80*(11), 2283–2302. https://doi.org/10.1002/jclp.23735

Hertenstein, M. J., Verkamp, J. M., Kerestes, A. M., & Holmes, R. M. (2006). The communicative functions of touch in humans, nonhuman primates, and rats: A review and synthesis of the empirical research. *Genetic, Social, and General Psychology Monographs, 132*(1), 5–94. https://doi.org/10.3200/mono.132.1.5-94

Hess, U., & Blairy, S. (2001). Facial mimicry and emotional contagion to dynamic emotional facial expressions and their influence on decoding accuracy. *International Journal of Psychophysiology, 40*(2), 129–141. https://doi.org/10.1016/s0167-8760(00)00161-6

Hewitt, P. L., & Flett, G. L. (1991). Perfectionism in the self and social contexts: Conceptualization, assessment, and association with psychopathology. *Journal of Personality and Social Psychology, 60*(3), 456–470. https://doi.org/10.1037//0022-3514.60.3.456

Hock, M., & Krohne, H. W. (2004). Coping with threat and memory for ambiguous information: Testing the repressive discontinuity hypothesis. *Emotion, 4*(1), 65–86. https://doi.org/10.1037/1528-3542.4.1.65

Hoenig, F., Batliner, A., Noeth, E., Schnieder, S., & Krajewski, J. (2014). Automatic modelling of depressed speech: Relevant features and relevance of gender. *Proceedings of the Annual Conference of the International Speech Communication Association* (INTERSPEECH), 1248–1252.

Horstmann, G., & Bauland, A. (2006). Search asymmetries with real faces: Testing the anger-superiority effect. *Emotion,* 6(2), 193–207. https://doi.org/10.1037/1528-3542.6.2.193

John, O. P., & Srivastava, S. (1999). The Big Five Trait taxonomy: History, measurement, and theoretical perspectives. In L. A. Pervin & O. P. John (Eds.), *Handbook of personality: Theory and research* (2nd ed., pp. 102–138). Guilford Press.

Johnson, J. G., Smailes, E. M., Cohen, P., Brown, J., & Bernstein, D. P. (2000). Associations between four types of childhood neglect and personality disorder symptoms during adolescence and early adulthood: Findings of a community-based longitudinal study. *Journal of Personality Disorders, 14*(2), 171–187. https://doi.org/10.1521/pedi.2000.14.2.171

Kaul, T. J., & Schmidt, L. D. (1971). Dimensions of interviewer trustworthiness. *Journal of Counseling Psychology, 18*(6), 542–548. https://doi.org/10.1037/h0031748

Kavanagh, E., Whitehouse, J., & Waller, B. M. (2024). Being facially expressive is socially advantageous. *Scientific Reports, 14*(1). https://doi.org/10.1038/s41598-024-62902-6

Keltner, D., Young, R. C., & Buswell, B. N. (1997). Appeasement in human emotion, social practice, and personality. *Aggressive Behavior, 23*(5), 359–374. https://doi.org/10.1002/(sici)1098-2337(1997)23:53.0.co;2-d

Keltner, D., Capps, L., Kring, A. M., Young, R. C., & Heerey, E. A. (2001). Just teasing: A conceptual analysis and empirical review. *Psychological Bulletin, 127*(2), 229–248. https://doi.org/10.1037/0033-2909.127.2.229

Kernis, M. H., & Goldman, B. M. (2006). A multicomponent conceptualization of authenticity: Theory and research. In *Advances in experimental social psychology* (Vol 38., pp. 283–357). Elsevier. https://doi.org/10.1016/S0065-2601(06)38006-9

Kochanska, G., & Knaack, A. (2003). Effortful control as a personality characteristic of young children: Antecedents, correlates, and consequences. *Journal of Personality, 71*(6), 1087–1112. https://doi.org/10.1111/1467-6494.7106008

Kraus, M. W., Piff, P. K., & Keltner, D. (2009). Social class, sense of control, and social explanation. *Journal of Personality and Social Psychology, 97*(6), 992–1004. https://doi.org/10.1037/a0016357

Lakin, J. L., & Chartrand, T. L. (2003). Using nonconscious behavioral mimicry to create affiliation and rapport. *Psychological Science, 14*(4), 334–339. https://doi.org/10.1111/1467-9280.14481

Lakin, J. L., Jefferis, V. E., Cheng, C. M., & Chartrand, T. L. (2003). The chameleon effect as social glue: Evidence for the evolutionary significance of nonconscious mimicry. *Journal of Nonverbal Behavior, 27*(3), 145–162. https://doi.org/10.1023/a:1025389814290

Lang, K., & Tchanturia, K. (2014). A systematic review of central coherence in young people with anorexia nervosa. *Journal of Child and Adolescent Behaviour, 2*(3). https://doi.org/10.4172/2375-4494.1000140

Lang, K., Lopez, C., Stahl, D., Tchanturia, K., & Treasure, J. (2014). Central coherence in eating disorders: An updated systematic review and meta-analysis. *The World Journal of Biological Psychiatry, 15*(8), 586–598. https://doi.org/10.3109/15622975.2014.909606

Laurenceau, J.-P., Barrett, L. F., & Pietromonaco, P. R. (1998). Intimacy as an interpersonal process: The importance of self-disclosure, partner disclosure, and perceived partner responsiveness in interpersonal exchanges. *Journal of Personality and Social Psychology, 74*(5), 1238–1251. https://doi.org/10.1037/0022-3514.74.5.1238

Linehan, M. M. (1993). *Cognitive-behavioral treatment of borderline personality disorder.* Guilford Press.

Linton, S. J., & Shaw, W. S. (2011). Impact of psychological factors in the experience of pain. *Physical Therapy, 91*(5), 700–711. https://doi.org/10.2522/ptj.20100330

London, B., Downey, G., Bonica, C., & Paltin, I. (2007). Social causes and consequences of rejection sensitivity. *Journal of Research on Adolescence, 17*(3), 481–506. https://doi.org/10.1111/j.1532-7795.2007.00531.x

Lopez, C., Tchanturia, K., Stahl, D., & Treasure, J. (2008). Central coherence in eating disorders: A systematic review. *Psychological Medicine, 38*(10), 1393–1404. https://doi.org/10.1017/s0033291708003486

Lopez, C., Tchanturia, K., Stahl, D., & Treasure, J. (2009). Weak central coherence in eating disorders: A step towards looking for an endophenotype of eating disorders. *Journal of Clinical and Experimental Neuropsychology, 31*(1), 117–125. https://doi.org/10.1080/13803390802036092

Losh, M., Adolphs, R., Poe, M. D., Couture, S., Penn, D., Baranek, G. T., & Piven, J. (2009). Neuropsychological profile of autism and the broad autism phenotype. *Archives of General Psychiatry,* 66(5), 518. https://doi.org/10.1001/archgenpsychiatry.2009.34

Lundqvist, D., & Öhman, A. (2005). Emotion regulates attention: The relation between facial configurations, facial emotion, and visual attention. *Visual Cognition, 12*(1), 51–84. https://doi.org/10.1080/13506280444000085

Lynch, M. P. (2004). *True to life: Why truth matters.* MIT Press.

Lynch, T. R. (2018a). *Radically open dialectical behavior therapy: Theory and practice for treating disorders of overcontrol.* New Harbinger Publications.

Lynch, T. R. (2018b). *The skills training manual for radically open dialectical behavior therapy: A clinician's guide for treating disorders of overcontrol.* New Harbinger Publications.

Lynch, T. R., Mendelson, T., Robins, C. J., Krishnan, K. R. R., George, L. K., Johnson, C. S., & Blazer, D. G. (1999). Perceived social support among depressed elderly, middle-aged, and young-adult samples: Cross-sectional and longitudinal analyses. *Journal of Affective Disorders,* 55(2–3), 159–170. https://doi.org/10.1016/s0165-0327(99)00017-8

Lynch, T. R., & Aspnes, A. (2001). Personality disorders in older adults: Diagnostic and theoretical issues. *Clinical Geriatrics, 9,* 64–70.

Lynch, T. R., & Cheavens, J. S. (2008). Dialectical behavior therapy for comorbid personality disorders. *Journal of Clinical Psychology,* 64(2), 154–167. https://doi.org/10.1002/jclp.20449

Lynch, T. R., Cheavens, J. S., Morse, J. Q., & Rosenthal, M. Z. (2004). A model predicting suicidal ideation and hopelessness in depressed older adults: The impact of emotion inhibition and affect intensity. *Aging and Mental Health, 8*(6), 486–497. https://doi.org/10.1080/13607860412331303775

Lynch, T. R., Hempel, R., & Clark, L. A. (2015). Promoting radical openness and flexible control. In W. J. Livesley, G. Dimaggio, & J. F. Clarkin (Eds.), *Integrated Treatment for Personality Disorder: A Modular Approach*, 325–344. The Guilford Press.

Lynch, T. R., Hempel, R. J., Whalley, B., Byford, S., Chamba, R., Clarke, P., Clarke, S., Kingdon, D. G., O'Mahen, H., Remington, B., Rushbrook, S. C., Shearer, J., Stanton, M., Swales, M., Watkins, A., & Russell, I. T. (2020). Refractory depression – mechanisms and efficacy of radically open dialectical behaviour therapy (RefraMED): Findings of a randomised trial on benefits and harms. *The British Journal of Psychiatry, 216*(4), 204–212. https://doi.org/10.1192/bjp.2019.53

Macdonald, K. (2009). Evolution, psychology, and a conflict theory of culture. *Evolutionary Psychology, 7*(2), 147470490900700. https://doi.org/10.1177/147470490900700206

MacDonald, K., Figueredo, A. J., Wenner, C., & Howrigan, D. (2007, May). Life history strategy, executive functions, and personality. In A. J. Figueredo (Chair), *Correlates of life history strategy.* Symposium presented at the Annual Meeting of the Human Behavior and Evolution Society, Williamsburg, VA.

Mackinnon, S. P., Sherry, S. B., Antony, M. M., Stewart, S. H., Sherry, D. L., & Hartling, N. (2012). Caught in a bad romance: Perfectionism, conflict, and depression in romantic relationships. *Journal of Family Psychology, 26*(2), 215–225. https://doi.org/10.1037/a0027402

Maclean, J. C., Xu, H., French, M. T., & Ettner, S. L. (2014). Mental health and high-cost health care utilization: New evidence from axis II disorders. *Health Services Research, 49*(2), 683–704. https://doi.org/10.1111/1475-6773.12107

Marean, C. (2015). An evolutionary anthropological perspective on modern human origins. *Annual Review of Anthropology, 44*, 533–556. https://doi.org/10.1146/annurev-anthro-102313-025954

Marvel, F. A., Chen, C.-C., Badr, N., Gaykema, R. P. A., & Goehler, L. E. (2004). Reversible inactivation of the dorsal vagal complex blocks lipopolysaccharide-induced social withdrawal and c-Fos expression in central autonomic nuclei. *Brain, Behavior, and Immunity, 18*(2), 123–134. https://doi.org/10.1016/j.bbi.2003.09.004

Matsumoto, D., & Willingham, B. (2009). Spontaneous facial expressions of emotion of congenitally and noncongenitally blind individuals. *Journal of Personality and Social Psychology,* 96(1), 1–10. https://doi.org/10.1037/a0014037

Mauss, I. B., Tamir, M., Anderson, C. L., & Savino, N. S. (2011). Can seeking happiness make people unhappy? Paradoxical effects of valuing happiness. *Emotion, 11*(4), 807–815. https://doi.org/10.1037/a0022010

McDonald, C. C., & Richmond, T. R. (2008). The relationship between community violence exposure and mental health symptoms in urban adolescents. *Journal of Psychiatric and Mental Health Nursing, 15*(10), 833–849. https://doi.org/10.1111/j.1365-2850.2008.01321.x

Miller, A. G. (1986). *The obedience experiments: A case study of controversy in social science*. Praeger Publishers.

Mineka, S., Watson, D., & Clark, L. A. (1998). Comorbidity of anxiety and unipolar mood disorders. *Annual Review of Psychology, 49*(1), 377–412. https://doi.org/10.1146/annurev.psych.49.1.377

Mizushima, L., & Stapleton, P. (2006). Analyzing the function of meta-oriented critical comments in Japanese comic conversations. *Journal of Pragmatics, 38*(12), 2105–2123. https://doi.org/10.1016/j.pragma.2006.05.002

Molnar, D. S., Sadava, S. W., Flett, G. L., & Colautti, J. (2012). Perfectionism and health: A mediational analysis of the roles of stress, social support and health-related behaviours. *Psychology and Health, 27*(7), 846–864. https://doi.org/10.1080/08870446.2011.630466

Montgomery, K. J., & Haxby, J. V. (2008). Mirror neuron system differentially activated by facial expressions and social hand gestures: A functional magnetic resonance imaging study. *Journal of Cognitive Neuroscience, 20*(10), 1866–1877. https://doi.org/10.1162/jocn.2008.20127

Moody, E. J., McIntosh, D. N., Mann, L. J., & Weisser, K. R. (2007). More than mere mimicry? The influence of emotion on rapid facial reactions to faces. *Emotion, 7*(2), 447–457. https://doi.org/10.1037/1528-3542.7.2.447

Morse, J. Q., & Lynch, T. R. (2004). A preliminary investigation of self-reported personality disorders in late life: Prevalence, predictors of depressive severity, and clinical correlates. *Aging and Mental Health, 8*(4), 307–315. https://doi.org/10.1080/13607860410001709674

Neuberg, S. L., & Newsom, J. T. (1993). Personal need for structure: Individual differences in the desire for simpler structure. *Journal of Personality and Social Psychology, 65*(1), 113–131. https://doi.org/10.1037/0022-3514.65.1.113

Palinkas, L. A., Wingard, D. L., & Barrett-Connor, E. (1990). Chronic illness and depressive symptoms in the elderly: A population-based study. *Journal of Clinical Epidemiology, 43*(11), 1131–1141. https://doi.org/10.1016/0895-4356(90)90014-g

Park, N., Peterson, C., & Seligman, M. E. P. (2006). Character strengths in fifty-four nations and the fifty US states. *The Journal of Positive Psychology, 1*(3), 118–129. https://doi.org/10.1080/17439760600619567

Parkinson, B. (2005). Do facial movements express emotions or communicate motives? *Personality and Social Psychology Review, 9*(4), 278–311. https://doi.org/10.1207/s15327957pspr0904_1

Perren, S., & Alsaker, F. D. (2006). Social behavior and peer relationships of victims, bully-victims, and bullies in kindergarten. *Journal of Child Psychology and Psychiatry, 47*(1), 45–57. https://doi.org/10.1111/j.1469-7610.2005.01445.x

Pittam, J., & Scherer, K. R. (1993). Vocal expression and communication of emotion. In M. Lewis & J. M. Haviland (Eds.), *Handbook of emotions* (pp. 185–197). The Guilford Press.

Porges, S. W. (1995). Orienting in a defensive world: Mammalian modifications of our evolutionary heritage. A polyvagal theory. *Psychophysiology, 32*(4), 301–318. https://doi.org/10.1111/j.1469-8986.1995.tb01213.x

Porges, S. W. (2003). The polyvagal theory: phylogenetic contributions to social behavior. *Physiology and Behavior, 79*(3), 503–513. https://doi.org/10.1016/s0031-9384(03)00156-2

Porges, S. W. (2007). The polyvagal perspective. *Biological Psychology, 74*(2), 116–143. https://doi.org/10.1016/j.biopsycho.2006.06.009

Porges, S. W. (2011). *The polyvagal theory: Neurophysiological foundations of emotions, attachment, communication, and self-regulation*. W. W. Norton & Company.

Ross, L. D., Amabile, T. M., & Steinmetz, J. L. (1977). Social roles, social control, and biases in social-perception processes. *Journal of Personality and Social Psychology, 35*(7), 485–494. https://doi.org/10.1037/0022-3514.35.7.485

Russell, I. T. (2018). Radically open dialectical behaviour therapy for refractory depression: The RefraMED RCT. *Efficacy and Mechanism Evaluation, 5*(7), 1–112. https://doi.org/10.3310/eme05070

Russell, J. A., Bachorowski, J.-A., & Fernández-Dols, J.-M. (2003). Facial and vocal expressions of emotion. *Annual Review of Psychology, 54*(1), 329–349. https://doi.org/10.1146/annurev.psych.54.101601.145102

Scambler, D. J., Harris, M. J., & Milich, R. (1998). Sticks and stones: Evaluations of responses to childhood teasing. *Social Development, 7*(2), 234–249. https://doi.org/10.1111/1467-9507.00064

Schauer, M., & Elbert, T. (2015). Dissociation following traumatic stress. *Zeitschrift für Psychologie [Journal of Psychology], 218*(2), 109–127. https://doi.org/10.1027/0044-3409/a000018

Schore, A. N. (2021). The interpersonal neurobiology of intersubjectivity. *Frontiers in Psychology, 12*. https://doi.org/10.3389/fpsyg.2021.648616

Schug, J., Matsumoto, D., Horita, Y., Yamagishi, T., & Bonnet, K. (2010). Emotional expressivity as a signal of cooperation. *Evolution and Human Behavior, 31*(2), 87–94. https://doi.org/10.1016/j.evolhumbehav.2009.09.006

Schupp, H. T., Junghöfer, M., Weike, A. I., & Hamm, A. O. (2004). The selective processing of briefly presented affective pictures: An ERP analysis. *Psychophysiology, 41*(3), 441–449. https://doi.org/10.1111/j.1469-8986.2004.00174.x

Schupp, H. T., Öhman, A., Junghöfer, M., Weike, A. I., Stockburger, J., & Hamm, A. O. (2004). The facilitated processing of threatening faces: An ERP analysis. *Emotion, 4*(2), 189–200. https://doi.org/10.1037/1528-3542.4.2.189

Segura-García, C., Ramacciotti, C., Rania, M., Aloi, M., Caroleo, M., Bruni, A., Gazzarrini, D., Sinopoli, F., & De Fazio, P. (2015). The prevalence of orthorexia nervosa among eating disorder patients after treatment. *Eating and Weight Disorders–Studies on Anorexia, Bulimia and Obesity, 20*(2), 161–166. https://doi.org/10.1007/s40519-014-0171-y

Shaw, A., & Olson, K. R. (2012). Children discard a resource to avoid inequity. *Journal of Experimental Psychology: General, 141*(2), 382–395. https://doi.org/10.1037/a0025907

Shenk, C. E., & Fruzzetti, A. E. (2011). The impact of validating and invalidating responses on emotional reactivity. *Journal of Social and Clinical Psychology, 30*(2), 163–183. https://doi.org/10.1521/jscp.2011.30.2.163

Sherry, S. B., Hewitt, P. L., Flett, G. L., Lee-Baggley, D. L., & Hall, P. A. (2007). Trait perfectionism and perfectionistic self-presentation in personality pathology. *Personality and Individual Differences, 42*(3), 477–490. https://doi.org/10.1016/j.paid.2006.07.026

Sherry, S. B., Mackinnon, A. L., Fossum, K.-L., Antony, M. M., Stewart, S. H., Sherry, D. L., Nealis, L. J., & Mushquash, A. R. (2013). Perfectionism, discrepancies, and depression: Testing the perfectionism social disconnection model in a short-term, four-wave longitudinal study. *Personality and Individual Differences, 54*(6), 692–697. https://doi.org/10.1016/j.paid.2012.11.017

Steklis, H. D., & Kling, A. (1985). Neurobiology of affiliative behavior in nonhuman primates. In M. Reite (Ed.), *The psychobiology of attachment and separation* (pp. 93–134). Elsevier.

Szczepek Reed, B. (2012). Beyond the particular: Prosody and the coordination of actions. *Language and Speech, 55*(1), 13–34. https://doi.org/10.1177/0023830911428871

Tchanturia, K., & Lang, K. (2015). Cognitive profiles in adults and children with anorexia nervosa and how they have informed us in developing CRT for anorexia nervosa. In K. Tchanturia (Ed.), *Cognitive remediation therapy (CRT) for eating and weight disorders* (pp. 1–13). Routledge/Taylor & Francis Group.

Thompson, M. M., Naccarato, M. E., Parker, K. C. H., & Moskowitz, G. B. (2001). The personal need for structure and personal fear of invalidity measures: Historical perspectives, current applications, and future directions. In *Cognitive social psychology: The Princeton symposium on the legacy and future of social cognition* (pp. 19–39). Lawrence Erlbaum Associates Publishers.

Van Der Gaag, C., Minderaa, R. B., & Keysers, C. (2007). Facial expressions: What the mirror neuron system can and cannot tell us. *Social Neuroscience, 2*(3–4), 179–222. https://doi.org/10.1080/17470910701376878

Vrana, S. R., & Gross, D. (2004). Reactions to facial expressions: effects of social context and speech anxiety on responses to neutral, anger, and joy expressions. *Biological Psychology, 66*(1), 63–78. https://doi.org/10.1016/j.biopsycho.2003.07.004

Watson, D., & Naragon-Gainey, K. (2010). On the specificity of positive emotional dysfunction in psychopathology: Evidence from the mood and anxiety disorders and schizophrenia/schizotypy. *Clinical Psychology Review, 30*(7), 839–848. https://doi.org/10.1016/j.cpr.2009.11.002

Williams, G. C., Lynch, M. F., McGregor, H. A., Ryan, R. M., Sharp, D., & Deci, E. L. (2006). Validation of the "important other" climate questionnaire: Assessing autonomy support for health-related change. *Families, Systems, & Health, 24*(2), 179–194. https://doi.org/10.1037/1091-7527.24.2.179

Wilson, A. T., & Miller, C. B. (2018). Virtue epistemology and developing intellectual virtue. In H. Battaly (Ed.), *The Routledge handbook of virtue epistemology* (pp. 483–495). Routledge. https://doi.org/10.4324/9781315712550-40

Wirth, J. H., Sacco, D. F., Hugenberg, K., & Williams, K. D. (2010). Eye gaze as relational evaluation: Averted eye gaze leads to feelings of ostracism and relational devaluation. *Personality and Social Psychology Bulletin, 36*(7), 869–882. https://doi.org/10.1177/0146167210370032

Yang, Y., Fairbairn, C., & Cohn, J. F. (2013). Detecting depression severity from vocal prosody. *IEEE Transactions on Affective Computing, 4*(2), 142–150. https://doi.org/10.1109/t-affc.2012.38

Zucker, N. L., Losh, M., Bulik, C. M., Labar, K. S., Piven, J., & Pelphrey, K. A. (2007). Anorexia nervosa and autism spectrum disorders: Guided investigation of social cognitive endophenotypes. *Psychological Bulletin, 133*(6), 976–1006. https://doi.org/10.1037/0033-2909.133.6.976

Index

A

B

C

D

E

F

G

H

I

JKL

M

N

O

P

R

S

T

U

V

W

Thomas R. Lynch, PhD, FBPsS, is professor emeritus of clinical psychology at the University of Southampton school of psychology. Previously, he was director of the Duke Cognitive Behavioral Research and Treatment Program at Duke University from 1998-2007. He relocated to Exeter University in the UK in 2007. Lynch's primary research interests include understanding and developing novel treatments for mood and personality disorders using a translational line of inquiry that combines basic neurobiobehavioral science with the most recent technological advances in intervention research. He is founder of radically open dialectical behavior therapy (RO DBT).

Lynch has received numerous awards and special recognitions from organizations such as the National Institutes of Health-US (NIMH, NIDA), Medical Research Council-UK (MRC-EME), and the National Alliance for Research on Schizophrenia and Depression (NARSAD). His research has been recognized in the Science and Advances Section of the National Institutes of Health Congressional Justification Report; and he is a recipient of the John M. Rhoades Psychotherapy Research Endowment, and a Beck Institute Scholar.

J. Nicole Little, PhD, is registered with the B.C. Association of Clinical Counsellors as a therapist and supervisor. She is a senior RO DBT trainer and supervisor, and regular RO DBT blog contributor. She maintains a private practice where she focuses on treating those with overcontrol (OC), and has been featured as an outstanding clinician for youth in *Insights Magazine*. In 2006, she received the inaugural Vance Peavey Award for Counselling Excellence, and has been the recipient of the prestigious Social Sciences and Humanities Council of Canada scholarship. She is the author of several peer-reviewed articles.

Did you know there are **free tools** you can download for this book?

Free tools are things like **worksheets**, **guided meditation exercises**, and **more** that will help you get the most out of your book.

You can download free tools for this book—whether you bought or borrowed it, in any format, from any source—from the New Harbinger website. All you need is a NewHarbinger.com account. Just use the URL provided in this book to view the free tools that are available for it. Then, click on the "download" button for the free tool you want, and follow the prompts that appear to log in to your NewHarbinger.com account and download the material.

You can also save the free tools for this book to your **Free Tools Library** so you can access them again anytime, just by logging in to your account! Just look for this button on the book's free tools page.

+ Save this to my free tools library

If you need help accessing or downloading free tools, visit **newharbinger.com/faq** or contact us at **customerservice@newharbinger.com.**